Praise for *Lion Taming*

"Steven L. Katz's own experienc[illegible] in both the government and the private sectors has given rise to this origin[illegible] [illegible]hat will give you insights on how to work [illegible] your own next steps up the ladder of a[illegible]

—*Joh[illegible] [illegible]ronaut*

"Steven L. Katz has successfully faced more than [illegible] [illegible]ions in the workplace. Consider this the world's best instruction manual for using your own whip and chair effectively!"

—*Paul B. Brown, coauthor of the international best-seller* Customers for Life

"Finally a book that acknowledges that the world of CEOs and top executives really can be a lion's den! A must-read full of meaningful insights on how to thrive with the big cats in the center ring at the office!"

—*Manuel N. Sousa, Senior Vice President, Saks Fifth Avenue*

"Brilliant! I immediately read my own experiences into every page-turning chapter. The image of the lion tamer exists in all of our minds—NOW we have the secrets and strategies to step into the lion tamer's shoes in our jobs and in life!"

—*John Corrigan, Senior Vice President, Hughes Network Systems*

"There has always been an acute need inside corporations and organizations to understand how to be an effective 'Number 2.' This is true whether or not you are an executive, manager, or assistant. *Lion Taming: Working Successfully with Leaders, Bosses, and other Tough Customers* is both rare and timely in addressing this critical subject."

—*Gail Schulze, CEO, Exime Inc.*

"If you have ever thrilled at the sight of a lion tamer inside a steel cage facing a pyramid of lions, this book is for you. Here you will learn the secrets of lion tamers and see those secrets deftly applied to relationships in the work place. Most importantly, you will learn that it is the teaming of the tamer and the lions that produces extraordinary results and how that can be achieved."

—*Marvin Zonis, professor, Graduate School of Business, University of Chicago, coauthor of* The Kimchi Matters: Global Business *and* Local Politics in a Crisis-Driven World

LION taming

Working Successfully with Leaders, Bosses and Other Tough Customers

Steven L. Katz

Sourcebooks, Inc.®
Naperville, Illinois

Published by Sourcebooks, Inc.
P.O. Box 4410, Naperville, Illinois 60567-4410
(630) 961-3900
FAX: (630) 961-2168
www.sourcebooks.com

The Library of Congress has cataloged the hardcover edition as follows:
Katz, Steven L.
Working successfully with leaders, bosses and other tough customers! / Steven L. Katz.
p. cm.
Includes bibliographical references and index.
ISBN 1-4022-0217-2 (alk. paper)
1. Managing your boss. 2. Conflict management. 3. Teams in the workplace. 4. Interpersonal relations. 5. Psychology, Industrial. I. Title.
HF5548.83.K38 2004
650.1'3—dc22

2004006855

Printed and bound in the United States of America
VP 10 9 8 7 6 5 4 3 2 1

For my parents,
Stanley and Frances Katz

Voices we hear
Laughter we miss
Souls we share
Dreams we wish
Yours

"Writing is thinking.
That's why it's so difficult"
—F.R. Katz

Contents

Acknowledgments ix

Part One: Lions Are Never Tame

Chapter One: Lions Are Never Tame 3

Chapter Two: Getting Inside the Lion's "Skull" 25

Chapter Three: The Top of the Food Chain 53

Chapter Four: Bringing Out the Lion Tamer in You 71

Part Two: The Art of Lion Taming

Chapter Five: The Art of Lion Taming 85

Chapter Six: Courage, the Whip, and the Chair 111

Chapter Seven: The Lion's Pedestal 137

Chapter Eight: Sticking Your Head in the Lion's Mouth . . 161

Chapter Nine: Lion Taming in Action 181

Part Three: Lion Taming Is Really Lion Teaming

Chapter Ten: Lion Taming Is Really Lion Teaming. 191

Chapter Eleven: Bringing Out the Lion *Teamer* in You! . . . 211

Chapter Twelve: Performing in the Center Ring 225

Chapter Thirteen: Building the Lion Team 245

Conclusion: Take Your Bow 271

References 275

Notes 277

Summary of Secrets of the Lion Tamers 283

Index 287

About the Author 291

Acknowledgments

Throughout my career I have worked with some of the best possible people—a cavalcade of lions and lion tamers in the workplace—leaders and executives, professionals across the ranks, and many terrific colleagues across the public and private sectors.

Melanne Verveer unwittingly inspired the idea for this book, characteristic of the many ideas and good works she has fostered throughout her own career. Thank you for the inspiration, education, and opportunity to realize that being a "lion tamer" in the workplace is a very important part of every job.

The team at Sourcebooks, Inc. deserves much credit for sharing this inspiration and education with the reading public. Taylor Poole has contributed an artist's eye and a craftsman's touch to the presentation of this book, and is responsible for letting *Lion Taming* leap to the attention and into the minds of the reading public—from cover to conclusion! Publisher Dominique Raccah heads a tight knit organization, and my editor Peter Lynch played a strong leadership role in bringing the book to life. Peter has demonstrated the patience and artfulness of a lion tamer: a willingness to learn and an eye for the natural strengths and talents of a subject; an appreciation of ironies and essential detail; together with good instincts and intuition.

Mark Pattis shared his personal and professional knowledge about publishers and getting published. Author and business writer Paul Brown generously gave of his time, knowledge, insights, and contacts "from proposal to publication." Ed Gold provided a "cold read" and valuable editing assistance.

Bringing the metaphor of "lion taming" to life as a way to better understand how to act, communicate, and work more effectively with people required a substantial education in the world of real lion taming—or "lion training" as it is professionally termed.

Kevin Patton, biologist, college professor, and former lion and wild animal trainer, generously shared his personal knowledge, understanding, and insights.

Other experts in animal behavior and training took time from their busy schedules and livelihoods to share their experiences, knowledge, and insights that contributed to this book. I am indebted to Jorge Barreda and his family, including his father Jose Barreda, for sharing their time and knowledge from decades of working with lions. Expert animal trainer Wade Burck was extremely helpful and insightful, enabling me to watch him work as he drew upon his talent, respect, and high standards for working with big cats. Juergen and Judit Nerger enabled me to observe and learn from them as they trained and worked, and provided thoughtful answers to as many questions as I could think to ask. Finally, I wish to thank lion trainer Jason Peters, who in 2004 began presenting the largest all-male lion act in the world for Ringling Brothers and Barnum and Bailey Circus. Jason provided many insights about lions and lion training and the parallels to the workplace.

Fred Dahlinger, Jr., director of collections and research of the Wisconsin Historical Society's Circus World Museum and his archival staff were extremely helpful in providing information, history, and photographs and guiding me to people with first-hand experience in "the steel-caged arena.” Fred D. Pfening, Jr., publisher of *Bandwagon,* has been a generous source of photographs. Bill Biggerstaff of the *Circus Report* was also very helpful in providing information and photographs, as was the Columbia County Historical Society of Bloomsburg, Pennsylvania. Murray Horwitz—good friend, former Ringling Brothers clown, cultural historian, artist, and an impresario in his own right—shared a wealth of vivid experiences, observations, knowledge, and ideas.

Thank you to “the people of Deloitte” for understanding, appreciating, and enabling me to have the dedicated time I needed to complete *Lion Taming: Working Successfully with Leaders, Bosses, and Other Tough Customers.*

Numerous people including friends, colleagues, and associates who work in many different occupations, companies, and organizations and live across the United States and in other parts of the world generously shared their own experiences and stories about life at work. They provided invaluable feedback over the several years that this book was being researched and written. I am grateful for their continuous interest and encouragement. I especially want to thank Walt Anderson, Jim Brink, Craig Collins, John Corrigan, Margaret Crenshaw, Andrew Decker, Ed Gleiman, Judy Green, Steve Francisco, Bill Hensel, Handy Lindsey, Gerry McAree, Gregg Prillaman, Julie Robertson, Gail Schulze, Tom Sisti, Lisa Slagle, Bernice Steinhardt, Harland Stine, Dr. Johanna Tabin and Scott Taylor for sharing their time, candor, experiences, and insights. Thanks for pushing me into the lion’s cage to write the book!

Books are lived as they are being written and shaped by those closest to the author.

I am deeply grateful to my wife Leslie for her years of *unending* patience, reading, listening, editing, and support. No one could have been a better sounding board and “first read" of a book—from the initial spark of the idea through the many drafts of the proposal, and every chapter through to publication! Our children Aaron and Nina deserve very special credit. Aaron and Nina have patiently listened, talked, cheered me on, produced beautiful artwork, and have been a fountain of terrific ideas! Thank you Leslie, Aaron, and Nina.

My very creative siblings—Marianne, musician and lyricist; Michael, writer and photographer; Bonnie, ceramic and visual artist—have been excited and encouraging as the book has evolved.

Lastly, I wish to express the deepest gratitude *in memoriam* to my loving parents, Stanley and Frances Katz. I hope that this book would have brought a smile to their faces and contributed to some late-night reading. On dad's nightstand was always stacked Rex Stout's Nero Wolfe and mysteries by Ngaio Marsh, Tom Clancy, Dick Francis—as well as Charles Goren on bridge. Mom's side of the bed overflowed with books by her favorite writers, including Saul Bellow, Sylvia Plath, John Updike, Amos Oz, and Cynthia Ozick; as well as literary journals and issues of *The New Yorker*. Perhaps *Lion Taming* would have found a place on their nightstands too, providing some good stories, solving a few mysteries, and imparting a little wisdom. May it still be so.

PART I

Lions Are Never Tame

1

Lions Are Never Tame

> **Secrets of the Lion Tamers**
> *Lions are never tame. You need strategies to deal with that.*

Do you feel that you need a whip and a chair to work effectively with your boss, client, customers, or others? You know the dangers—a growl if you throw them a compliment and a roar if you ever look for thanks! One minute you are stroking them and praising them for an accomplishment, the next minute you suddenly wish you were not standing so close.

It's as if there is an invisible world of perceptions surrounding your actions, and you never know what will cause them to roar. You may have unwittingly shared information or even just struck up a conversation with someone who is seen as an enemy or a competitor. Or, you may have become too visible on a project while just trying to get it done, and are perceived as seizing an opportunity for yourself. The next thing you know—WHAM—you are up to your neck in teeth! Shoulders squared, jaws tense, eyes sizing up everything and everyone around them. What is their next move? Where do you fit in? How should you behave?

Following the lions in the workplace in order to find out how to act, and as importantly when to act, leads to a twisting trail. You'll find behavior full of ironies and emotions that are unexpectedly complex.

Familiar Traits of the Lions

Do any of these qualities of lions in the workplace seem familiar in people you deal with every day? If you find yourself nodding your head, you may be more aware of the lions around you than you had believed!

- Projecting dominance but always needing to know where they stand
- Displaying a tough exterior yet interpreting everything personally
- Preferring to act instinctively, even if they have to prepare in advance to do so
- Being creatures of habit who react quickly to new developments
- Isolated by power, yet reigning from wherever they stand
- Instinctively commanding, yet wanting to be understood
- Approachable and appreciative one-on-one, while rebuffing or ignoring you in a crowd
- Capable of attacking everything but the problem
- Ruling the kingdom yet depending on the loyalty, skills, and agility of others to serve and protect them
- Possessing an agility of reserve that is more worrisome than what they are doing at the moment
- Keeping others off balance while they remain surefooted

The only thing you can be certain of is that they are predictably enigmatic!

The Lions All Around Us

You have probably seen more than a few lions in the workplace and heard them roar. They are the people all around us with power, responsibility, authority, talent—not to mention the people who may simply be preoccupied with gaining *more* power and authority. Leaders and bosses. Executives and professionals. Managers at all levels. Owners, partners, and boards of directors. Elected and appointed officials. Colleagues, customers, clients, and employees. Lions roam freely everywhere, across all occupations and professions—throughout life.

We have all stood back from the lions in the office, the boardroom, or wherever they appear on the scene. Who hasn't been afraid of getting their head bit off at work? Who hasn't admired the strength of the lions in the workplace yet feared their ability to wreak havoc in the blink of an eye?

Many lions look to seize the advantage, even if it is by taking many small unobtrusive steps closer to power over a long period of time. They will patiently plan, wait, and make their move. Still others are nomadic lions, working alone or in coalitions. Some team to work, others team to kill. They're on the prowl for opportunities to consume, often benefiting from the energies of others, rarely seeking ownership or responsibility. Lions thrive on whatever they get, whether it is information, intelligence, compensation, authority, territory, budget, headcount, or recognition.

However, we need lions. And we need people who are good at being lions, particularly those who can become great lions as leaders. We look to the lions as being vital to the success of any company or organization. We need them to use their persona to lead in a new direction, face challenges head on, expand the territory, and put their strength, power, or position to use—to seize the opportunity and *pounce!*

Preparing to Work with the Lions

In the workplace, you do not always have time to plan your encounters with lions. And, for many people, if you are working inside any organization you can assume that you are already in the steel-caged arena with the lions. Sometimes you get tapped for a promotion or recognized for your knowledge or special skills. Sometimes the role is temporary, even pinch-hitting for someone else; other times it becomes a permanent responsibility. Ready or not, you may suddenly find yourself face to face with the lions at work—even though as it is happening, you may be wishing in the back of your mind that something might save you. Real lion tamers, including some that became world famous, first entered the cage just as suddenly.

Lessons of the Lion Tamers

"Hey, Can't I Just Watch from Out Here Once or Twice?"

Charly Baumann began what became an illustrious circus career working as a young man training and presenting horses. He had no plans to be a lion tamer, or even get close to them, although he ultimately became world renowned for his artistry and skill as a big-cat trainer. How did it begin?

On a morning off, Baumann walked through the big top and passed by the lion cage. Rehearsal was just starting and the lion tamer, a man named Michon, waited impatiently with his lions for an assistant to arrive. Michon asked Baumann to pick up a pole, reach through the bars, and nudge one reluctant lion onto a pedestal. Baumann tried without success, attracting only a deadly stare. He quickly handed the pole to the assistant as he arrived.

Minutes later, Baumann was only steps outside the tent when he heard the screams. Running back inside he saw a storm of flying dust and paws inside the lion cage—three large male lions were attacking Michon.

(continued)

The roars shook the steel bars and the nerves of the cage hands that stood frozen, watching. Baumann, who had never been in a lion cage, ran inside and fought the lions back to their pedestals, then dragged the bleeding and bitten body of Michon out of the cage.

Baumann's bravery earned him a reputation—and an offer to replace Michon. He declined the offer, but that winter agreed to replace a lion tamer who was leaving another circus. Arriving at his new job, Baumann was greeted by his new boss and was asked to change into his trainer's clothes. Returning quickly, he was handed a long, thin stick. "What's that for?" Baumann asked. "You're going in with the lions, that's for cueing," his new boss answered.

"Going into the lion's cage?" he asked. He later recalled, "We were distracted briefly by the clank of metal as a workman let six male lions into the steel cage." Waiting by the cage door stood the lion tamer that Baumann was hired to replace, beckoning him inside.

"Hey, can't I just watch from out here once or twice?" Baumann asked.

Lions at Work Are a Different Species

As Baumann's story tells us, it wasn't the cage that gave him pause, it was the sight of the lions.

And of all the realities that must now frame your outlook as a lion tamer in the workplace, it is that *you* are dealing with lions too. As a senior executive who spent twenty-five years working his way to the top of a large company observed about the company president, "*He's a different species,* and that's how I treat him." The lions in the workplace really are a different species, and we will describe in detail just what makes them different, how they think and act, and the techniques that will make you effective in dealing with them.

However, it is much more than a mental exercise. You need to *feel* that you are a lion tamer before you walk into the equivalent of the steel-caged arena at work. As one astute lion tamer observed: "I know that I am about to enter a cage full of lions, and I think carefully about it before, during, and after I go in. But people in businesses and organizations don't quite see that beforehand, do they? They are more likely to get caught flat-footed just when someone who is a lion is coming at them!" He's right. It does little good to realize that your job may at times make you feel like a lion tamer because of all the things you are unable to control, including your own desire to run for safety! You need to be in possession of the self-image and strategies that put you on top of the situation as both a participant and an observer.

For now you need to remember one rule about the lions that you encounter every day. How should you approach and communicate with them? Person to person? NO! Mammal to mammal? YES!

This is not meant to sound harsh. Rather, it is respectful and realistic. Lions are a different species, and it is okay to think of them that way. Think how differently you might act if you were dealing with a real lion, and you will begin to get the idea. So ingrained is this reality in the minds of real lion tamers that they can instantly recite from memory their rules for working with lions—even decades after they last set foot in the ring!

Rules for Working a Lion Act

- Lions are a different species.
- Respect their power.
- Recognize the danger.
- Pay attention.
- Always maintain visual contact—keep them in front of you.
- Don't be thinking of anything else.
- Remain alert.
- Be determined.
- Patience is essential.

These rules help in the workplace, too. Keep them in mind as you learn to identify and understand the lions in your organization.

The Lion's Traits

> **Secrets of the Lion Tamers**
>
> *Social animals need a clear decision about their social position.*

Let's look further at what makes lions in the workplace a unique species. Lions in the wild and the workplace share four important traits:

- Lions need to be dominant and be secure in the feeling that they are dominant.
- Lions need to control territory and know when and how to preserve, protect, and expand it.
- Lions need to know where they stand in the social hierarchy.
- Lions are fine-tuned to any potential threat to their survival.

When we hear such phrases as "lions are social animals," it is usually to grasp that lions in the wild parallel human society—from the family-like prides to the male lions who remain with the lioness and the cubs that they father. However, if you really want to understand why "lions are social," it is the workplace that most closely parallels lion society in the wild.

In both the wild and the workplace, there is always a hierarchy and a competition—and there is always a bigger lion. This is true for all kinds of organizations or companies: blue chip or microchip, for-profit or non-profit, government, the military, and more. It is true regardless of the organization's size, design, or way that it is structured—whether it is a traditional corporate hierarchy or one that has been reorganized, right-sized, or, as is increasingly common in modern organizations, "flattened" to reflect fewer management levels. Lions in the workplace are always highly aware of the people they encounter and the environment that surrounds them, and they see through any organizational framework to compete for a place in the hierarchy.

Secrets of the Lion Tamers

Hierarchies control competition.

Professions have their own hierarchies. Some hierarchies are more clearly demarcated than others are. For example, in medicine it exists between administrative staff, nurses, physicians, and surgeons. In industry, there are workers and crew chiefs, supervisors and managers, executives, chief executives—and often unions and other organizations in between! The president of the United States has Congress, public opinion, the media, and the voters on the one hand, and the Cabinet and a cavalcade of executives and employees below. CEOs have boards of directors, Wall Street, the media, and shareholders—and are subject to government oversight. All the while they must handle their own executive suite, perhaps today even an audit committee, and a range of energetic and often street-smart employees.

Hierarchies are particularly prominent in both the social lives of lions and the social order of the workplace, and have deep and often invisible effects on everyone.

- Hierarchies exist regardless of an organization's size, design, or structure.
- Hierarchies determine who is an insider eligible for the privileges and support of the pride, or in our case the organization.
- Hierarchies are designed to control competition and control access to the lions that hold the power.

The result can sometimes be an unintended irony. The lions may persevere over the competition, yet risk becoming isolated at the top. Organizations often devise many systems and even implement the "theory of the month" to improve communication, management, and performance. However, few such approaches recognize the underlying drive for hierarchies that keep the lions caged off from everyone and almost everyone caged off from the lions!

The lions themselves often make the effort to operate beyond their existing terrain. But when they do, it is not to interact with just anyone—it is to satisfy their impulse to know where they stand as a lion. They have a need to validate to themselves and others that they are lions—and this above all else is something that they must leave the isolation of their own hierarchy to achieve. We can watch this play out every day of the week at work. Lions seek each other out, even if they have to go outside of their organizations to do so. They have a need for contact with each other, including the need to act aggressively with other lions. It is not just anti-social for them to do otherwise, it is "unbiological," as one scientist noted in the context of real lions. It is equally true in the workplace.

Why do the lions in the workplace do this? Here are some of the reasons:

- To find other lions
- To reinforce that they belong in lion society
- To exercise their lion-like personality traits
- To be with their own kind

After all, a single individual can only take its place in a social hierarchy among the animals with which it lives. In this case, that means other lions in the workplace.

Overkill Is an Adaptive Behavior in Lions

Secrets of the Lion Tamers

Lions don't bargain or reason, they fight.

To the leaders, bosses, and other tough customers, it is *their* survival that always counts, even if to others their words and their behavior seem like overkill. After all, the term "overkill" might just have come from observing the way real lions behave. As the noted naturalist George Schaller witnessed in his studies of lions in East Africa:

> With snapping jaws and flashing claws, lions assert themselves, and it is not coincidental that 6 percent of the animals I studied had only one eye. The vigor of the disputes often seemed excessive, especially if there was ample meat, and I frequently had to remind myself that such behavior was adaptive or it wouldn't have persisted in evolution.

Indeed, when we see similar behavior displayed by lions in the workplace it seems so natural to their makeup, connecting their viscera, mind, and personality. The briefest instinctive actions—even a sign that something is about to happen—creates a primal emotional climate that absorbs everyone's attention. Overkill is adaptive and purposeful to the lions in the workplace too.

What is the adaptive purpose that overkill serves for the lions in the workplace? Overkill is a form of communication that the lions use to preserve their territory and maintain order. It is triggered when the lions in the workplace feel the need to stand their own ground, defend their status, and establish and oversee their territory. It is part of how they govern behavior around them. For some it is their modus operandi, while for others it is triggered more randomly.

As lions, they view their domain and the responsibilities,

resources, and relationships within it to be theirs to control. They live by a simple rule that seems perhaps ironic to everyone else: ***Anything they give away is still theirs.*** As a result, they react very personally to people who seize for themselves responsibilities, resources, or relationships that the lions perceive as theirs to give. The challenge to others is that the lion's reaction is not predictable according to discrete boundaries, but rather their expectations, rules, policies, protocols, or processes for how they want people who are in their territory to perform their job. You may have experienced this when provoking a reaction of overkill not because of what you did, but because of *how* you went about it—even in situations when the result was the desired result.

Lions Can Assert Themselves without Uttering a Word

> **Secrets of the Lion Tamers**
>
> *The signs of imminent attack are these: switching of the tail brush, sudden enlarging of the eyes with a marked increase in green color, a sudden adjustment into a crouch...*

How do real lion tamers characterize the politics of such behavior as it plays out between real lions in the arena? "It may be all bluff and bluster, but it is never a bluff you want to call." In fact, as zoologist H. Hediger noted in his research of lions more than fifty years ago, even the outcome of a fight can be foreshadowed by a clear and simple message:

> When two creatures meet, the one that is able to intimidate its opponent is recognized as socially superior, so that a social decision does not always depend on a fight; an encounter in some circumstances may be enough.

You have probably seen this for yourself in the workplace: a deadly stare, a friendly and powerful handshake, or the kind of tail-pounding warning that says if you want to fight, they are ready—go ahead, pick your subject. The people who are the lions around us do not always need to establish themselves in ways that are the most flashy or blustery. And sometimes it is the ones who are gripped in a grimace of insecurity and fear about their status that come off the strongest.

What drives the lions around us to act this way? It is not simply a pecking-order issue. Unlike how it often looks, they are not trying to kill someone. Ironically, it precedes whatever they do next, but is not always linked to what they do next. It is something deeper, a biologically driven impulse to know where they stand. They are trying to *establish* where they stand and determine their status in lion society. It can happen in the blink of eye or longer, depending on who is involved. They file the instinctive urge away along with what they have sensed, for the moment, registering the experience in their minds. The lions know among themselves exactly what it all means, even though to the rest of us it spells t-r-o-u-b-l-e.

Identifying the Lions around You

> **Secrets of the Lion Tamers**
>
> *There is always a bigger lion.*

As one executive commented, "Being a lion is not a specific position, it is a state of being." So it is too for lion tamers in the workplace. Almost everyone has lions they must deal with regardless of their own job, whether you are a special assistant, manager, senior manager, or upwards through the ranks of executives and the CEO. The lions are at all levels, and that means so are the lion tamers.

As people rise in an organization, a chain of command, or a power structure, more and more lions become visible. The people they report to are lions and the people who report to them, even people they already know, suddenly resemble lions. Often it is when people begin to be promoted and advance up the executive food chain that they are suddenly surrounded by the people who resemble lions. They are everywhere, and there are far more "people" issues of this sort to deal with. A mid-level executive who was relatively new to the upper ranks of management commented with exasperation, "I spend 90 percent of my time getting my boss and her boss where they need to be just so I can do my job!"

When CEOs and high-ranking executives reflect on their own experiences, they often acknowledge the presence of so many lions around them. Interestingly, however, they often remark that "I deal with the lions every day," and when asked who the lions are, the answer is likely to be "my employees"—even though there may be bigger lions to acknowledge! It's all a matter of perception. Their answer is also revealing because it has triggered a different and important set of questions in their own minds—questions that lion tamers in the workplace need to answer about the lions they are working with: What do I want to be perceived as the lion king of? Who are the people to whom I most often must demonstrate that I am the bigger lion?

No lion likes to acknowledge that they may have to play lion tamer to a bigger lion—even though it could be the smartest on-the-job skill they ever master. In fact, one of the greatest challenges in the workplace is to function both as a lion at your own level and as a lion tamer with the bigger lions above you.

Many people cannot do it because of their ego. Yet what it requires is not a smaller ego, but a more multidimensional ego, one that allows you to suppress the negative side of your ego in order to function effectively with others with more power, rank, or status than you have—and still remain effective in a different role. In fact, real lion tamers face this challenge every time they enter the ring. They cannot possibly be dominant as another lion, but for the time that they are in the ring with the lions they can have significant influence—some would even say dominant—as the lion tamer!

The Good Lions...and the Bad Lions

> **Secrets of the Lion Tamers**
>
> *The lion tamer's advantage is having the intelligence to study the lions individually.*

One of the first tasks of a real lion tamer is ironically one that is often never done by people who step into the role of lion tamer in the workplace. There is a mixture of individuals in the lions available to work with, and real lion tamers would never choose to keep a lion that they could not work with or feared as a killer in the act. Yet in human society we spend a good deal of our time at work ignoring these realities, even when they consume some of the most valuable energy we have to give in our jobs. We assume that we are powerless. But we're not, and therefore we need to be able to tell the difference between good and bad lions.

Just because someone is a lion does not mean that he or she is a difficult person. Again, we need lions, and we need people who are good at being lions. Most often we recognize people as lions in the workplace because they possess and display qualities that we associate with leadership—from instinctive thinking to emotional energy and charisma. If the lions at work share any trait, regardless of the level within the organization they operate, it is that they hold some kind of power. Power magnifies everything in the lion's personality for the people who wield it and the people who perceive it in them. A controlling CEO? CEOs are hired to be in control. A passionate and charismatic leader? Emotional energy is part of their package. These are the positions that engage their personalities.

Yet many people who encounter the lions at work universally treat these qualities as a challenge, not an opportunity. They draw a line in their minds that cages the lions off from everyone and also cages everyone else off from the lions. They don't realize that their ability to work more effectively with many people will produce things they had never thought possible: results that leaders, bosses, and customers need.

Perhaps the least optimal consequence of our reaction to the people who are the lions derives directly from the assumption that they are unapproachable—whether because of title, status, personality, or even the retinue that may seem to exist to protect them. As a result, paradoxically, we keep our distance from the good lions and work harder at tolerating and often accommodating the bad lions. The people, particularly other high-level executives who think that they have dodged a lion at work, ignore the effect such people are having on others.

One senior vice-president faced with a particularly ferocious company president explained: "I trained the lion to avoid me." This was the wrong approach, because instead of harnessing the lion's skills, he was setting the lion loose on everyone else. You can only imagine how much trouble the company president was causing all over the rest of the organization, popping up at meetings, grilling personnel, and invading business relationships. Ultimately when the viability of the company was impacted, it took two senior vice presidents and a board member to try and tackle the lion and get things under control.

Recognizing the Difference

People instinctively run so fast from the lions in the workplace that they never distinguish the good lions from the bad. Real lion tamers make that distinction quickly—so should you! They know the lions in the wild and the workplace will always be lions, but at the same time lion tamers look for specific differentiating traits, qualities, strengths, and capabilities that cannot be taken for granted. These are the traits that signal whether you can work together or not. No lion tamer will keep a killer lion in the act. If they are too dangerous to work with, out they go.

The lion tamer is looking for the opportunity to work with the lions in ways that are proactive and productive, not reactive and perhaps disruptive. People who recognize this also know that stepping into the shoes of the lion tamer is something that they do well, and requires the right lions to work with. Even if they have been burned once or twice, they work to avoid what can be the kind of working relationships that mean-swinging lions can produce—and the feelings range from simply unhealthy to being abused and tormented.

The Closer You Draw to the Good Lions...

How do you identify the good lions in the workplace, and how do you distinguish them from the bad? Surprisingly, when people have been asked to identify the qualities of the many "good" lions throughout society and the workplace, the list of traits to look for and seek out is considerably longer and more detailed than in the "bad" lions. As one executive noted of his own boss, "The closer I work with him, I see more and more qualities that I am impressed by, but you have to get closer to see them."

Here is a substantial and helpful, though still incomplete, list of the traits of good lions collected from a range of experienced people—from executive assistants to mid-level manager and executives to CEOs themselves. No single person has all of these qualities, and it is better to think of these traits along a wide spectrum instead of a checklist. These traits can be divided into **Leadership and Character**, and **Respect and Communication**.

Leadership and Character

- Has the ability to learn something new, internalize it, and adapt
- Is accountable to someone besides themselves, including the organization and the people in it
- Admits mistakes, does so in time to correct them, and is capable of self-correcting
- Is aware of what they know and do not know
- Is conscious of what they are learning, though not necessarily how
- Creates a climate of doing things
- Delegates authority and responsibility
- Demonstrates commitment through active involvement
- Gives people freedom to discover
- Enjoys their job
- Helps others accomplish their goals
- Leads by example
- Lets other people shine
- Is not there to oversee the status quo
- Recognizes that people need leaders but do not want dictators
- Recognizes egos—determines how smart people really are and are not
- Serves as a role model and mentor without knowing it
- Sets ambitious and reachable goals
- Uses, but does not abuse, position and authority

Respect and Communication

- Is aware of how other people are being treated
- Is aware of whether people have the right resources, people, training, and expertise
- Puts employees and customers before themselves
- Enables and trains others
- Encourages open communication
- Energizes others
- Identifies, helps illuminate, and fuels priorities
- Listens
- Is sought by people who want to work for them
- Promotes openness and communication about change
- Puts themselves on a par with others when possible
- Speaks to employees "like people," and gets to know them personally
- Respects people, positions, and responsibility above and below their own level
- Rewards performance
- Shares information

How to Spot the Bad Lions

Secrets of the Lion Tamers

The best offense against a lion attack is a dodge.

Despite the fact that there are many "good lions," the "bad lions," including the "mean-swinging lions" are out there, and they can be very, very difficult. Ironically, these are often qualities that are visible from far away, even made known over great distances by word of mouth. Yet some people are right up close before they realize what they are dealing with.

Naturalist George Schaller found these lions in the wild as well. He called them "despots who take what they want—whose existence lacks all subtlety." If you want to work with leaders, bosses, and others, then find the lions that want to work with you because you have skills and abilities that will make them successful in new ways. Otherwise, you may be simply viewed as someone else's breakfast, lunch, or dinner.

Do not enter a job blindly, and do not remain in one blindly. These are some of the characteristics most frequently identified in the lions that you want to avoid—a list compiled from people who wished they had avoided such people, and who in many cases found better lions to work for after experiencing many hardships. Bad lions are:

- People with an anger and a temper that is uncontrollable
- Autocratic
- Bullying
- Demanding to a degree that interferes with other people's work and lives
- Discriminatory
- Harassing
- High maintenance yet ineffective and unproductive
- Lacking in respect for others
- Manipulative
- Mean and demeaning to others
- Micromanagers
- Needlessly aggressive
- Obstructionist
- The only ego in the room
- Paranoid
- Perfectionists
- Self-serving
- People who take all the energy and drive out of the room
- Ones who treat anyone who is not perfect as defective
- Underestimating others, overestimating themselves
- Unethical
- Unwilling to admit making mistakes

A Privileged Few Lead the Pride

The range of people around us, including the people who are the lions, is always more varied than any list, and you will likely decide which balance of the great, the good, and the bad are tolerable. However, the number and scope of the lions is always larger than people first think. While only a privileged few lead the pride, many others compete aggressively up and down the ranks whenever the opportunity arises. From their standpoint, whether they are conscious of it or not, the number-one job is to hold their own in lion society. All lions in the workplace behave this way to varying degrees—the good lions, the bad lions, and everyone in between. Those who have power, authority, or territory will work hard at preserving and expanding it. Those who don't have enough will want their "pound of flesh."

Recognizing that lions are a separate species of people at work provides a foundation for finding out what makes them tick. They act differently because they think differently, and it is essential to follow the advice of real lion tamers and "get inside the lion's skull" to deal with them more effectively. As we will see, instinct plays a more pronounced role in their thinking and behavior than almost any other type of person, and as a lion tamer in the office your own "reverse animal instinct" must be operating at full power. Let's see how it unfolds in the next chapter, "Getting Inside the Lion's 'Skull'."

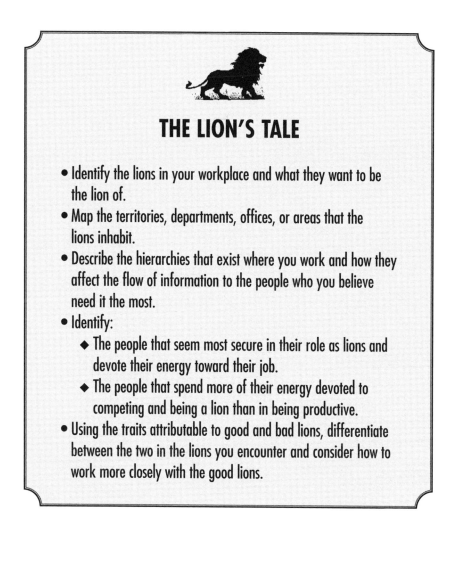

THE LION'S TALE

- Identify the lions in your workplace and what they want to be the lion of.
- Map the territories, departments, offices, or areas that the lions inhabit.
- Describe the hierarchies that exist where you work and how they affect the flow of information to the people who you believe need it the most.
- Identify:
  - The people that seem most secure in their role as lions and devote their energy toward their job.
  - The people that spend more of their energy devoted to competing and being a lion than in being productive.
- Using the traits attributable to good and bad lions, differentiate between the two in the lions you encounter and consider how to work more closely with the good lions.

2

Getting Inside the Lion's "Skull"

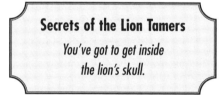

> **Secrets of the Lion Tamers**
>
> *You've got to get inside the lion's skull.*

Some lion-taming experts compare respect and understanding for the lion—the core of the lion tamer's thinking—to the insight and knowledge that teachers and writers must have to connect with their audiences. Anyone who is effective in working with leaders, bosses, or other tough customers will acknowledge that in some way they "*connect.*" To others it is a blend of intuition, common sense, and psychology. It is equally applicable in the workplace and in the center ring. After all, the lions at work act differently because they think differently. In order to understand why and how to communicate and behave, "You've got to get inside the lion's skull."

Prey, the Enemy, or Ignored

Perhaps the most primal and instinctive place to begin is also the place where most of us find ourselves when we come face to face with the lions at work. We immediately think, "Where do I stand, what should I do?"

You first must understand what shapes the lion's perception of the people and the world around them. Is there a way to decode their thoughts? Yes. Lions, including those at the office, make a simple and instinctive calculation the minute any living thing comes into view. ***You are either prey, the enemy, or ignored***. Prey they eat. The enemy they kill. Everyone else they disregard.

The first two options seem like the most dangerous. However, in the workplace being ignored is far more prevalent, challenging to deal with, and often fatal to the careers of many people. It is not that the lions in the workplace have any compunction about eliminating a problem permanently. But to do so, the problem must first appeal to them as necessary—as either something they need to aggressively make their own, or believe is an untenable threat to their survival. If it does not, then they tend to ignore it.

Ignoring is sometimes the simplest response because it requires the least amount of effort. The lions in the workplace are focused on putting their energies somewhere else, into something that they are personally interested in sinking their teeth into. As a result, it is always surprising when bosses who are capable of some of the most visible displays of power hesitate to take action in situations that are having an adverse affect on many other people in the organization. Yet from their standpoint, it is perfectly natural to ignore a person or problem that is neither something they need to make their own nor are threatened by. Many may often assume that the lions are so well insulated by their power or persona that they simply distance themselves from the cause.

People who are the targets of being ignored die a slow death in the workplace because they are not taken seriously. If the lions do not take you seriously, the message quickly spreads around the organization, and others at the colleague level begin to treat you as if, as one executive put it, you are "radioactive."

Some who feel that they are ignored treat it as a blessing, because they believe that it allows them to get their job done. Yet even in the best of circumstances, it does not pay to be invisible. With the lions in the office, if you do not say anything, they will ultimately assume that you have nothing to say, and they simply place you in the "ignore" category. One vice president came to this realization after successfully establishing himself in his organization, with his clients and professional community, and even as an expert who board members liked to seek out. Yet when it came to the CEO and the senior vice president whom he reported to, he appeared to have no standing, a fact increasingly evident from his shrinking budget and headcount.

In order to work closely and effectively, even if situationally, with leaders, bosses, and other tough customers, you cannot afford to be considered either prey, the enemy, or ignored. Yet, how do you deal with that? Surprisingly, it is more up to you than to the people who are the lions. You use your lion-taming skills to change your own focus from reacting as if you may be prey, the enemy, or ignored. Instead, you make it your goal to communicate to the lions—by establishing rapport, trust, and mutual respect—that it is to their advantage to have you working in support of their objectives. *You are aiming to be part of the lion's pride in the office.*

The Lion's Four Senses

> **Secrets of the Lion Tamers**
>
> *I would never understand the actions of animals unless I knew and took into account the extent to which their senses were different from mine.*

What are some of the other motivations and senses coursing through the lion's skull? How can it help us understand what the lions in the workplace are really doing and saying? Lions in the workplace of course share the senses of sight, sound, taste, touch, and smell with everyone else. But in addition they possess other special sensory abilities. It is a built-in radar system lions use to scan everyone in their path, and it works almost as well as a tool for the lion tamers to anticipate and guide the lion's thinking and behavior.

The *Lion's Four Senses* are: Dominance, Territory, Social Standing, and Survival.

Let's step closer and see the world from the mind's eye of the lions themselves. As we will see, even though they use lightening-fast instincts to react to the people and situations around them, it is based on a highly specialized intelligence that drives their perceptions and motivations, and often their beliefs and actions. These four senses form the basis for how lions in the workplace determine where they stand and whether something is a good fit for them personally.

The Lion's Four Senses

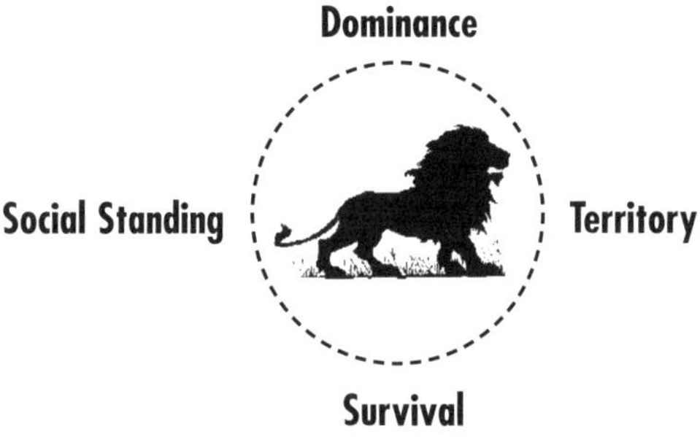

You can use the *Lion's Four Senses* as a secret decoder. Ask yourself how Dominance, Territory, Social Standing, and Survival may operate in the minds of the people you deal with. As we examine this template in greater detail, here are the four questions that the people who are the lions are asking themselves:

- What do I want to be the lion of? What do I want to reign over?
- What territory is mine to preserve, protect, or expand?
- Who knows that I am the lion?
- Do these answers raise fears about my survival?

Dominance

Dominance translates most directly into the span of authority, influence, and advantages that the lions at work perceive that they have or wish to have. It is usually seen as a privilege of rank or position. The easiest way to assess the dominance needs of the lions you encounter is to ask these questions: What does this person want to be the lion over? Is it an issue, an organization, resources, responsibility, or something else entirely?

Territory

Territory to the lions is something that they are motivated to protect, preserve, expand, or even conquer. What is it in the case of the people you work with? People, decisions, budget, clients, policies, actual physical property, perhaps even access or rights. It is often the most concrete and identifiable foundation for the influence, control, and power that they use to exercise dominance or reign over others.

Social Standing

Social standing reveals the most fundamental truth about being a lion in the workplace. There must be a social context to make the status meaningful for someone who is a lion. It answers the species-driven question of "Where do I stand as a lion?" and the broader questions of who knows that the lion is dominant and over what territory.

The issue of social standing is so interwoven with the *Lion's Four Senses* that sometimes it seems to be the purpose of being a lion at all. For some that is true, while others do not need such constant reminders that they are a lion. Yet, as we will discuss, never assume that it is out of the lion's mind, particularly in situations where you shift from one-to-one working scenarios to appearing together in public or in a group. At that point even the lion's closest allies may be seen as a threat to their social standing.

Survival

Survival underlies every one of the *Lion's Four Senses,* and in many ways is emblematic of how the lions in the workplace define success. On the one hand it could be said that dominance, territory, and social standing are the essential ingredients of anyone's survival as a lion. Any significant fear that these other elements are deficient will raise concern in the lion's mind about his or her survival, because it also is seen as a threat to their success.

Test this approach on people in the news, for example, when:

- Sports team owners fire the head coach or manager and hire another
- School superintendents fight with the mayor

- CEOs combat regulators and prosecutors
- Congress and the White House are in battle
- Political candidates take aim at one another

Since news reporting is often based on events stemming from conflict and tension between people, see if you can identify the *Lion's Four Senses* at work behind what people are saying and doing in the stories.

Now consider the *Lions Four Senses* with people you encounter at work. What do they want to reign over? What do they consider their territory to preserve, protect, or expand? Who knows that they are the lion, and what is their place in the hierarchy? How assured is their survival?

When you begin to apply the *Lion's Four Senses* to the people you encounter every day, you may begin to see ways to communicate with them that were not visible before. As a general rule, applying the *Lion's Four Senses* is a good baseline analysis of how the lions are feeling and acting. You can use it to make your own determination as to whether they should feel confident about their degree of dominance, territory, social standing, or survival—including what may need to done to shore up support in any of the four areas.

Additionally, the *Lion's Four Senses* are useful to pinpoint and possibly remedy feelings of insecurity or uncertainty. If you can help someone see that their dominance, territory, social standing, and survival are well established, they are likely to feel and act more confident.

Lastly, the *Lion's Four Senses* can be used to help the person who is the lion honestly gauge the wisdom of an idea through the way it may affect their position as a lion. While the lions may not like others telling them how to behave, they do appreciate it when people tell them that all the good things that they are doing to maintain their dominance, territory, social standing, and survival may be placed at risk because of an idea or approach they are about to undertake. In many cases, this is an advantageous way of saying "no" and still have the people who are the lions respect that you are looking out for their best interests.

Being a Lion Is Personal

What are the lessons we learn from understanding and applying the *Lion's Four Senses* in working with leaders, bosses, and other tough customers? For something to be credible to the lions in the workplace, it must be presented in a form that they can judge first-hand and assess in terms of its impact on their dominance, territory, social standing, and survival. The more concrete, the better. Lions learn whether something is good for them by sinking their teeth into it, and it is the four senses of Dominance, Territory, Social Standing, and Survival that is the first threshold test.

The result of this approach is a very personalized outlook and way of organizing the world around them. You have probably heard people say that the best way to convince the boss of something is to make it his or her idea. There is more than a kernel of truth to this, and the *Lion's Four Senses* help explain how they process something so that it does become their idea. This is not because they are trying to steal someone else's valuable thinking, but because they are deciding from first blush whether something is good for them. It happens in one swift gulp—when they sink their teeth into something to determine its relationship to their dominance, territory, social standing, and survival, they just as quickly digest it and make it a part of themselves. It is no joke—making something their own idea or rejecting it is exactly what they *are* doing!

All of the Answers, None of the Questions

Secrets of the Lion Tamers

The wonder is not that so many are killed but that so many remain alive.

Roman Proske's life as a lion tamer had a story-book beginning—he ran away from home to join the circus and become a lion tamer. As a teenager, Proske secretly left his prosperous Austrian family in the middle of the night. By the time he was twenty he had traveled to Africa, collected and trained lions, and formed his first act. He then returned to Vienna to headline in his hometown, only to be disowned by his family.

During his long career, Proske had many close calls, including almost being chomped in half. Nevertheless, he always returned to the ring. When he ultimately retired in good health and "in one piece," he admitted that he was addicted to "the drug we know as danger, the sensation of fear." Yet what did Proske think the biggest danger was to anyone entering the ring? *"Having all the answers without knowing any of the questions."* Unfortunately, this danger is also present in the workplace: ego, impatience, and overconfidence keep us from gaining the knowledge we really need to work effectively with lions.

What is the mystery to learning what makes a lion tick? How do you learn what the right questions are? Whether you are in the center ring or the boss's office, you are dealing with a different species. Let's face it, you cannot get inside the lion's skull simply by asking the usual questions: "What are they thinking? What's on their mind?" And the lions in the workplace do not believe that it is their job to tell you.

One top executive earned her position by coming up through the ranks, and as a result had the reputation of working well with her managers and the rank and file. However, she also believed in holding everyone else to the same standards she applied to herself, "because it worked for me."

What happened when people did not understand what she expected of them?

> It's the little things as much as the big ones. I am intolerant of people who hear me say that I don't like the idea or approach they have suggested but keep trying to sell me on it. I'm not going there. I like the people who get it the first time.

She knew the value of being persistent but did not believe this was one of those situations where persistence was paying off for anyone. Those who did not "get it" were left hovering in front of her desk, as she either sat expressionless or simply said, "Next idea?" When asked if she ever clues people into her likes and dislikes, she replied "No, are you kidding? That's not my job!"

So what part of the mind of the lions in the workplace gives us the clues to how they think and act? As one seasoned right-hand executive considered the question, he looked back on decades of working with different heads of companies and organizations: "Their behavior," he quickly concluded. "It isn't conscious, is it? It's instinct." *Exactly.*

Instinctive Thinking

> **Secrets of the Lion Tamers**
>
> *They are killers because they know their own strength.*

Lions in the wild and in the workplace operate by instinct. It is a unique and primal strength, both conscious and unconscious, that is shared by the lions that we encounter every day. Dictionaries define instinct as innate, unalterable, and unlearned. However, as we will see—especially in the people whose instincts are so pronounced in their thinking and their leadership—instinct is not so much unlearned as it is *self-learned.* In its most primal form, it is a highly personalized sense of knowing. It is the very core of the lions' confidence, and often is what propels them into our lives!

Anthropologist James T. Brink had the benefit of observing real lions on the plains of Africa and then spending years working among and observing the hungry denizens of New York's Madison Avenue business community. He said:

> Instinctive thinking is the core component of how the people who resemble lions in the office operate. They know what works for them and what doesn't. They know the line between what they want to do and what they don't want to do. Everything else is irrelevant. They are not looking for a paradigm. They are the paradigm!

For such people, it is not their only way of thinking. In leaders, it is not their only form of leadership. Yet it is much more than a sign of active intuition. Instinctive thinking and behavior is a dominant characteristic, significantly more pronounced and critical to their existence than in anyone else we encounter. As a result, it is worthwhile to magnify the characteristics and significance of instinct in the leaders and bosses around us, and the impact they have on everyone around them.

Every lion tamer in the office needs to be acutely aware of this. It is an important part of the lion's personal tool kit and its ability to simultaneously explore, learn, decide, and act. Even curiosity has consequences, sometimes serious ones. After all, with a lion's curiosity comes the whole lion!

There is a speed to how lions assess something, passionate and devoid of patience, sinking their teeth in to get the information they need as quickly as possible. It explains why real lion tamers recognize that "intense curiosity leads to quick attacks." In the office, a lion's curiosity can be punctuated by quick decisions, even important ones. To others it can appear that they are jumping to conclusions. But in their minds, the lions have sensed something, rolled it around in their brains, created a specific response, and BOOM! The gap between observation and action is much smaller than in most people. They map situations and act very quickly. One mid-level manager described her leader's style like this: "He's usually right, but he just leaps!"

A word of caution: while the primacy of instinctive thinking and behavior is crucial to appreciate, it may also take some time, careful observation, and a variety of experiences to do so. This is not because it is difficult to grasp; rather, it is because instinctive thinking and behavior is manifested as part of the personalities of the lions—revealed in the course of their actions and reactions.

To avoid the fate of the lion tamers who rush into the cage without preparing—the ones Roman Proske described as "knowing all the answers without knowing any of the questions"—do not rush to grab the idea of instinctive thinking and behavior and to categorize it. Let it become absorbed into your way of thinking about the leaders, bosses, and other tough customers as you interact with them. We can sometimes hear and see it acknowledged. Looking and listening for it will help you do your job, including how to tell the difference between good instincts and bad.

Take, for example, a prominent executive speaking at a leadership conference. Without any notes, yet standing before an audience of almost 1,500 executives and managers, he succinctly defines his own style: "I like to operate by instincts—our gut often tells us the right thing to do." Or consider the CEO who handpicked a new senior vice president to "take control of strategy, people, and customers." Yet within weeks, the CEO bypassed the new vice president's authority to assign special projects to his best staff, recruited a new mid-level manager for the vice president's division, and berated a major customer. When the vice president got up the courage to ask the CEO to explain all these moves, he candidly responded, "That's how I think. I react. I do."

It is evident in politics as well, where a candidate in a tight election race was asked how he calculated his chances of winning or losing into his strategy: "I actually usually don't envision myself losing or winning. I just envision the next step."

In these cases and others, instinctive thinking is not simply innate and involuntary, it is automatic and purposeful. Rather than thinking that instinct is essentially reactive, it is perhaps useful to recognize instinct as the engine that drives people in a direction. It takes the lions where they want to go in life. In fact, they cannot live without instinctive thinking and behavior. It may be their most valuable tool.

For survival purposes, the lions in the workplace must be able to gather themselves together just that quickly—from a deep sleep to a fighting stance in the blink of an eye. "Uncuddly but decisive" is how one boss was described. Another was nicknamed "The Stiletto" because, "He could turn on you at any second, and no one knew what the motivation was." Sometimes you don't know what prompts their behavior—remember, lions act differently because they think differently. But if you keep an awareness of instinctive thinking in your mind, you will begin to better understand the lion's behavior.

The Instinctive Identity

> **Secrets of the Lion Tamers**
>
> *They don't have to be mad at you to go after you. It's just instinct.*

Inside the lion's skull, instinct drives their behavior not merely to live another day but to survive and live *as a lion in lion society*. After all, the lions are not trying to establish themselves among the antelope, zebras, and wildebeest—*they* already "get it." The political battles are not between predator and prey, but over the social order—dominance, territory, and standing—among the predators themselves and in relation to the hunt, the kill, and the spoils. In the workplace, that often means that the lions react to the people in the same organization who are lions.

Nonetheless, as people we must work together, sometimes closely. Therefore, it is essential to recognize some of the characteristics that differentiate the lion's instinctive thinking and behavior. Doing so is also essential to fostering a unique ability that is fundamental to lion taming in the center ring or in the office.

The Instinctive Identity

The people who are the lions around us have an *Instinctive Identity* that enables us to recognize instinctive leaders in all professions, occupations, and walks of life by the way they think and act.

- They are multidimensional thinkers.
- They are adaptive learners.
- They are focused on doing.
- They must demonstrate their strength with speed and quickness in an up-front manner.

It is important to note that instinctive thinking and behavior is a cumulative phenomenon and these four parts must add up. When they do, these qualities distinguish the true lions around us—especially from the people who are merely impulsive, unscripted, or spontaneous, or worse, the people pretending that they are acting instinctively when in fact they are just "winging it."

The lions at work who are truly instinctive in their thinking and behavior display an intelligence, a *modus operandi* tested repeatedly by experience, which they rely on to ensure a continuous series of successful transitions throughout life. It often is not conscious, except to the extent that they are aware that they have a way of getting things done that is their own—unique and invaluable to the task at hand.

Their instinctive and adaptive thinking enables them to take on the world, sense the value and use of what they see and hear, and, if necessary, replace or add to the catalog of information on which they rely. They quickly integrate ideas and action to address whatever is at hand. Inside their minds, instinct and adaptation work together at a speed that allows the lions in the workplace to form a complex and specific response and then impose an interpretative framework on what strikes others as merely disparate facts and events. All the while a lion's mind is quietly busy, and when it is time, the lion acts!

Let's take a closer look at each of these qualities: multidimensional thinking; adaptive learning; focus on doing; and up-front behavior.

Multidimensional Thinking

> **Secrets of the Lion Tamers**
>
> *That lions have a good visual and auditory memory is an established fact.*

Many people have broad interests, can focus on several things at once, and can "multitask" effectively. Instinctive thinkers grasp every detail combining and connecting facts, information, and events into something meaningful in the blink of an eye.

While often our own instinct and respect for bosses is not to be too nosy about the details behind their work and lives, the best lion tamers in the office have a radar system that is always on. They have an active information-and-intelligence network. However, what they are looking for is not simply advance information and intelligence, but rather information, strategies, and decisions that arise from many sources of experience to integrate with their own thinking. For instinctive thinkers and leaders, the true context of a discussion is not necessarily confined to that moment in time, that day, or even the four walls of the room. Such people can sometimes amaze others precisely because they can, as one Fortune 500 CEO described, "digest unfamiliar facts, balance complex competing claims with little or no context, and make a snap decision."

They think in multiple issues, such as a member of Congress debating what seems like a narrow issue of a commuter tax. It sounds one-dimensional, but in her mind the outcome must be analyzed in terms of costs to businesses and workers, impact on the environment, and even local issues of traffic congestion.

Their minds are multidimensional in other ways, traversing a wide range of people, facts, places, experiences, and thoughts from the past, present, and into the future. For example, the chairman and chief executive of a large and well-known company found his successful but tradition-bound company at odds with the dot-com era. Acknowledging that the world had changed quickly, he still needed to reconcile his personal doubts about the permanence of the new economy:

> I didn't believe the hype around the Internet, but people kept telling me, "You just don't get it." But I saw parallels to the real estate bubble in Manhattan in the 1980s when...I lost a lot of money. That helped me get through by refocusing our mission.

That meant a new strategy, direction, and use of technology. But he also focused the mission on a society technologically changed in a less prosperous economy. He factored his doubts about the economic bubble into his thinking, and as a result refocused the company but did not overextend it or abandon its core mission to keep pace with the dot-com revolution. When the bubble burst, the company was well positioned.

How did the CEO know that he had all the right information and knowledge to make the decision, refocus the company, and time it successfully as he did? The same question could be asked a million times of people who make important decisions. He used multidimensional thinking.

Adaptive Learning

> **Secrets of the Lion Tamers**
>
> *Lions have a faultless eye.*

While instinct is defined as inherited and unalterable, we often see people using their brains and abilities to learn to do something so naturally that it *becomes* instinctive. As former Boston Red Sox manager Jimy Williams once quipped, "It takes years of practice to be able to do something instinctively." He was not far off. Instinct can be learned and enables us to adapt, compensate, and handle new and changing situations. In fact, adaptive learning can make a guess an educated one or make a decision an informed one. It may be among the least visible and most important reasons why people who are instinctive leaders and thinkers are constantly collecting and processing new information. It is often their way of continuously preparing in advance. It reflects an adaptive intelligence that is an important component of instinctive thinking and behavior.

It helps explain how such people seem to absorb new experiences and information as the world unfolds before them. They learn from everyone, and seem to have a sixth sense. The closer you get to them, the more there is to discover. What you see from up close is exactly how they have absorbed the world unfolding before them, sorted it out, and adapted it to their own rich and multidimensional view of the world.

Focus on Doing

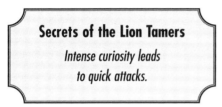

Secrets of the Lion Tamers

Intense curiosity leads to quick attacks.

If you ask the lions what makes them tick, they can tell you a great deal about themselves, relate experiences, and recall many details of what they have learned and who they know. However, it is hard for lions who rely so heavily on instinct to explain how they think. They are focused on *doing*.

However, this does not mean that they do not see the value of understanding how people learn, train, and prepare to do their jobs. Having people with the right education, specialization, training, and resources is widely accepted as one of the best practices of successful organizations of any kind. If anything, the idea of the office becoming a "learning organization" is becoming a strategic necessity, resulting in recent years in hiring in-house experts at the executive level called the Chief Learning Officer.

This, however, only adds to the mystery of understanding and working with the lions in the workplace. Lions as individuals, even those who run organizations and hire Chief Learning Officers, do not concentrate on how they are learning something or formulating ideas. In their minds, it all transacts too quickly and too intuitively to explain. It would be like asking a jazz musician who improvises to repeat the exact notes and explain why the sounds interrelate. It would take all the art out of it—so too with leaders, bosses, and others who think instinctively.

However, there is another important and less visible dimension to the fact that the lions in the workplace are focused on doing. Some would say it is just impatience, and that the lions are too eager to move quickly. Their moves are not for the sake of movement alone. In fact, they may be to gain more experience to be prepared when they really must demonstrate their instinctive speed and strengths. Doing is a form of preparing, because *the lions in the workplace learn from doing.*

Unlike others, they are not afraid to act, because they know they have to sink their teeth into something to feel what it is. As a result, they are sometimes much more comfortable than others with getting into real situations to apply their minds to it as they become involved. They consider learning as a profitable experience in and of itself. This explains why the best lions seem to have so many more experiences that taught them lessons, many of which they share with others.

Up-front Behavior

> **Secrets of the Lion Tamers**
>
> *A lion's power is so much a part of its character—it is overpowering.*

Lions place so much value on acting instinctively because so much of what is involved in being a lion happens "up front." It is visible on the surface of their personality and behavior, yet it is not superficial at all. It is linked to something much deeper inside of them, inside their souls, and inside their skulls.

As writer Evelyn Ames observed and wrote about lions and humans in her book *A Glimpse of Eden:*

> Lions are not animals alone: they are symbols and totems and legends; they have impressed themselves so deeply on the human mind, if not its blood, it is as though the psyche was emblazoned with their crest.

The human psyche is indeed emblazoned with the lion's crest, worn on the chest of those we encounter, expressed through instinctive thinking and behavior.

There may be no other way to describe it but to say that lions have an instinct to act instinctively—sensing from deep within them that their speed, behavior, and credibility are linked as an equation in the eyes of others. It is visible in lightning-fast reactions to complex relationships and dynamics. It can quickly add up to success or failure, and everyone knows it.

Importantly, however, the determining factor between success or failure is not simply whether the lions think or act instinctively, but whether they can act and think when others need to see them do so. Such behavior energizes others, gets people charged up, and connects with them at their gut.

How does it play out before us? When selecting or following people to resolve conflict or ease crisis around us, an up-front display of speed, strength, and thinking is so primal, powerful, and essential in our own minds. Perhaps one reason that the talent in leaders, bosses, and other tough customers for instinctive thinking and behavior remains less visible to the naked eye is ironically because we are the ones who consciously or unconsciously look for such qualities when we need them. Conflicts and crises trigger this effect in us, but so do some inherent and even subconscious qualities of our own. It is a hidden indicator in our own minds, not just the minds of the lions around us. In the people we choose to follow, we often must see the lion emblazoned on their chest.

It is a tendency that is neither bound by country, language, or culture. In some ways, it is as primal as the instinctive behavior of leaders and bosses themselves. It may even explain how leaders get elected or chosen, how executives get hired—from CEOs to school principals—how we react to lions in the workplace, and who we are. As one seasoned and philosophical executive succinctly observed, "When we sense a need for energy, momentum, or leadership, we look elsewhere."

We look for these qualities in people and often find them. Sometimes this means assenting without acknowledging all the consequences that will follow—even when we have the knowledge or experience to do so. As another experienced executive observed:

> There are traits that we expect the leaders and bosses to exhibit. We expect some strong impulsive instinctive behavior. It's part of how they evolve. We have respect for "action" not passivity, even when they make the wrong choice or decision.

People still have a need to "see it to believe it." Consider this example.

Executive Rite of Passage

A company needed to select a new division chief for an important and untapped market. The selection process created such a brutal internal succession battle, which exposed deep loyalties, that the CEO decided to hire someone from outside the company.

Several weeks into the job, this new division chief was asked to present his own market strategy to the company's top executives—including two internal candidates who battled for his job and lost. No one wanted to miss this meeting, though no one knew what would happen. Some people even suspected that "the new guy is being ambushed."

Indeed, the new division chief was aware that while technically he had the job, he also needed to win the confidence of the corporate suite on a live stage, with the unspoken requirement that he must do so with a display of up-front speed and strength. The meeting was a primal ceremony, although everyone was wearing a suit and tie. The new executive was a consummate professional, friendly, even willing to be overlooked.

When he started the meeting, he surprised everyone by asking his inside competitors to provide their perspective on the challenges ahead. The most senior of the two—the one everyone thought "deserved the job"—began to speak.

The new division chief calmly waited, watched the room until the executives relaxed, being put at ease by the familiarity of the board room, the arrangement of everyone in their usual seats around the table, and the voice of a familiar colleague. Suddenly but smoothly, the new division chief stood up and politely sliced the air, interrupting the executive. He rapidly shifted everyone's attention, making eye contact only with the CEO, and panning the room. Never looking the executive who was speaking in the eye, even when he tried to regain the floor, the new division chief simply held one arm outstretched, like a traffic cop calmly waking into a busy intersection as if to say, "I'll take it from here." And he did.

When the meeting ended, no one remembered much about the new strategy or vision, but they unanimously concluded, "*He's* the guy!"

While instinct goes well beyond the innate ability to divine between life and death, instinctive thinking is necessarily born from the drive to survive. When displayed, it is always imbued with the sense that something more is at stake. The lions of the workplace share the same image as the lions who lead the prides on the African plains—providing protection, getting fed, creating an organization in their own image, and engendering fear and respect in others.

Working with Instinctive Thinkers

Instinctive thinkers are exciting people to work with and for. Make it easy for them to work with you—even if you are already working right in front of them. Recognize their instinctive qualities and needs, learn where they are headed, and be the person who helps them to prepare in advance so that they can act instinctively and successfully. Be a valuable source of information and experiences for the lion to incorporate into his or her instinctive thought and behavior, but do so in a way that is compatible with the four dimensions of instinctive thinking and leadership.

As ***multidimensional thinkers*** they are capable of juggling a variety of related perspectives and interrelationships between people, information, and events. Be clear and organized in how you present something to them, but do not be one-dimensional. Include perspectives from others whose opinion they might respect or want to consider, and do not be boring.

As ***adaptive learners*** they are keenly interested in how change will affect them and are often interested in how they can use change to their advantage. Always be up front about the possibility of change, the factors that you believe are determinative, and the opportunities and advance preparation that may be required to be ready. Then be ready to help them prepare in advance so that they can both act instinctively and absorb new information while moving at the same time. From their standpoint, *some part of everything they learn about will be assessed and possibly extracted for its intrinsic and instinctive meaning and application.* How they search for and detect such information may be more telling about how you help inform and prepare them than many other qualities about their care and feeding.

As people who are ***focused on doing*** they are not afraid to do things, and while they have their own sense of risk related to their position and status as lions, they are much more prone and interested in learning by doing. Since they do not spend time analyzing their own learning process, when you work with them it is not productive to spend as much time explaining how you are going to do something, or how they are going to do something. Instead, put them into the action as quickly as possible. If there is a role for them to play from either a strategic or implementation standpoint, turn these into action steps for them to be involved in. They are more willing to take risks in many situations because they know that by sinking their teeth into something they will learn, even if it is not considered a success. Do not spoon feed a lion. They will lose interest quickly. As one person found out after emailing his boss a brief but direction-setting memo on an issue: "It was not so much the brilliance of the idea but the fact that I got it to him first, in time for him to make it his own." Sometimes you need to give them the chance to do so. If you can help it, avoid hovering and trying to elicit a response.

As people who must demonstrate their instinctive speed and strength up front, it is crucial that these lions use but do not abuse the opportunities to demonstrate their instinctive thinking and behavior publicly. This includes on the internal level amongst the people who consider them to be the executive or person in charge, and in an external and more public arena, even among other lions. The crucial point to remember—especially if you are dealing with a lion that is content, insular, isolated, or lacks visibility in their role—is the social importance of instinctive thinking and leadership. The value of the lions that fall into this category is not simply the triumph of a brilliant or intuitive mind, but the degree and manner in which others learn to look to them. It may result from the way they run a meeting where people walk away saying "I like the way she thinks" or seeing someone in a more public capacity and concluding that "I trust him."

Different Learning Styles Require Patience and Adjustment

There have been presidents of the United States who preferred to be briefed by videos. Others were famous for spending late hours sifting through documents in the Oval Office and calling their Cabinet members in the middle of the night to provide the answer to a question. The range is equally as broad elsewhere.

For example, one CEO preferred to work and meet with his top executives at his desk in a stream-of-consciousness fashion using people to punctuate his thoughts. As one executive commented, "We felt like commas in his day." But one of the senior executives figured out how to break that train of thought. It was a surprising technique but it worked. The CEO did not mind having executives come in and out of his office. So one day the senior executive simply went into the CEO's office, and instead of interrupting him, he wrote a number on the CEO's whiteboard and walked out. Sometime later, the CEO called and asked him to come in. When the executive sat down, the CEO leaned back fully relaxed and said, "Okay, tell me why I need to know this." This became an important and effective part of their communication repertoire.

However, the head of another organization judged the value of the information she was fed by its weight. Her Monday morning "executive session" was clearly feeding time. As one of her top executives related:

> The boss thought it was her right to know and her job to understand any information that was guiding the direction of the organization. On Monday mornings her eyes lit up as she opened the meeting with "What do you have for me today?" She was very thorough, and it was amazing what she could do with what you gave her, but it wore a lot of people out in the process.

As you consider the style of the people you work with, keep in mind how they think, what their instinctive strengths and tendencies are, and what they are likely to glean from what you give them. Is it what you intended? How do you think they might expand or extrapolate from the material, and whether they expect it or not, will they need additional help once they do so?

Recognizing that the instinctive qualities of the lions in the workplace are an important part of what makes them unique is a vital step. Now that you understand this, let's find out how it puts them at the top of the food chain and what this means for the lion tamers in the workplace.

THE LION'S TALE

Prey, the Enemy, or Ignored

- Identify the people that the lions view as prey, the enemy, or ignored.
- Acknowledge how you are viewed and how you want to be viewed.
- Identify the people who are viewed in another category, such as part of the lion's pride, and the role that they perform.

The Lion's Four Senses: Dominance, Territory, Social Standing, and Survival

- Describe the Lion's Four Senses in the lions you work most closely with.
- Identify how others would evaluate them using the Lion's Four Senses.

The Instinctive Identity

- *Instinctive Thinking and Leadership.* Help the lions prepare in advance so that their instinctive thinking can be used more effectively.
  - ◆ *Multidimensional thinking.* Always be able to discuss and approach issues by presenting several ideas, perspectives, and even competing approaches. However, it is just as important to avoid being confusing as it is not to be one-dimensional. If you do, you will risk losing their attention and confidence.
  - ◆ *Adaptive learning.* Treat change as an opportunity for the lions to demonstrate their instinctive thinking. However if they are unprepared for change to occur, they consider it both an unwarranted surprise and a lost opportunity to maintain their presence as a lion, or even seize an advantage in a new situation. This will draw their anger and distrust.

(continued)

- *Focused on doing.* Remember that "doing" includes learning by doing. Do not spend inordinate amounts of time describing process, either a process for them or for you. Even if working on a plan together, put them into the action first, then cover the specifics of what they will be doing and the desired result or outcome. Do not hesitate to provide them with opportunities to learn by doing, whether it is sinking their teeth into a subject at a meeting, in a discussion, meeting new people, or leading a new project or issue.
- *Demonstrating up-front instinctive and intuitive strength and speed.* Others need to "see it to believe it." People need to see the lion emblazoned on the person's chest! Identify the specific role and context in which they must demonstrate their instinctive and intuitive strength in an up-front manner to establish credibility with others both internally, to command respect for how they think, and externally so that others see an authentic leader worth following.

3

The Top of the Food Chain

> **Secrets of the Lion Tamers**
>
> *The lion is at the top of the food chain and has no need to be afraid. The lion has a "big cat mentality."*

The higher up people are in the food chain at work, the more opportunities there are to apply instinctive talents and abilities. In fact, people who hire leaders look for that quality, even if subconsciously. Does it appear in job descriptions? No. Does it appear on resumes? No. It is something much more palpable yet subtle: chemistry.

The crucial components of instinctive behavior in leaders and bosses—*multidimensional thinking, adaptive learning, focus on doing, and an "up front" show of speed and strength*—constitute the profile of people who rise through the ranks. It is their credential for joining the other lions on the pyramid. Indeed, it is often the ability of such people to handle themselves instinctively among the other lions that gets them the job—especially if they present themselves as one of the lions but do not challenge the hierarchy of lions. In some situations, "all other things" are not really equal—skills, experience, expertise, or the person's track record—but the person still gets the job. What has happened? The lions that are handling the interviewing and doing the hiring get the sense from meetings and often from references provided by others at their level (other lions) that the person is "one of us." Sometimes it is a good result, and sometimes it is not.

Nature versus Nurture

Secrets of the Lion Tamers

It is self-confidence in your mastery of the traits and behavior that you need, not self-confidence that you can control the lion.

The fact that instinctive traits are often perceived as an eligibility requirement at the top of the food chain is only part of the equation. There exists something of a nature-versus-nurture puzzle.

Positions at the top of the food chain bring out the instinctive and lion-like qualities in people. We sometimes see it in people that we may not have thought were lions in the workplace, but somehow a promotion upwards in the food chain breathes new fire into them. In fact, in many cases, from corporate and other organizational executives all the way to candidates for the president of the United States, we want to be assured that the job will transform them into a lion when it is most needed.

The lions in the workplace pursue the positions that move to the top of food chain because they want the opportunity to apply their instinctive strengths, knowledge, and ability to work. It is not merely a freedom that they seek, but a sense that they need it to be at their best. Their instinctive capabilities are also part of their persona, and they know it. They know that these qualities make them unique, make them who they are. As a result, they are looking to throw themselves into their jobs. They take ownership of the position because the position absorbs, is transformed, and is identified with their persona.

Instinctive thinkers and leaders recognize that the top of the food chain enables them to be lions, operate instinctively, and do so to a degree that will be recognized and rewarded as a talent. They want to have the freedom to do what they instinctively think and recognize is necessary. That knowledge is something they come to the job already possessing, a set of actions honed in another context, and it is embedded in their personality. Even in specific situations where an executive is hired at the top of the food chain to get a job done or lift a heavy weight, the lions hired for such jobs need the creative freedom to do things the way they think are necessary. It is no small coincidence to see articles in business journals with titles such as "Successful Execs Create Their Own Opportunities." What have we learned that is really driving these people? The lions in the workplace negotiate a territory and an area of influence and authority. They create opportunities in part because it is an opportunity to be themselves, to use their business personality. Regardless of the occupation, it is the personality that makes them who they are in their profession. Whether consciously asked or not, it comes down to one gut threshold question: *Do I have the freedom to operate instinctively, and, if so, to what degree?*

At the top of the food chain the lion has a "big cat mentality" and has no need to be afraid. In the workplace, the "big cat mentality" is visible in the lion's confidence that he or she has the ability and freedom to be instinctively decisive and that this is a prerequisite, not an entitlement, of the job. For the good and great lions in the workplace, it is also a responsibility to use appropriately. Instinct complements the lion's other personal qualities, strengths, and experiences.

Instinctive thinking is one of the most distinct and important "species characteristics" of the lions. As one lion tamer observed, "The whole art and science of lion taming revolves around species characteristics."

Lessons of the Lion Tamers

Lion Tamers Accept the Lion's Inherent Traits, But Not Blindly

Lion tamers study the lion's inherent traits, simultaneously weighing the lion's individual manner, and use this knowledge to satisfy the lion's needs in order to get to the next step. They develop knowledge of how lions will act and interact with other lions, *and with people.*

Let's look at how our understanding of the lion's trait of instinctive thinking can help us satisfy the lion's needs and get to the next steps in working more effectively together.

The Lion Establishes the Territory

Secrets of the Lion Tamers

Lions can run 100 yards in three seconds—when you are in a forty-foot cage they can nail you before you can say 'oops!'

The primacy of the lion's instinctive abilities poses an important irony that explains why the lions in the workplace need good lion tamers around them. The lions establish their territory, but it is your job to create the environment for them to be effective, feel safe, and perform well. That includes scanning and interpreting the world around the lion, even applying the lion's own two-tier radar of *prey, the enemy, or ignored* and the *Lion's Four Senses* of dominance, territory, social standing, and survival. All the while, the people who are the lions are honing in on their own meaningful stimuli and variables. Others around them must provide institutional knowledge, clear descriptions of the status quo, and "how things really are," because the lions in the workplace are often more focused on how the world around them *should* look.

The lion tamer's role also includes knowing when it is most appropriate for the lion's instinctive thinking and behavior to be demonstrated. Sometimes it is not, and your job is to candidly but respectfully say so. Do not forget that even though in the complete cycle of instinctive thinking and behavior it is the "up front" display of speed and strength that convinces others, such behavior is also public and visible. That can create consequences you need to consider. When the CEO acts, it is a much more celebrated fact than if someone less conspicuous carries it out. Sometimes you want that bigger emphasis, and sometimes you do not. You need to know when to keep the lion in the cage!

In the process of assessing the lion's instinctive strengths, you will also begin to recognize the weaknesses, and the challenging role that this creates. When should you take steps to minimize or subdue these behaviors? There may be times when this can and should be done. However, just as in real lion taming, it can be very dangerous. Sometimes when it seems most blatant, reacting might make it even more blatant and more dangerous. Sometimes a good lion tamer will just have to let the boss's weaknesses go. Other times these traits must be dealt with—sooner rather than later.

The Lion Tamer Creates the Environment

> **Secrets of the Lion Tamers**
>
> *Movements must be quick and sure, an important thing to remember.*

The lion's instinctive drive can be a strong influence on everyone. However, it does not necessarily manifest itself the way you would think, and for many reasons you cannot afford to just sit and wait for orders. The lions in the workplace are self-starters, and they expect others around them to be self-starters too. However, it is a combination of your individual assistance and your ability to help facilitate a larger state of organizational readiness that makes a difference to them.

Your job is to create an environment in which the lion feels comfortable operating. As one executive described the job of the people working closest to him, "I need people who can create situations where leadership can see where to go and not feel threatened getting there." Even the lions recognize that the more times they get things right, the more secure their own territory and position becomes. The lion tamer helps them build on their instinctive abilities, adapt successfully, and create new strengths to be displayed. Just like real lion tamers, you are building confidence, shaping leaders not followers, and then standing back as they leap through the hoop of fire. ***You are always presenting the lion, not the other way around.***

Watch your boss in action. Observe his or her strengths and weaknesses. Ask yourself what your boss's instinctive traits are—both positive and negative. Apply the *Lion's Four Senses* at both the macro and micro level, including seeing what the boss is personally and instinctively attracted to. At the same time, be prepared to answer some tougher questions. Where necessary, appropriate, and helpful, ask others who are involved to come up with some useful answers. Lion tamers in the office bring the lion's instinctive strengths to life in their job by effectively doing some of the following:

- *Using multidimensional thinking.* Feed them the information, updates, and intelligence they need and are interested in.
- *Learning adaptively.* Help them continue to be learning, adapting, and preparing in advance so that they can operate instinctively to a greater and more responsive degree. Give them the freedom to use their adaptive intelligence.

- *Focusing on doing.* Identify, suggest, lead, and provide opportunities to get involved and feel, sense, and sink in their teeth. Create opportunities for them to "do" something as a way for them to train and to learn—from meeting people to considering an issue or a problem. Even a meeting on an issue is a way for them to be learning while doing.
- *Displaying their behavior up front.* Create opportunities for the lions to show their instinctive strengths up front, visible to others, especially others whom the lion wants to be seen by. Know who those people or what those situations are.

Considering the Environment

What are some of the conditions of the environment? To the lions in the workplace, an environment that has opportunities in which they can operate instinctively is extremely important. Remember that being a lion in the workplace is personal. They select the jobs to perform according to their personal interests and potential, and they measure success in terms of themselves. They often perceive organizations or the world in which they work as the platform for them to be the lion and as the territory that they reign over.

Perhaps even more important is how they see everyone's job around them. It is reflected in the specific responsibilities, duties, or actions they are prepared to undertake, those they do not choose to handle, and the ones they need other people to perform. As we have emphasized, one of the secrets to the success of instinctive thinkers and leaders is that they prepare in advance to be successful. They often use the people and organizations around them to achieve that state of personal readiness.

Leaders, bosses, and other tough customers are driving, commanding, and often demanding that the people around them help them achieve. The best bosses go one step further, constantly urging workers—through expectations, strategy, and leadership—not just to support their bosses but to achieve a high level of organizational readiness. Consider the number of people and positions dedicated to both of these channels of activity every day where you work.

So, before you can accurately determine how lions learn, discover what kind of information they need, and communicate with them effectively, you must be able to close the gap between *attention getting* and *attention using.* You must know how to get their attention and hold it, and then together with the person who is the lion, be able to do it on cue.

As we will see, it is one of the very first steps in real lion taming, and comes as a surprise to many people because it explains why lions are put on a pedestal. Instead of creating the impression that the lions are even bigger and more invincible, it is the lion tamer's way to meet the lion's primal need for dominance and being secure in that feeling. Then, and perhaps only then, will the lion begin to pay attention.

If the environment is not right, the lions at work may avoid situations even where others see a great fit between the lion's instincts, effectivencss, and new opportunities. It is not only found in weighing initiatives, decisions, and actions, but also alliances, relationships, and responsibilities—including some that everyone assumed the lions were hired to handle. It can be puzzling to people around them.

The Lion in the Daisies

In the following story, a group of employees receives some unexpected results from a proposal to a top executive and leader that they work for, but also learns something in the process that is characteristic of the lions in the workplace.

Instinctive Opportunity Knocks

The head of a major think tank is known for his ability to focus lawmakers and other leaders on future obligations of government to society and the world in changing times. A major address to leaders in Washington is being prepared to that very audience, and in the course of his preparation his staff recommends using the speech to attract a wider audience—the lawmakers and leaders who make decisions about spending and programs, plus the people outside of Washington who are the first to feel the impact of such policies.

His top staff sees the speech as an opportunity to expand his territory and to bring together and prevent some of the problems that are so difficult to reverse once set into motion. However, the staff's proposal elicits only red lines drawn through the "new" names that are added to the list of invitees.

Why wouldn't this leader stray from the heart of his territory, as his staff had hoped? The parallels to the lions in the wild, especially their physical occupation and use of space, can provide some very valuable insights. It is as if we are watching ourselves operate in a primal state. Lions in the wild, particularly the males who lead the prides, become intimately familiar with every hill and contour that forms the heart of the territory over which they reign. That knowledge comes from focusing their time and movement on a specific part of the area, using other means such as their deep resonant roar or other lions in the pride to establish and maintain larger territorial boundaries.

They know the smaller area so well that they can respond physically to threats, maintain their position without hesitation, know the terrain, and literally know which way the wind is blowing at any moment to detect the movements of friends and enemies. Studies show that the pattern of male lions' travel is a *daisy* pattern, keeping the heart of the territory the center of their focus and sense of security, and making short forays outward and back.

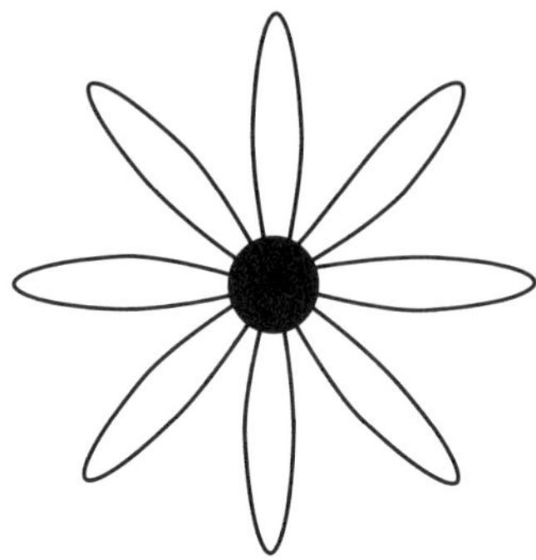

Is this sounding familiar? If we step back and look at leaders and bosses, we can often see well-defined and sometimes confined patterns of movement and relationships, well-worn routes to get to places, and even specific zones for particular activities. The lions of the workplace have a very vivid sense of their own domain. *It is a topography that is embedded in their minds.* The daisy pattern is their strategy for defending their position. But also, in their minds, it is a strategy against isolation. It may sound simple, but it is a lesson from the lions in the wild: know the terrain and inhabitants closest to them. If they are much further away, you may not be able to do anything about them anyway. Leaders who fail to adhere to this lesson are sometimes the first to fall.

The daisy pattern shows the intensity and frequency of the pattern of interaction with people in close proximity that can provide information or assistance. This can include people both inside and outside the organization. Lion tamers in the office are often perplexed by this behavior and believe they have to break the lion of the pattern. Instead, they need to make sure that the daisy includes the right people, and adjust or broaden it when it doesn't.

But suppose there is no daisy pattern, or just a very small one—maybe just a few petals of the pattern? This can be a sign of either extreme isolation or the exact opposite—a boss who roams all over the territory. The roaming boss may need help from the lion tamer to feel secure in his position and learn to make more effective use of resources and his presence in the office. Are the resources lacking? Are the means of establishing such a presence unavailable? If their primary world really is external to the organization, you can help them be more effective as lions by ensuring that they also have people in their daisy pattern who are internal to the organization.

Realities, Limits, and Dangers

> **Secrets of the Lion Tamers**
> *With lions, you just never know!*

As we have said from the outset, lions are never tame. This applies equally to the leaders, bosses, and other tough customers we encounter every day. There are always certain nonnegotiable realities that you have to be prepared to accept and deal with. While many of the ironies of their predictably enigmatic traits can provide insights into how to work more effectively with the lions, other qualities remain a challenge. For example, as important as instinctive thinking and abilities are to the lions, this can also create limitations.

Individual instinctive strengths can sometimes be weaknesses. Instinctive thinkers can pull information from many sources and directions all at once. However, some people are capable of pulling the information or searching for it without having the ability to organize it. Some may simply have too much information—past, present, and even a sense of the future—swirling in their minds to focus or make a timely decision. They may be more perceptive and insightful than is necessary to arrive at the right answer. Just as in real lion taming, the lions in the workplace need others around them who know their strengths and weaknesses, help them prepare in advance, and focus and channel their energies so they can leap through hoops of fire without any visible assistance.

Others who may have all the right ideas and understanding cannot organize themselves to display their strengths convincingly to others. Others still may be all show and no substance.

Instinctive leadership that is effective in crisis may breed a climate of crisis. Some lions are good leaders in a crisis. But no viable organization or situation can remain stable and successful in a constant state of crisis. There are people who specialize in leading organizations through crises (such as corporate turn-around specialists), and others are better as overall leaders in the day-to-day management and operations of stable organizations. The needs and forces that surround the need for leadership often attract a range of people, including those whose best instincts do come out in a crisis. Whether they know it or not, in some cases these people are prone to create a crisis mentality around themselves.

Such people tend to use conflict and crisis to resolve a problem whether it is called for or not. In some cases, crisis is used as a distraction, to avoid dealing with the real problems. Everyone around them is kept off-balance, sometimes even fighting with each other. Others truly go to war to showcase the instinctive thinking and behavior we equate with leadership; it amounts to feigned "up-front" behavior. Of course, the worst leader creates a crisis and can't lead anyone out of it or end it.

The same instincts and intuition, even genius, that give rise to a great idea can limit its viability and success. Perhaps one of the most fatal weaknesses of leadership is the inability to adapt to change. "Founders Disease" is an excellent example. Founders of companies or organizations have been known to maintain a stranglehold on their businesses by continuing to rely on instincts that were essential to start the venture, but not to grow it. The approach and style that worked at the beginning unfortunately become outmoded, and everyone is aware of this but the founder. Their personal paradigm is no longer the organizational paradigm, but from where they sit nothing has changed.

They Stayed at the Table Too Long

High-tech start-ups in the dot-com era in Silicon Valley provide some of the most recent examples of this. Some people had the instinctive ability to launch companies, but could not run them. Failure could be just as fast-paced as success. One Silicon Valley executive observed it all from inside the executive suite at the height of the dot-com revolution: ten years, four companies, start-ups, IPOs (initial public offerings), mergers and buy-outs, stock-price highs, stock-price lows, bone-chilling stock-price crashes, and even one company that made a phoenix-like rise from the ashes. What was the barometer for success? "It was not so much the genius of the idea," explained the executive, rather "*how long the founders stayed at the table.* Most stay too long." They put ideas in play—from the simple to the complex—but were frequently mystified by the highly dynamic environments in which they were operating.

The inherently personal nature of being a lion in the workplace can lead people in positions high up on the food chain to forget that there is always a supporting structure, framework, or organization that also defines their dominance as the lion.

Sometimes in the name of accruing more power, these very people bypass the need to become intimately familiar with their existing terrain, to be realistic and honest about the support that they need in order to remain in place, as well as to detect potential threats. Here is one good example in which the head of one organization just barely saved himself from sacrificing his entire reign and every inch of his terrain—all in the name of giving himself greater control and influence over the means by which decisions were made in his organization…or at least so he thought.

The Solar-Powered Board Chair

The chairman of a federal regulatory agency worked together with a board of fellow regulators and policy makers—all appointed by the President of the United States and confirmed by the United States Senate. The chairman was the chief executive, but any regulation, policy, or action had to be voted on with his fellow board members.

Nonetheless, the chairman felt restrained from having what he considered were frank and "off the record" discussions with other board members. The culprit as he saw it were the "open government" laws, passed by Congress in the wake of Watergate. These laws, including the Government in the Sunshine Act, required all the agency meetings of its board to be held in public. The chairman could call a closed meeting, but that too required public notice, and all of the board members still must be present.

The chairman's solution was to ask Congress to exempt his agency from the Sunshine Act so that they could have "general policy discussions" without a public meeting or notice. The amendment to the Sunshine Act was quietly slipped into a larger bill being prepared in a congressional committee. However, within weeks and without any official action on the bill, the amendment was suddenly removed without a trace.

What happened? The chairman learned that if the provision became law, not only could he meet with board members without being observed by the public or the media, but that any of the board members were now also free to meet *without him!* His next call was to Capitol Hill to "please pull the amendment from the bill." Little had he realized that his survival as chairman was solar-powered by the Government in the Sunshine Act!

End of Discussion

Lastly, as is the fear of everyone who is dealing with powerful people at the top of the food chain, there is the potential for them to act powerfully, so powerfully in fact that the only thing that people can say in retrospect is that whoever it happened to "never saw it coming."

Here is an unforgettable story related by the lion tamer known as Professor George Keller and his act, Keller's Jungle Killers, that in this case truly lived up to its name.

Lesson of the Lion Tamers

"He Never Saw It Coming"

A large male lion named Regal had a dominating presence in the center ring, but that did not stop a puma in the same act from showing his resentment. At the end of every performance, as the big cats returned to their cages, the puma passed Regal's pedestal and reached up, quickly clipping Regal on the leg.

This continued for many weeks. As the lion tamer described: "I knew that real trouble was building, but I couldn't think of any way to stop it. The animals are trained to leave the arena in a certain order; I couldn't send Regal out first and so get him out of the puma's way. I was afraid to interfere directly between the two animals; if I should chase Regal down from his seat, there almost certainly would have been a fight."

Ultimately, "Regal decided to end the annoyance."

"This time, when I cued the puma to go back to his cage, Regal was ready. Just as the puma was passing but before he had time to reach up and clip the lion, Regal leaned down and swung with such a haymaker as I have never

(continued)

before seen. He caught the puma on the side of the neck, striking with such force that he severed the head from the body as cleanly as though it had been cut off by a headsman's ax. The puma's body fell limp at the foot of Regal's pedestal, and the head flew across the arena, struck the bars on the far side and rebounded, to drop on the ground like a spent ball…

"Regal was still on his seat. I cued him to go to his cage, and he got down, stepped across the blood that was flowing from the puma's body, and returned to his cage. His attitude was that of one who has performed a necessary, though perhaps unpleasant duty. He had removed an annoyance, and there was no more to be said on the subject. When he returned to the arena for the next performance, he never even glanced at the place where the puma had been."

This is not meant to scare you, but to point you in the right direction. While life at the top of the food chain does represent significant challenges and nonnegotiable realities in the instinctive behavior of lions, as a lion tamer you have to be aware of their entire range of behavior and how to deal with it. The lion establishes their territory, but the lion tamer, as the person who is responsible for creating the right environment for them to operate in, must maximize the display of the lion's strengths, while managing the risks associated with their possible weaknesses.

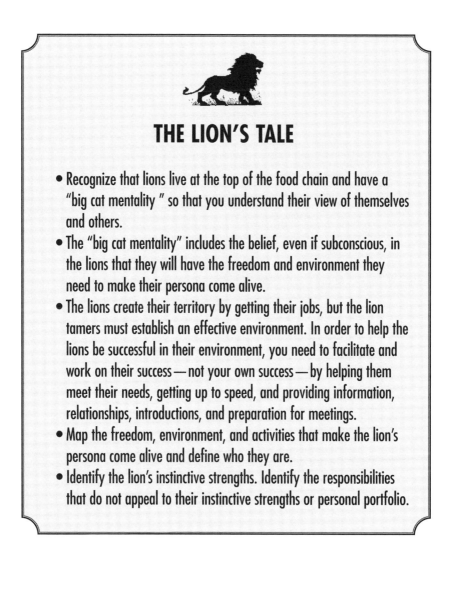

THE LION'S TALE

- Recognize that lions live at the top of the food chain and have a "big cat mentality " so that you understand their view of themselves and others.
- The "big cat mentality" includes the belief, even if subconscious, in the lions that they will have the freedom and environment they need to make their persona come alive.
- The lions create their territory by getting their jobs, but the lion tamers must establish an effective environment. In order to help the lions be successful in their environment, you need to facilitate and work on their success—not your own success—by helping them meet their needs, getting up to speed, and providing information, relationships, introductions, and preparation for meetings.
- Map the freedom, environment, and activities that make the lion's persona come alive and define who they are.
- Identify the lion's instinctive strengths. Identify the responsibilities that do not appeal to their instinctive strengths or personal portfolio.

4

Bringing Out the Lion Tamer in You

> **Secrets of the Lion Tamers**
> *The number of accidents suffered is in direct proportion to the lion tamer's attentiveness.*

Are you ready to take a step or two in the lion tamer's shoes? Can you begin to change your self-perception and self-image to that of a lion tamer and identify those around you who are the lions? This is one part of the lion tamer's approach that you can adopt quickly. You do not have to tell anyone you are doing it. It is your decision. You are merely adding another professional dimension to the way you think while you are at work, not overtly changing it. However, you will see that it does change your job because of your approach, the response, and the results. It is not role playing. Your personality and that of the people who are the lions will come out.

The metaphor of lion taming has a way of helping because you can already visualize it in your mind, gaining the intellectual distance you now need.

How do you do it? As we will begin to see, many of the lessons and experiences of the lion tamers apply directly to the steps we all need to follow in the workplace.

Lessons of the Lion Tamers

Lions May Have Your Full Attention, But It's Not Easy Keeping Theirs

Evidence that lion tamers possess unique wisdom lies in their ability to distill knowledge from every bead of sweat earned in the ring. Kevin Patton trained lions and then acquired his own formal graduate education in biology. Perhaps only a college professor who trained as a lion tamer could be so succinct, precise, and accurate in describing the ways in which working with lions and people in the workplace are parallel experiences:

"Choose your battles. Know the difference between when it is vital to have the lion's attention and when it is just convenient. If you see every situation as vital, all your energy will be spent on 'attention getting' and both the lion tamer and the lion will burn out quickly. Lions are not going to simply be soldiers on parade for you. Work on the steps essential to achieving goals and leaping through the true hoops of fire in the arena!"

"Animal Instinct in Reverse"

Just like real lion tamers, you must have the intuition to react faster than the speed of thought to handle a variety of situations and characteristics. "Animal instinct in reverse" is what lion tamer Dave Hoover has called it. You use all of your senses—visual, physical, emotional, intellectual, and psychological—just as you would in building any relationship. But in working with lions, there is less room for error. Get your points across quickly, but if you do not talk to them they will assume that you have nothing to say. Lion taming requires a highly focused, disciplined, and self-aware approach. You must be in control of yourself to a greater degree than you are ever in control of the lion. The footwork can be intricate, the setting dynamic. Keep in mind that you must achieve this from up close, from where the lion can smell you and reach you!

You can't fake it. The lion's own instincts and split-second reactions are at work. You must stand your ground without causing them to flee, bluster, or attack. You must do so consistently and repeatedly. Just as in the wild, whether we see a lion standing still or on the move, we know that they have the capacity to change reality, to restructure the social order—sometimes permanently. They know it too. As any lion tamer will tell you: ***Lions are never tame. You need strategies to deal with that.***

Lions Like to Use Their Strength

Secrets of the Lion Tamers

Lions look for opportunities to test.

Lion tamers in the workplace must be sensitive to how the lions handle groups of people in whose eyes they want to establish that they are the lion. This is continually part of the lion's focus. Lions are distracting in a very powerful way, and lion tamers both in the center ring and in the workplace can lose their focus. Sometimes even the most skilled and practiced real lion tamers can face trouble. When things are going well with the lions, it is possible to forget how changes in the atmosphere, setting, or others around them instinctively change the lions' outlook and cause reactions much faster than a lion tamer can process what has happened.

Consider the common situation in the office when the lion tamer assumes that the one-on-one relationship that takes place in the privacy of the boss's office will prevail with the lion in public. As one executive commented on the president of his company: "He's great one-on-one, almost acts like a friend, but with a group of us he's a completely different person—watchful, chest out, ready but we're never sure for what!"

Even in working with some of the best bosses, the truly good lions, the difference between working one-to-one compared to being in a group can lead to misinterpretation, misjudging, and falling into a deep and invisible crevice—the equivalent of the lion's jaws. As soon as others are involved, both the lions in the steel-caged arena and in the workplace shift into hierarchical high gear. You and everyone else are a potential challenger to their reign. This extends to the lion's other interests related to their status and prerogatives.

In the workplace, not all the vulnerabilities are created by the lions. Sometimes we create the vulnerability and the lion pounces! Unfortunately, things can go terribly wrong even if the lion tamer is someone who possesses an in-depth catalog of information, experience, risks, and strategies in their minds. Even such highly skilled people are capable of misjudging the lion as "tame." For that reason, so many real lion tamers who are injured are often heard commenting, even as they are carried off on the stretcher, "It is a good animal. It wasn't the lion's fault, it was mine."

Lessons of the Lion Tamers

"Nero's Crush"

Even some of the most experienced lion tamers, such as Clyde Beatty, have unintentionally landed in harm's way. Beatty's favorite lion for many years was a large male named Nero. When Beatty and Nero were alone in the arena, Beatty could get as close as he wanted to, even "riding" the lion around the ring. However, as soon as Nero was part of a lion group, his senses of dominance, hierarchy, and other natural lion desires kicked in, including sexual dominance—a known and very serious hazard in lion taming.

(continued)

Unfortunately, Beatty was not aware that Nero had developed a crush on one of the lionesses, and Beatty innocently stood too close to the object of Nero's passion. In what became a famous attack that almost ended Beatty's career, Nero instantly leapt down from the top seat in a fit of jealous rage, tearing into Beatty and almost ripping his midsection apart. Beatty lived, returning to the arena after a long recovery. He even reenacted the attack for a scene in the movie *The Big Cage*.

What lessons can we learn from this story? We must be aware of our own learned behavior so we can anticipate the behavior of the lions in the workplace and respond properly. This includes whether the lion is standing still, saying something, or heading for the door. The ironies abound: just when the lions seem to be a paragon of strength and ferocity, they can also display a sense of raw hurt, pain, or anger. You have to listen carefully to even the loudest roar to make the right interpretation!

Lions Need to Roar

Secrets of the Lion Tamers

The quiet ones may take the most handling; the roaring ones are often not so bad.

Lions in the wild and workplace like to roar. We have all heard it, but we do not always interpret it for what it means in lion language. The volume is unmistakable, but the meaning is not always clear. Sometimes its very nature and the related emotions even prevent us from listening. Where does that leave us, and what are some of the best ways to react?

Understanding what the lions are really saying goes a long way toward providing the knowledge of how or whether to answer back. When people in the office roar, are they hurt or angry? Are they hungry or getting excited? Are they attacking to kill, as it seems, or merely roaring as a reaction to even the simplest thing—at the unexpected, or at someone encroaching into their space or their "turf"? Are you the target or merely the nearest set of ears?

Take, for example, the company president who acknowledged economic pressures that might slow the company's growth, but ignored the advice of his financial executives and business strategists to refocus the company, significantly reduce the number of employees, and close most of the sales offices. Their advice was to shift from being "the cutting-edge company that keeps its customers out front" to a more targeted market with a few solid products that "gives its customers staying power in tough times." The president roared at every idea, lashing out, threatening to "begin the downsizing right here!"

What should the executives have done? (a) Do nothing; (b) Hurt the company president back; (c) Go around his back and prove he was wrong. You have probably witnessed all three happening, but the correct answer, for the moment, is (a) Do nothing. Let him roar—he's a lion! It is at that very moment that the communication is really beginning, not ending as some people believe. Even if you have to let the lion cool down or give both the lion and the subject a rest, you have captured their attention. Don't let the matter die! They know there is a problem. That is one of the first things that lion tamers learn to listen for. Stay close enough to sense what the lions are reacting to, what are they telling you. If the roaring made you stop listening, walk away, and never come back, then you are not doing your job as a lion tamer.

> **Secrets of the Lion Tamers**
>
> *They like the sound of their own voices.*

Real lions roar to communicate—roaring a deep resonant sound on a regular basis to strengthen their communal bonds. Their roar is perhaps most deep when they want to mark their territory, keeping the interlopers out while helping stray members of the pride find their way back. They roar to make sure their own reign is recognized, all the way to the boundaries of the kingdom and beyond.

Capitol Hill in Washington, D.C., home to the United States Senate and House of Representatives, is a veritable island of lions. Hundreds vie every day to rule a far-away land. They roar day in and day out on the floor of the House and Senate, in the lions' dens of offices, and in committee and subcommittee rooms stacked one on top of each other. Press releases and statements fly left and right as the lions in Congress declare their territory—show interest, take credit, preserve, protect, or destroy.

In the workplace, the lion's roar manifests itself in many ways. Consider the senior manager who likes nothing more than talking on the speaker phone with his door wide open. Or the boss or CEO who likes to spontaneously call people on the organization's staff—at all levels of the "org chart"—at home, just because he or she can. Or the new boss who requires everyone to read a favorite "best selling" management book. Other lion's roarings are heard, seen, and read about every day: companies staking out markets, politicians and other leaders establishing their cause. The press release is the megaphone for roaring. From individuals to companies and organizations—is the roar for real? Is it bluff and bluster to keep others away or is there a true capability and commitment?

The "Reorg Roar"

People and organizations roar in order to stake out their territories all the time. Many people throughout companies and organizations feel the roaring as the leaders and executives try to govern and manage. It is not always obvious what is going on. Even experienced managers and executives have lost valuable time before recognizing that they are dealing with a lion—a roaring lion. In fact, not too different from the lions in the wild who take over a pride and territory, one of the first things any new leader or boss in a company or organization does is begin to change the social order to their liking.

Consider the case of the vice president who successfully led and managed a large division of a well-known international company. That is, until a new senior executive arrived and decided that nothing was right: responsibilities, turf, positions, divisions, and technology. Morale dropped, projects drifted, and growth stalled, and it was everyone else's problem except the new boss.

As a new reorganization plan takes shape, the lion's territorial roar will echo through every hallway, phone call, and email—and back again to the lion's ears. Sometimes it begins subtly in a roar that builds with a rumbling sound, other times it is a forceful swipe of a claw or even produces a bigger fight.

The vice president was consumed by the internal turmoil of the reorganization. His meetings with his new boss were even more tumultuous as he tried to explain the impact of the restructuring and identify past successes that may be jeopardized. Many lion-like traits were apparent. But one in particular—the lion's roar, in this case the territorial roar—finally sparked the realization for the vice president that he really was dealing with a lion.

In this case, the realization in the mind of the vice president that he was also dealing with a lion meant one thing: you don't realize that you are a lion tamer in the office until you have to say "no" to the lion! However, the challenge that he found himself facing also provided opportunities. The vice president needed to achieve several objectives at once—goals that began to define him as a lion tamer to the lion he recognized sitting at his boss's desk. He was one of the few people with regular access to the new boss. So he realized that there was a mutual need between them, and did not have to be negative when saying "no."

Don't Take It All Personally

One immediate psychological and emotional benefit of stepping into the shoes of a lion tamer is that you will learn not to interpret so much of what the lions say and do personally. Let them roar—they're lions! It is only then that you may gain a sense of why they are roaring. Are they angry, hurt, afraid, confused, or hungry? When there is a "blow up" in the office, should you flee or determine the cause and enable yourself to understand what is going on? In some situations, you simply need to gain some distance perspective, and determine how to keep the stress that drives other people from consuming you.

To do that, you need intellectual distance to observe and think as a participant observer when you are in the ring, and objectively explore the problem when you step outside to safety. ***The Office Lion Tamer's Checklist*** offers some starting points:

- ❑ Act quickly and intelligently.
- ❑ Balance the scales or "level the playing field" of the working relationship.
- ❑ Avoid the feeling of powerlessness or subservience.
- ❑ Demonstrate the strength, nerve, and equanimity to tackle the situation.
- ❑ Become an ally to the boss without becoming everyone else's opponent.
- ❑ Create the opportunity to be influential.
- ❑ Maximize the boss's perception that he is a player in his own right.
- ❑ Assess the boss's needs and who can help fulfill them—including you.
- ❑ Establish a foundation for working together and establishing rapport, trust, and mutual respect.
- ❑ Make the boss successful in new ways that advance his business objectives or goals.

- ❑ Provide candid but respectful and constructive feedback.
- ❑ Say no without getting your head bit off.

You cannot achieve this if you are consumed with frustration, pained at something the boss said to you, or plotting how to get around them. "Practiced ignoring" is how one person, a senior operations manager, described part of her strategy, and learning not to take personally everything that executives did around her was an essential component.

How did she deal so effectively with the many different department heads and others she had to interact with each day? Her outward calm and equanimity were part of her secret:

> At first their attitude was always one of being too busy to work together. I was viewed as a "support executive" and they viewed themselves as the "business executives." I assumed that since I held the keys to improving the infrastructure of the company, that they would understand how it would help them perform and profit. No way. So I learned—don't take it personally, just maintain the confidence that what I am doing is just as important but not in a way that needs to be seen as competing in importance to what they are doing. Think about the pressures they might be under, at that minute, during a particular time of month or year, and find a way to collect information from other people who work with them to learn more about their work, schedule, traits, and needs. I have found that they respect that I have respect for my work and therefore I don't have to be trying to get them to respect what I do and what I think. It has helped me as well. Even if they roar, I do not take it personally.

Indeed, it has probably crossed your mind many times that the lions in the workplace do not play by the same kinds of rules that everyone else does—even if they are supposed to be setting an example at the top of the organization. The questions about how to communicate and work with bosses often outpace the answers: “How do you talk to her?” “What kind of information does she need?” “Does the boss really want to hear other people’s ideas or is she just saying that?” Often, people’s observations about the boss’s behavior became mythology, but nothing adds up. That is because even though they may very well have a particular personality and style of communication, you need to engage them for yourself and find out what works *between you and them!* As we have said, lions are never tame, you need strategies to deal with that. In the next part of the book, “The Art of Lion Taming,” we offer a number of valuable strategies that real lion tamers use to create a one-to-one rapport and working relationship in the center ring that also apply directly to the workplace.

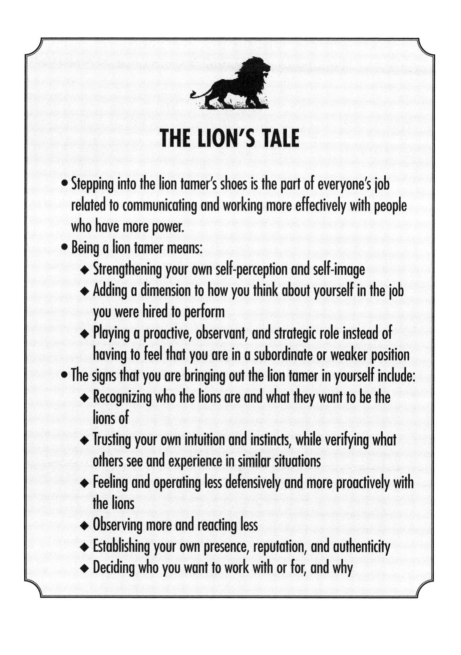

THE LION'S TALE

- Stepping into the lion tamer's shoes is the part of everyone's job related to communicating and working more effectively with people who have more power.
- Being a lion tamer means:
  - Strengthening your own self-perception and self-image
  - Adding a dimension to how you think about yourself in the job you were hired to perform
  - Playing a proactive, observant, and strategic role instead of having to feel that you are in a subordinate or weaker position
- The signs that you are bringing out the lion tamer in yourself include:
  - Recognizing who the lions are and what they want to be the lions of
  - Trusting your own intuition and instincts, while verifying what others see and experience in similar situations
  - Feeling and operating less defensively and more proactively with the lions
  - Observing more and reacting less
  - Establishing your own presence, reputation, and authenticity
  - Deciding who you want to work with or for, and why

PART II

The Art of Lion Taming

5

The Art of Lion Taming

> **Secrets of the Lion Tamers**
>
> *They come to see death.*
> *I don't think they wish it.*
> *That would be too horrible.*

"Oohs" and "aahs" and the excitement of close calls will always characterize lion taming for the masses. To the audience, the ringmaster is heard barking:

> This daring young man is about to enter the den, the steel-bound arena, with Nero, that ferocious, untamed African lion direct from faraway jungles. He will fight his way in, he will fight his way out, and remember, friends, no matter what happens, the steel bars are there for your protection.

The lion tamers hear a different voice. To their ears, the ringmaster's call echoes the lion tamer's inner thoughts: "*And nowwww, in the center rrrrring, journeying from the Himalayan heights of harrowing honesty, having dived to the death-defying depths of soul searching, transcending awareness of even the most astute, the most acute...a spectacle of superhuman self-control revealing not a single secret of their trade!"*

Contrary to popular ideas and circus posters, the art of lion taming is *not* about driving lions into a snarling frenzy, winning a battle of "man over beast," or sticking your head into the lion's mouth! The most exciting acts to watch—the fighting acts—are not the ones you want to recreate in the office. Lion tamers use brains not brawn, and thinking that you can muscle your boss is a bad idea. Even if you have the ability to escape from the ring unscathed, you still do not have the option of sending the lions at work back to their cages after their act. They are roaming free, and the things that they can do and say will have an impact on you and everyone around you for a long time to come.

Lion tamers have a sober prescription for the essentials of their craft. They must first reach inside their own minds, their own hearts, and know their feelings all the way down to their toes. There is more: at the core of every lion tamer is an acute awareness founded on their respect and understanding of the lion. Without this, no matter how deeply you have plumbed your own mind or exercised your innermost thoughts, when you approach a lion all the images of greatness will quickly disappear down a drain in the middle of your stomach.

Secrets of the Lion Tamers

To be considered one of them you must respect their code as they do.

Lion tamers must think on their feet before, during, and after they have gone into the ring with the lions. To do so, they must succinctly capture in their own minds the information that is most real and most important—distilled by the ounce, by the bead of sweat from every encounter. Out of necessity, they have created a pragmatic philosophy for a profession in which there is little room for error. Some would say that is what the art of lion taming is all about.

The wisdom of lion tamers bridges the arena and the workplace, providing valuable insights, strategies, and steps to help us work more effectively with the powerful people around us.

If a lion tamer could take a checklist into the ring, it would probably look something like this:

- ❑ Remember that the lion is a member of another species.
- ❑ Approach the lion with the aim of getting the lion to approach you.
- ❑ Recognize the need for an adjustment period or adjustment agenda.
- ❑ Respect, study, and understand the traits that make them lions.
- ❑ Recognize the strengths, weaknesses, and idiosyncrasies of each lion.
- ❑ Establish your presence, reputation, and credibility.
- ❑ Gain and hold their attention.
- ❑ Engage their interest in working with you.
- ❑ Achieve mutual trust and respect.
- ❑ Interpret their needs as keys to learning.
- ❑ Build confidence by finding the path of least resistance, gradually adding new challenges.
- ❑ Observe what they can do instinctively and then help develop it.
- ❑ Make them successful in new ways.
- ❑ Help them look strong in the eyes of other lions.
- ❑ Minimize negative or destructive abilities.

How closely do real lion tamers' experiences parallel the encounters that unfold in the office? Very closely. How soon does it happen? From the moment the lion tamer and the lion lay eyes on one another. The similarities between the center ring and how people react to the lions that they encounter in the workplace is striking—whether it is entering the boss's office, heading into a client meeting, or numerous other situations. Some have equated the symptoms with standing before a large group to speak. The most important parallel is that the feeling courses through your mind and body even if it is a job or responsibility you have always wanted.

Why Lion Tamers Don't Rush into the Cage

The telling difference between real lion tamers and those in the workplace is whether the effect of approaching the lion is an enervating rush of energy and heightened awareness that puts you on your toes, or the freezing sensation that all your blood has run cold! Alex Kerr of Great Britain always knew that he wanted to work as a wild animal trainer, and one day his wish was granted to enter the lion's cage.

Lessons of the Lion Tamers

Entering the Ring!

As I slipped through the door, my feelings were not those I had expected. The small cage, which from the outside had looked so full of space, seemed suddenly to have shrunk to a tiny cell. I did not know it then, but it is a common reaction when facing wild cats for the first time. Two lionesses eyed me from the far end of the cage.... I did not understand the breathlessness in my throat—surely not fear? And I was surprised to feel a tightening of my brain, a consciousness of nothing in the world but the small cage and its occupants.

No lion tamer ever rushed into the cage just to test his or her agility and footwork, at least no one who wanted to live. Similarly, just "standing up" to a lion can be suicidal. Only the lion tamer that understands how and where to stand his or her ground while shielding their personal fears can take the next steps. These steps are establishing their presence and reputation in the eyes of the lion, and building rapport, trust, and mutual respect in order to work together. And remember these are steps, not leaps. Just imagine what would happen if a real lion tamer leapt at the lion as they began to work together. End of story.

Lion "Rushes" at the Office

The irony is that as the lion tamer, even if you tame yourself from the kind of display of bravado—the "know your stuff and show your stuff" attitude that sometimes seems triggered in people who get in front of leaders, bosses, and other tough customers—the lions themselves do not hesitate to "rush" you! Sometimes your first step in establishing yourself with the lions is to survive not by challenging them, but by sidestepping situations where they are instinctively challenging you, then bringing them back to focus on the work at hand. Mabel Stark, a legendary and experienced trainer of big cats whose career spanned more than fifty years, described how she dealt with the lions that charged or "rushed" at her in the ring:

> Lion rushes I never minded much: They're just big woof-woof bluffers. If I stand my ground or side step them, they don't try it again.

Yet how did she know what to think and how to react, even if she arrived at the right conclusion intuitively? How did she spoil the surprise that the lion had in store for her? How did she undo the lion's motivation and replace it with something positive?

In the workplace, "lion rushes" happen all the time. Maybe you've run into some of these lions:

- A CEO who devours his senior executives at every weekly meeting around the conference-room table.
- An executive director that charges around the office "just trying to help."
- A department head who reacts to strategic suggestions by screaming, "Why are you trying to do my job?"
- A boss that has a million great ideas but no concept of the time, people, or resources needed to implement them.

No doubt you and others you know have had their own experiences. It's easy to say that you should just stay out of their way, but that is never a permanent solution. When you run into lions like these, do you know whether they're bluffing or why? Do you understand the crucial difference between standing your ground and standing too close? When is the right time to get out of the way? If your boss is roaring, what is she saying? Is she establishing her territory; expressing anger; reacting to being hurt, threatened, hungry; or in need of everyone's attention? To begin the process of working with the lions, you need to consider the environment around them.

Adjusting to a Dynamic Environment

One of the characteristics of a good lion tamer, both in the center ring and in the office, is the ability to accept that the environment is complex and dynamic. It means actively sensing and sorting out what is unfolding around you and why. Some of what you observe and learn is about you; but much is also revealed about the nature of others.

You might think that given the danger, a lion tamer's focus would be on themselves. But it is not. The same is true in the workplace. Your mind cannot be preoccupied with simply understanding how you feel. You must be more acutely aware of the dynamics of relationships between people around you—from the passive to the explosive.

Here are just a few questions to keep in mind:

- Where are the energies and actions of the lions you are working with directed?
- What are the influences that are visible and invisible—including your own words and behavior—and what reactions are being triggered?
- How can you sharpen the focus on what you are working on together?
- When is it necessarily to adjust the pace and speed—sometimes slower, sometimes faster?

The last point may be surprising. Faster, are you kidding? We are often afraid of situations in which the pace can accelerate without our control. Studying and learning seem easier in slow motion. But lion tamers have no choice. The intensity and complexity of a dynamic environment produces something new. More important, the lions around us are instinctively attracted to opportunities that require them to demonstrate their mastery of speed of thought and action—just like real lions. That is the environment you need to help foster. By putting the lions in action, you help them learn and pursue something in a new and more effective way. Success does not come from the equivalent of just posing with the lion. As Alfred Court, the revered French lion tamer and animal trainer, wrote:

> When does the lion tamer think most productively? When the muscles are warmed up...the body steams with sweat...the mind is busy...a new idea emerges!

It is true in the office as well. To reap these benefits, however, you must first learn to approach the lion.

Approach the Lion So That the Lion Will Approach You

> **Secrets of the Lion Tamers**
>
> *Getting the lion to approach you, including when you need them, is really what it's all about.*

Lion tamers are practical and realistic about how and what to accomplish with lions. As a result, they are tuned in to the fact that you are building a two-way relationship—not just issuing commands, cracking a whip, and standing back. Just like in other relationships, there are incremental stages of growth. You need to be introduced, get acquainted, adjust to one another, learn each other's styles, and take some time to overcome hesitations, inhibitions, and fears. It cannot be achieved instantaneously. Even good chemistry assures nothing more than the possibility of more fluid next steps, but you still must take them one at a time.

> **Lessons of the Lion Tamers**
>
> **Approaching the Lion**
>
> When a lion tamer approaches a lion, his aim is to get the lion to approach him. You can never take for granted the need of a lion and a lion tamer to adjust to each other's presence; work gradually to resolve any fears, inhibitions, and resistance in the lion's mind; and avoid creating new ones. In the end, the lions must have confidence in approaching the lion tamer, and not only sense that there is nothing to fear, but possibly a direct benefit for them to do so.
>
> Consider our discussion of the *Lion's Four Senses* as part of the analytical screen that the lions around you are using to make judgments as they adjust to others around them. That includes you!

Having an Adjustment Agenda

> **Secrets of the Lion Tamers**
>
> *This separates the good from the bad: Do you have the patience to take it slowly?*

Lion tamers recognize the need to create an opportunity for the lion and the lion tamer to adjust to each other. It is a core requirement in approaching the lion with the aim of having the lion approach you. Lion tamers have an adjustment agenda that precedes, helps establish, and serves as a foundation for working toward rapport, trust, and mutual respect.

In real lion taming, the first item on the trainer's agenda is to sit outside the lion's cage, getting the lion accustomed to the lion tamer's presence and voice. One experienced trainer who was about to tackle putting a new act together was asked if he was ever charged by the animals when he would enter the arena for the first time. His response was blunt but honest: "I'm not stupid. I spend a lot of time outside the cage watching them, talking to them, just getting us all used to each other." In the workplace, unfortunately, we often forget how important this is. We assume that "we're all people," when in fact some of us are lions.

For real lion tamers, the adjustment process continues even after the first encounter in the arena. One lion tamer had a specific procedure he would follow with any new lion. He would spend two to three hours a day for several months simply entering the lion's arena. With the new lion sitting or pacing on one side of the large steel cage, the trainer would sit in a chair on the other side, near the door. As the lion grew more comfortable, usually indicated by when it stopped pacing, he would move closer to establishing a working distance.

Secrets of the Lion Tamers

Don't use any forcing tactics.

Another story illustrates this approach. Jack Bonavita gained notoriety in the early 1900s working with groups of twenty or more lions. In a well-known photograph, Bonavita calmly sits in a specially built "armchair," reading a newspaper while surrounded by thirteen large male lions! (See pg. 191) The "armchair" had pedestals or platform like seats built all around it, and in the photograph four of the lions sit above Bonavita's head and shoulders; the remaining nine are at his sides and feet.

How did he do it? He extended the technique he used to help the lions first get accustomed to him. It began by sitting in a chair reading a newspaper outside the lion's cage. Working with each new lion individually, Bonavita would bring a chair and the newspaper into the steel-caged arena and sit on one side reading. Gradually, when he sensed that the lion was feeling safe and secure, Bonavita would move closer. Gradually he was able to use the adjustment agenda to create a unique performance by the lions. The same measured kind of approach and adjustment is applicable to the workplace as well. (Though as a note of caution: don't set up a reading corner in your boss's office!)

Secrets of the Lion Tamers

Be respectful in tone and approach. Everything works better when they are the lion.

Just as in real lion taming, the adjustment process is a continuous part of the relationship that builds and develops. In fact, when you can give your lion time to adjust and gradually build his or her confidence and trust, you are actually *creating time!* The secret is to ensure that you make the time—even if no one tells you it is part of your job description. The goal is to build a relationship. Here's an example.

CEOs Need Room to Adjust Too!

A large company chose a new CEO, and from his first day on the job a visible number of people quickly stepped forward to be "helpful." As the CEO later observed to a vice president who had kept a respectful distance, "Most were committed primarily to their own visibility."

The vice president had not been sure at first how involved to become in the process. Having survived mergers and reorganizations in the past, she had a good track record of success, but saw the danger signs. As an executive, she also knew that it was unwise to be invisible, so she requested lunch with the new CEO. To her surprise, he put it on his calendar immediately. She let him talk about his past experiences, his first impressions of the new company, his thumbnail vision, and some current needs.

In return, he asked her for her input and for a memo: "Tell me what you can do and what you want to do—let's follow up in two days." As her lunch confirmed, the new CEO was talented, proactive, and focused, but "he was drinking from a fire hydrant" of people and ideas.

In preparing the memo to the CEO, the vice president recognized that even if it was likely that her ideas might get washed away by the flood of information the CEO was receiving, the lunch and the memo had begun an important process of remaining in parallel contact with the CEO and his world. Still, she wanted to be helpful, even essential to his transition into the company. She thought that maybe he was serious about the follow-up in two days.

She hand-delivered the memo to the CEO's office, introducing herself to his longtime personal assistant, who had come with the CEO to the new job. She quickly learned whether or not he used email, and whether the personal assistant screened the email. She was back at her desk within five minutes.

Two days came and went, and so did two weeks. No response. Her safe distance was beginning to feel unsafe. Other executives she knew were in meetings, preparing presentations and writing a new business strategy. Yet she still believed that it all seemed too random. She did her own job while informally touching base with the CEO and occasionally talking to his personal assistant to:

- Request a follow-up meeting to discuss the memo
- Provide some historical documents
- Send occasional emails with competitive information that had been useful to the past CEO
- Support others who were getting more "face time" with the new boss

After three weeks, just as she became convinced that the CEO was not interested, the CEO's office called to set up lunch. The CEO unfolded his napkin and at the same time told her, "I asked for things that should have taken hours and took weeks. I'm not sure the people who showed the most interest have what I need. What would you do?" He wanted help immediately and in concrete terms.

Without hesitating, she suggested an approach that she had used successfully as a right-hand executive in the past: the CEO should lead a three-to-six-month transition team. She volunteered to staff, help people, or manage it from behind the scenes—whatever he needed. He agreed and asked her to draft an outline and follow up in the morning. This time the vice president called the CEO's personal assistant to tell her what transpired at the meeting and asked that she confirm a meeting time with the CEO.

The vice president's patience had paid off. She gave the lion room and took the time that was necessary to come into focus as someone the CEO could trust, approach on his own, and not feel that he was being pressured, manipulated, or possibly threatened.

Small Steps to Building Trust

People in the workplace are very sensitive to being approached as they begin to establish relationships. This is particularly true for people trying to develop new working relationships both inside their own organization, and, perhaps more frequently, externally. It encompasses obvious pursuits such as sales, but is equally important in the context of networking, strategic alliances, and coalitions.

The number of small steps that you must take to build trust, gain knowledge, and get information—even before adding one or two new faces to discussions and meetings—must be small, numerous, measured, and never taken for granted. For people who are naturally good at this, these stages come quite easily. However, they are in the minority. This is not because they are such rare individuals, but because of the momentum and pressures of the workplace.

Most people are in some kind of rush, reflexively falling into the "hard sell" mode of thinking and acting. Their gut tells them that they must demonstrate that they "know their stuff and can show their stuff." Yet think how you react when someone tries either a self-justifying or high-pressure sales technique on you! Now you know how others in the workplace feel when you fail to examine and adjust your behavior as you approach them. A measured self-awareness is called for, whether you are moving fast or slow. What's the secret? ***Adjust to how you are impacting the lion, rather than reacting to how the lion is making you feel!*** The result is identical to walking into the lion's cage on the first day without taking the time to observe and adjust to one another. The lion backs off. He might even charge at you just to get you out of the way, giving himself a chance to escape. Sometimes the lion wants to escape by coming right in your direction!

These same issues apply as you interact with new bosses. And as one executive learned, it's just as important in how you handle employees when you become a boss. Looking back on a thirty-year career, a seasoned and highly respected mid-level executive noted that to this day, the dynamic of adjustment, tension, and fear is always a factor. He first noticed it as a new employee reporting to his very first boss, and it repeatedly came into play whenever he reported to someone new. Now, as a boss, he makes sure that people get adjusted to him. He makes time for it, and calls it the "adjustment agenda."

Here are this corporate lion tamer's rules for building trust:

- Don't bring anything to the table until you totally understand the lion.
- Work to create a first impression by getting to know the lion first. If you lose the first impression, it's over.
- Find out what makes them tick and what is important to them. Are they trying to accomplish something specific? Help them.
- Don't throw yourself at anyone.

Make a Personal Connection

Regardless of whether you are a part-time or full-time lion tamer, or someone who is both lion and lion tamer, there is an essential ingredient. You must make a *personal connection,* communicating and developing signals that have *emotional value,* taking them beyond their generic approach to screen out others. You don't want to be in one of the dangerous categories: the prey, the enemy, or the ignored.

Connecting means using a depth of thinking and a capability beyond what you were specifically hired to do. Be a person, not just a position. Do whatever it takes—listen, notice, share information, praise, acquire information in advance of needs, or help inform a potential decision. It is more than small talk. Your personalities and expressions must become linked at some level.

> **Secrets of the Lion Tamers**
> *Lions do not answer.*

Right from the start, real lion tamers think about the task of developing such mutual recognition and rapport with animals that do not use words. Gunther Gebel-Williams, considered among the most dedicated and hardest working all-around animal trainers in the last quarter-century, described the importance of mutual communication and rapport to his work: "Our relationships developed through talk, and not just on my part—some animals really do respond." But as he ticked through the list of animals from the most communicative to the least, he simply concluded, "***Lions do not answer.***"

Few other observations seem to resonate so strongly with people when they think of the leaders, bosses, executives, and other people they encounter at work. *"Lions do not answer."* Indeed, the ways in which such people are easy to read—a grimace, a growl, or silently turning away—reveals an inherent resistance to influence.

Although there are many extroverted lions in the workplace, even the best of them display this quality. They are hardwired to achieve objectives, and that is where their energies are devoted—often up until the last available second before shifting to a new subject or meeting, and then some! How many times have you arrived at a meeting to be greeted with: "Be with you in a minute," "Whaddya want," or plain silence while you stand there shifting in your shoes?

As a result, when people hear the phrase, *"Getting the lion to approach you, including when you need them,"* they react with part realization and part disbelief. It is simultaneously an "aha!" and a scary idea. "Have you ever met my boss?" they say. It is a natural reaction. Our own survival instinct as animals tells us to keep our distance, often to keep to ourselves, and we have reinforced this throughout society. You do not have to look very far to see that the culture of most workplaces—from organizational charts to office architecture—is based on hierarchies that serve to demarcate leadership and status. Like all hierarchies, they are designed to preserve territory and control competition. The most obvious consequence in the workplace is isolation—at all levels—as the lions tend to be caged off from everyone else, and everyone is caged off from the lions.

One consequence is that we approach each other from our own frame of reference, our own point of isolation in the organization. Our natural inclination is to focus on simply whether we know our stuff and can show our stuff, not whether we have the sufficient rapport or the knowledge of the people we are meeting with to be most effective. We are focused on the event, and with virtually every event we start over. We start everything over, from the efforts to get and hold their attention to readjusting to each other's presence, to determining what the agenda is. Is it any surprise how often people leave meetings, turning to one another to ask, "Do you think he *heard* us?"

What kind of performance would it be to watch a lion tamer spending all of his or her time just getting the lion's attention, getting him up on a pedestal, holding his attention, and keeping him from jumping off, playing and fussing with the other lions on nearby pedestals? Not a very good performance. Now consider what goes on in your office. The goal is not to grab the lion's attention and rush them to the finish line of the discussion! The goal is to gain their attention, stretch it, engage them, and be able to repeat this all over again on cue. It requires patience and time to adjust to new people and new situations. What is it really all about? Overcoming fear—the lion's fear, not the lion tamer's!

Overcome the Lion's Fear of Lion Tamers

> **Secrets of the Lion Tamers**
>
> *Man is almost always seen as a challenger to their rights.*

Lion tamer Dave Hoover, a protégé of Clyde Beatty, said it simply enough: "If you're not afraid of 'em, you're in trouble." Yet lions are said to be at least afraid, if not more, of the lion tamer. Inhibited, resistant, or uncertain about who or what they are dealing with, and recognizing that lion tamers have some kind of power over them, lions want to know that you are not going to hurt them. The big bosses of the world are worried about this too.

If you remember the *Lion's Four Senses* of dominance, territory, social standing, and survival, you will be able to begin to understand what is going on inside the minds of the leaders, bosses, and other tough customers. To many that are already sensitive to these issues, keeping this framework in mind is helpful. Try to see yourself from the point of view of the *Lion's Four Senses.* Even though the lions need you, they may have significant fears about you:

- **Dominance:** Can you control something that they either want to control or appear to control?
- **Territory:** Are you challenging their information, contacts, experience, investment, and opportunity?
- **Social standing:** Is your visibility overshadowing their own?
- **Survival:** Do you have something they don't have that diminishes their strength?

In the workplace, the lion's inherent fear of new people and situations is not the result of raw fright. It is more elusive, and sometimes more dangerous, because it is usually connected to something else that is palpable only to them, not visible on the surface. We may see it as inhibition, resistance, arrogance, aloofness, self-absorption, or simply being "too busy all the time."

These can be frustrating reactions to deal with. Yet even resistance, unwillingness, or active opposition does not mean that the lions don't understand you. They may simply be moving away from whatever it is they are unsure of; preserving their existence as lions; maintaining the kind of distance, space, and territory they require. Even the people who may not normally display the typical lion behaviors in the workplace possess these traits and reactions. Some lions in the workplace react aggressively, and others seem not to respond at all. In either case, they act like they just want you to go away.

However, you cannot go away. Once the lion tamer and the lion meet, the relationship begins. There is an instant shift from the periphery of each other's lives to the center of it—from saying hello to sizing each other up, gauging space and territory, sparring to test, testing to judge, adjusting, and determining where things are going and on whose terms. The fact that they have asked to meet with you, personally hired you, or recognized that they really need your help is totally irrelevant. You still have to expect that they will surprise you. Also, you'll need to show patience to help them adjust and feel secure. Perhaps the lesson to be learned is simply this: ***Take the time to find the right way to approach each lion.*** Or as one observer said about real lion acts: "The people who rush into the cage are the ones who usually don't last very long." Here is a real-life lesson that reveals how that occurs in the workplace—even among serious people warned of the need to tread slowly.

Give the Lion Room

The executive vice president and the department manager of a large corporation were meeting to solve a serious problem that was costing the company three-quarters of a billion dollars a year. Ultimate accountability for the problem rested with the executive vice president, and he had asked a team of outside strategists and experts to listen to the company's approach to the situation, provide some comparisons to other companies with similar issues, and offer some new options and ideas.

One of the executive vice president's most respected qualities was his patience and his judgment, and in this case he was aware that the company was sensitive about revealing the guts of the problem to outsiders. The department manager was particularly sensitive and was keenly aware that outsiders would think that the company had waited too long to seek help.

So, the executive vice president decided on a two-meeting approach. One would be in private with just himself and the outside strategists. If that went well, he would hold a second meeting and include the department manager.

The first meeting was straightforward. The problem was presented, some strategic comparisons were provided, and everyone agreed that problems that evolve over long periods of time require a lot of time and hard work to resolve. "One last thing," the executive vice president concluded. "Our people are doing the best they can and you need to be good listeners and let them tell our story." Everyone nodded as if they fully understood.

The second meeting took place just a couple of weeks later, and everything went according to plan—that is, for at least a minute. No sooner had the executive vice president asked his department manager to "tell our story" when one of the senior members of the outside strategy team burst in like a salesman to say, "Let me tell you a little about our background and expertise." Needless to say, he might as well have held fifty pounds of raw meat up to his head!

Within minutes, the department manager tore the speaker to pieces. "You obviously have never done any work for our company!" he roared. "You have no experience under the kinds of regulations *we* have to live with!"

Weeks and months of preparation were quickly sacrificed. The executive vice president merely shot the strategists a look that said: "This was your meeting to lose, you just lost it." Efforts to reestablish contact failed.

It is stories like these, true stories involving experienced business people, that reveal that the people who you would think should "get it" often do not, even when there is much at stake. They do not seem to recognize that they are dealing with lions, and that lions need to adjust to you. They do not realize that they must step into the role as a lion tamer to handle the situation appropriately. Let's look at how to approach such situations by understanding where you should aim your efforts in order to become an accepted member of the lion's team.

Aim for a Place in the Pride

Secrets of the Lion Tamers

Lions are hardwired as pride animals.

Consider the world from the mind's eye of the people who are the lions. Like lions in the wild, the lions in the workplace are hardwired both for fighting for a place in the hierarchy and for living as pride animals. The "pride" is the family or group of lions that live together, hunt together, and work together to survive. Some like to lead the pride, yet it is important for them to know what their place is in lion society, while also knowing who else is playing a vital role.

As we have said, everyone else who is considered outside of the pride is in one of three vulnerable categories: *prey, the enemy, or ignored.* None of these are a realistic option to survive at the office. Being targeted as prey or the enemy is an obvious enough problem, but being ignored at work is a far more pervasive tactic and a particularly slow and progressive form of death.

That is why you aim for a place in the pride that gives both you and the lion something you each want and need. Why is this important in the workplace? Because at the outset many bosses may ignore almost everyone. They instinctively treat most employees as generic members of a generic category.

Lion tamers in the center ring and in the workplace must work hard to overcome this attitude. How do they do it? Some would say it is by out-bluffing the lion, but there is much more to it than that. There is a significant degree of authenticity that must be demonstrated. It is achieved by establishing your presence and reputation as an individual; recognizing the lion as the lion; supporting their objectives, goals, and needs; and establishing a strength and depth that they will respect—that will even keep them guessing that there is more they cannot see. Often, however, people who are the first to fall prey to the lions at work are the ones who rush into situations, driven by a "know your stuff and show your stuff" attitude only to be quickly sorted as either prey, the enemy, or ignored and dealt with accordingly.

Switching Roles: From Lion to Lion Tamer

Who has the most difficult time with these situations? Anyone who believes that he is a lion and fails to recognize when it is time to switch into the role of being a lion tamer. Virtually anyone whose position is located upwards on the food chain at work falls into this category. It happens to mid-level managers and department heads who do not want to show their own bosses that they are weak. It happens to presidents of companies and executive directors of organizations, to school principals and others who must deal with board members and others who are lions.

Lions must be made to feel that they are the lions over the world they reign over daily. Ironically, they believe that somehow they have to show the boss that they are worthy of their own position as a lion, expert, or whoever they are in the eyes of others, as if their job depends on it. They desperately want to show the lions that they are not weak, when in fact doing so triggers the undesired response in the lion.

Recognizing such traits as a failure of ego does not solve the problem. We all know that lions have a strong personal sense of themselves. The size of someone's ego as a lion is not the problem—and a smaller ego will not necessarily help. Remember what's needed is a more multidimensional ego, one that enables you to realize that there is always a bigger lion for whom you need to at least temporarily adjust your need to be dominant or be the expert, and instead become influential as a lion tamer.

How do you achieve that? As one executive found, "Perspective and a sense of humor can help." What did he mean? "My biggest hang-up was that I didn't want to appear subordinate or weak to my boss, jumping whenever she said 'jump!' However, one day when we were meeting together I realized, 'What have I got to lose, she already thinks I am weaker than her, but if that really matters then why am I am sitting in her office with an opportunity to be influential?'" Lions need your help to keep them in the role of the lion the same way you need the help of others below you. At the same time, you play a unique role as a member of the team who is invested in them.

As we have learned, the art of lion taming, both in the center ring and the office, requires a great deal of attention to building a foundation for any working relationship. Even if you know what it is you want to accomplish, there must be a comfort level and a degree of receptivity before any real communication can begin. And as we have just seen in the last example above, it is not just the lion that needs to be ready to work together in their role—just as often it is the person who needs to step into the role of a lion tamer.

With this awareness and sensibility at the forefront of your mind, you will be ready to take the next steps as a lion tamer in the office. You must first realize that lion taming is about controlling yourself to a greater degree than you can ever control the people who are the lions. Then the secrets and strategies that seem to give lion tamers the appearance of control can be put to use to work more effectively with the lions around you at work. We will examine the real meaning of the lion tamer's courage, their use of the whip and the chair, and even the lion's pedestal. You will see secrets and strategies that lion tamers use for closing the gap between attention getting and attention using, and for fostering the environment and opportunities for communicating and working more effectively with the lions as a team.

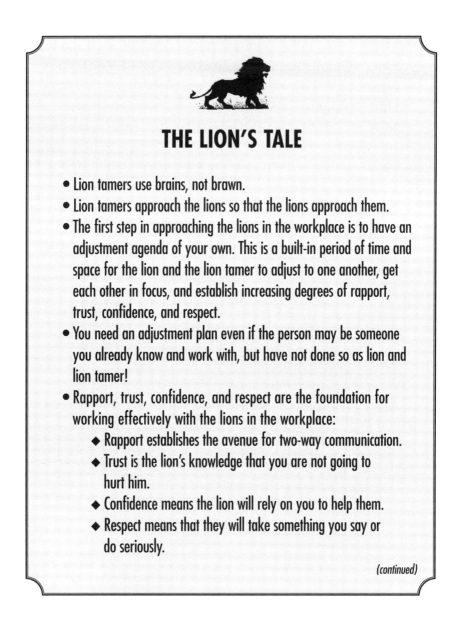

THE LION'S TALE

- Lion tamers use brains, not brawn.
- Lion tamers approach the lions so that the lions approach them.
- The first step in approaching the lions in the workplace is to have an adjustment agenda of your own. This is a built-in period of time and space for the lion and the lion tamer to adjust to one another, get each other in focus, and establish increasing degrees of rapport, trust, confidence, and respect.
- You need an adjustment plan even if the person may be someone you already know and work with, but have not done so as lion and lion tamer!
- Rapport, trust, confidence, and respect are the foundation for working effectively with the lions in the workplace:
    - ◆ Rapport establishes the avenue for two-way communication.
    - ◆ Trust is the lion's knowledge that you are not going to hurt him.
    - ◆ Confidence means the lion will rely on you to help them.
    - ◆ Respect means that they will take something you say or do seriously.

(continued)

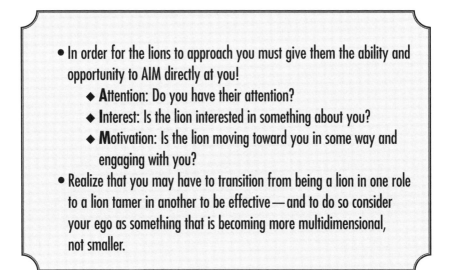

- In order for the lions to approach you must give them the ability and opportunity to AIM directly at you!
    - **A**ttention: Do you have their attention?
    - **I**nterest: Is the lion interested in something about you?
    - **M**otivation: Is the lion moving toward you in some way and engaging with you?
- Realize that you may have to transition from being a lion in one role to a lion tamer in another to be effective—and to do so consider your ego as something that is becoming more multidimensional, not smaller.

6

Courage, the Whip, and the Chair

> **Secrets of the Lion Tamers**
>
> *Lions can kill without killing to eat.*

Clyde Beatty, the legendary American lion tamer of the big top and the big screen, created the fighting lion-tamer image in popular culture that has lasted across many generations. Standing poised and seemingly fearless in a steel-caged ring full of roaring and ferocious lions, he was protected by nothing more than a slender whip and a wooden chair. Taking on five hundred pounds of muscle and teeth with such simple props seems hardly adequate to the challenge at hand, and every moment feels like a battle between David and Goliath.

We've all had days like that. You quickly muster your courage and look to the spot in the corner of your office where you keep the whip and the chair when these kinds of lions in the workplace register in your mind, or even on your calendar!

- The aggressive CEO who intimidates everyone in his path, shoulders squared against all comers, grilling everyone around the table, gulping down information.
- The boss who flares up when someone is missing from a meeting, when information is not at hand, or when things are not the way she expected.
- The executive who snarls irritably at an idea but never explains what is bugging him.
- The company president who seeks you out one-on-one, valuing the information and insights you have, but in a group is tough on everyone.

Certainly, not all lions are difficult. As we have articulated, the traits to look for in the good lions comprise a much longer list of attributes than the troublesome traits of the mean-swinging lions we encounter. Many lions are good lions, people whom everyone likes dealing with and who can impact the organization and others beneficially. They are among the quickest to work together and to recognize the value of the cues, guidance, and teamwork that can help them perform optimally and be more successful at their own jobs.

Also, the ferocity and power of the lions in the workplace is not always a negative. It can be a very purposeful exercise of their authority. Usually, the lions in the workplace are not one type or another, but display a spectrum of characteristics often triggered in reaction to different situations, people, and environments.

So how do you know how to handle yourself when face to face with a lion? Sometimes the only way to figure it out is by stepping into the shoes of a lion tamer.

More Chairs Have Been Devoured than Lion Tamers

> **Secrets of the Lion Tamers**
>
> *The steps you take and the movements you make actually provide many of the cues.*

After trying to stave off an attack by one very powerful lion, Clyde Beatty commented, "I use about a hundred of these reinforced kitchen chairs per season, and if Prince felt like putting a leg of this one out of commission, that was all right with me." More chairs have been devoured than lion tamers. Their skill and ability to survive is what draws us to their performances. Anyone becoming acquainted with lion taming cannot help but want to satisfy their own curiosity about the image of the lion tamer. It's what people see, mouths agape, every time a lion tamer enters the cage: "They're throwing themselves into their job." Literally, in this case!

As we begin to understand how the art of lion taming helps us get inside the minds of leaders, bosses, and other tough customers, we must ask ourselves what it is that we recognize in lion tamers that must also be operating inside our own minds in the workplace. It is the total involvement of the lion tamer's personality in his or her work that is crucial to engaging the lion and achieving results together. Is it sheer courage? Nerves of steel? Or do lion tamers possess a higher threshold for tension, stress, and pain? Is there an invisible whip and a chair that we can take into work? How do you use them to project your persona and ability in a controlled manner rather than reacting randomly? What behaviors does your behavior trigger?

As one lion tamer observed, "The people who just run into the ring are the ones who don't last very long." Yet how many people do you know who do just that every day, and how close have you come to doing it yourself?

Instead of rushing into the cage, you must carefully consider many questions that focus on your own mental state and preparation, including:

- What needs to be going on inside your mind?
- What skills and tools do you need to possess?
- How do you forge ahead in a way that is productive and effective, helping the lions leverage their position and resources most effectively?
- When should you be less obtrusive and when should you show your mettle?
- How far do you go and when?

One CEO, speaking to a large group about the value of working closely with leaders, offered this advice:

> You get stronger as you take on the problems of others. But how you do it is key. If you push too hard, it will come down on your ears. If you stop pushing, you betray the purpose of your mission.

Having the Courage Not to Show Fear

> **Secrets of the Lion Tamers**
>
> *It takes confidence, but not in the 'I can do anything' sense.*

Lion tamers must unquestionably have courage. They must command the arena in which any one lion can kill in the blink of an eye. You remember being introduced to big-cat trainer Charly Baumann in the story about his very first day entering the ring with lions. Years later, after he had moved on from working with lions to become among the foremost tiger trainers in the world, he was asked to comment on what is unique about the lion tamers who enter the steel-caged arena. "They've got guts," remarked Baumann with a bright twinkle in his eye. Another lion tamer, whose act was comprised of ten lions—"all males, the toughest"—described what it was like as the lions sauntered out of the tunnel looking up at him one by one: "You get bigger," he said slowly as if reliving the experience. "Maybe it's the rush of adrenaline. You just get bigger." Others have emphasized the need to "work big," "to be noticed in the spread of the arena," though in this case it is also to instill dimension in the eyes of the lion.

What gives lion tamers the inner strength they need? Physical stamina? Yes. An understanding of lion psychology? Yes. Courage and confidence? Let's take a look.

Alfred Court, a famous French lion tamer who lived into his nineties, had decades of experience performing with lions and other big cats. He summed it up this way in his autobiography:

> Contrary to the general belief, courage is the least important quality. I have taught a score or more trainers, men and women, and among them I have encountered young braggarts who prided themselves on their courage. They have always made me nervous, and they have generally ended their careers in the hospital. Others more reflective, fully realizing the perils of the business, even a little fearful, have nevertheless become experts.

Secrets of the Lion Tamers

To know fear is not to be a stranger to courage.

"Lion tamers have fear?" asked one business executive. They do. Lion tamers walk into the cage just like anyone else walks into their office. But because they address their fears, they are more focused on the possible accomplishments than the obvious dangers. Other careers may strike them as more dangerous. Take, for example, the lion tamer who originally intended to become an airline pilot in the early days of commercial airlines. He was saving his money for flight lessons until he learned that the airlines did not give their pilots parachutes. He decided to become a lion tamer instead.

In fact, it is not unusual to hear lion tamers address the issue of fear before ever hearing them mention courage—perhaps *that* is being courageous!

Lessons of the Lion Tamers
FEAR

"I have been asked thousands of times if I was not afraid in the cage with the animals," remarked one lion tamer. "I have always been able to answer truthfully. 'No.' Inside you don't mind it. You are too busy thinking about your business, but sometimes after you get out, your hair stands on end to think how near you came to having something happen!"

Dave Hoover, a protégé of Clyde Beatty whose favorite lion was said to have been a 714-pound male named Leo, put it simply: "If you're not scared of them you're in real trouble." After many years still working in the ring, Hoover added, "My teeth rattle now, but you just have to ignore that."

Is it understatement? Modest pride? Or is it evidence that lion tamers aren't daredevils or gladiators? Indeed, the job requires an acute understanding of everything going on in the environment and the internal dynamics between the human and the lion. Fear is without question part of that reality, and the lion tamer must deal with his or her fear.

Secrets of the Lion Tamers

When courage is self-conscious, it betrays great fear.

Courage and fear are inextricably tied together: one is used to manage the other. As Indian trainer Damoo Dhotre concluded dispassionately, "Fear is a mental process, not an emotional one." Few people, however, arrive at such a transcendent state of mind.

You cannot afford to reveal either courage or fear in a dramatic sense to the lion, because as one observer stated philosophically: "Courage that is self-conscious betrays great fear." Indeed, in the workplace the lions may interpret a display of courage as a direct challenge or competition and prey on your fear as a weakness. You will succeed in getting the lion's attention, but not in a way that is useful to anyone. The secret is found in the heart of every successful lion tamer: ***It is the courage not to show fear.***

Courage develops inside your mind as an organizing tool, both consciously and unconsciously. It is the way you confidently organize yourself mentally and physically to do the job. It is displayed through a heightened awareness of your own equanimity. Courage means entering the ring fully aware of the dangers you face while working to achieve specific goals and objectives with the lion. In lion taming, you need to be more in control of yourself than ever. You must believe that you are controlling the lion. You must be completely honest with yourself about everything: your observations, feelings, stress, dangers, and anything that could trigger danger. A truly courageous lion tamer is extremely aware and cautious.

When lion tamers list the attributes they consider essential, courage and bravery may be implicitly essential. But *patience* is at the top of the list, and *overconfidence* always ranks at the very bottom. You can look back over one hundred years of lion taming wisdom and you will hear that "nothing is as valuable as patience" and that "patience must be inexhaustible."

Add Stress and Stir

> **Secrets of the Lion Tamers**
>
> *When the lions come through the door you have three seconds to read them. Are they coming at you or going to their pedestal? And it changes every time. I am sweating. It can be thirty degrees outside and I am sweating from the physical tension, the mental stress.*

One element is missing from the equation—STRESS. We feel it in the boss's office or a client meeting, working things out with key employees who we depend on, or simply after a long day's work: *physical and emotional stress.* As one executive put it plaintively: "Sometimes you think so hard your hair hurts!" The real lion tamers feel the same way: "You're only in the arena for ten minutes, but you are sweating and aching as if you have just run your fastest mile."

There isn't a single job in the workplace that doesn't stress you out at times. Many a boss, just like the lions in the arena, can bring it about without moving a muscle. Sometimes it is challenging intellectually, emotionally, and physically just to stay in the ring, stand on your feet, and absorb the lion's emotions and moves. Alfred Court summed it up this way: "Have infinite patience, be calm and capable of great physical endurance, and have a little courage."

Adding the physical demands of lion taming to the equation gives us a tangible definition of courage. We can feel it in our bones. As lion tamer Frank Bostock stated at the beginning of the twentieth century, the key to the lion tamer's success is: "Nerve and plenty of it!" That still applies at the beginning of the twenty-first century.

Courage is many things, but in lion taming a simple equation will help you sort it out:

Mental Focus + Physical Stamina = Nerve

In stressful moments when people ask if you are "holding it together," this is what they mean. Some situations require more nerve than others, and some people have greater physical and mental endurance than others. Yet no one can or should do it forever. When you lose your nerve, you lose the courage not to show fear!

The Whip and the Chair

> **Secrets of the Lion Tamers**
>
> *It is most important that the primary movement of the cue is always the same, given from the same position, with the same stance and tone of voice.*

In lion taming, there is a practical purpose to everything, including where you stand, the look on your face, and your tone of voice. The same is true for your tools and equipment. After all, we use special equipment in many sports to extend our reach, power, and control. Tennis players use a racquet to extend their arms, hit the ball more powerfully, and keep their heads up and eyes on the game. Baseball players use a bat to hit the ball and a glove to field. Hockey players use a stick to control, pass, shoot, steal a puck, and block a shot.

Real lion tamers use the whip and the chair, or a long thick wooden stick, to enable them do what they cannot do with their bare hands. The lion tamer's tools achieve these important results:

- Making the lion tamer look bigger than it really is
- Extending their arms and bodies beyond the ordinary span of their reach

- Creating the space between them that both the lion tamer and the lion need
- When necessary, making the lion tamer a larger and more awkward target

The lion tamer also uses the whip and chair to project his presence and his personality. Together with his voice, the lion tamer can communicate from a distance that the lion needs and will accept. To get the lion to approach him without attacking, the lion tamer must respect this distance.

The crack of the whip cues the lion's attention, lets the lions know to begin a routine, corrects a misstep, or triggers a trained movement away from the sound of the whip. People sometimes have trouble believing that such detail can be communicated and understood without words. But not only is the whip an effective communicator, it also helps the lion tamer maintain pacing, speed, and finish! As one lion tamer observed, "The whip is like a walkie-talkie, popping the message, 'Yes, I mean you!'"

Lessons of the Lion Tamers

Cue the Band

British lion tamer Patricia Bourne described just how carefully she used her whip, almost as if she was sending a message and using the whip for punctuation. "Sevilla only needed to hear the crack of a whip close by her, and round she would swirl in a cloud of sawdust and chase me. And I would back up quickly to exactly the right place—quite near Guieto and his roars—and put out my stick. She would swipe that hard and begin a backward retreat, with me following her back to her stool. She snarled all the time, turning her head from side to side and really looking alarming. However, she knew the act as well as I did, and this was her party piece."

We use cues all the time without realizing which signals we send, their meaning, and how to use them again repeatedly to produce a specific effect. Few of us recognize the economy of gestures, body movement, and speaking as cues that can be recognized, learned, and repeated—on cue!

Cracking the whip to achieve movement away from the source of the sound is actually a technique people use all the time in the workplace, though not often consistently. We do it through language, the use of words, body movements, and in reverse psychology, moving people toward something when they think they are moving away from something else. You know how effective you can be in getting word around the office by just whispering in someone's ear: "This is confidential. Don't tell a soul…"

Conversely, striking a lion to inflict pain would only provoke an attack that the lion tamer could not stop. Being aggressive with lions arouses more aggression. And if the lion does not charge immediately, he files the experience away — the day *will* come. You have heard stories at work about the people who "didn't see it coming."

Pushing a lion too strongly also can arouse aggression. Successful lion tamers strive to develop and reinforce results they can reward, not behavior they are trying to correct by acting like a "lion tamer."

Lessons of the Lion Tamers

The Case of the Wobbly Lions

A new lion tamer took over a lion act in which the lions were trained to mount a set of pedestals arranged in a pyramid, then sit up, heads back, paws together skyward — a classic lion-act portrait. After several weeks of becoming acquainted and practicing, the lion tamer decided to address some of the problems in the act.

(continued)

With all the lions up on their seats, the pyramid looked good. When the lion tamer raised his arms and said, "Up," several of the lions struck a perfect Buddha-like pose with their paws clasped together prayerfully. However, two of the biggest lions near the top leaned back and forth in a wobbly manner. Their paws slipped in the air and they glared down with uncertainty at the lion tamer.

Again, the lion tamer raised his arms, "Up! Up!" He approached each of the wobbly lions, "Caesar Up, Caesar Up! Sampson Up, Sampson Up!" Each growled and snarled. When the lion tamer reached up with the whip to show them where to put their paws, they growled louder. The lion tamer motioned the lions down, signaled to the assistants outside to open the tunnel, and one by one called the lions, "Nero, house! Prince, house! Atlas, house! Jewel, house!" One by one, the lions returned to their cages.

The frustrated lion tamer turned to leave the arena. Another lion tamer who was watching asked if he could come inside. He said, "Their first trainer was too strong with them. He pushed the two lions before they were ready and now they are just trained to get angry. You're just the guy giving them the cue."

The first lion tamer asked how to change it. *"You have to help them learn to sit up with confidence.* They cannot do it just because the others can do it, and lions don't sit up by raising their paws in the air. When a teacher asks a student to raise their hands, do the kids stand up when they do it? No. You have to help the animal learn it by using the muscles in their backs—not their arms—then work on where you want the paws.

"Anyway, you can't do it standing so far beneath a towering lion on a pedestal. Why do you think they are staring down at you? There you are way below, talking up to them. They're confused and mad at you, they have to look down to see, listen, and tell you they're pissed off. First, stand on a tall pedestal and get up to their level. Then work individually until they learn the trick in stages, first with their back muscles, then with their paws. They will learn what 'Up' means when you are in a higher position to show them. Once they are confident, you can lead them somewhere new like putting their paws up and together, heads arched back. When you return to your position on the ground 'Up' means way up! Train confidence, not resistance. Train to reward lions, not to correct them."

Ernest Hemingway once visited Clyde Beatty in his dressing room after a performance. He told Beatty that his footwork and the way he used a chair to rebuff and move the charging lions around the ring reminded Hemingway of the bullfighters in Spain.

In lion taming, a chair or wooden stick is used at first to attract and guide the lions to a position by placing a reward of meat on the end of the stick. It is later used without meat to guide and playfully spar. For stopping a charging lion, kitchen chairs may blunt an attack or provide a second or two for the lion tamer to say a prayer, but only just barely. More likely, the lion tamer in the Clyde Beatty tradition uses the chair to quickly shift the focus of the rushing lion's thinking from "eat the guy in the white pants" to sorting out the four chair legs.

In some ways, a lion tamer is like an orchestra leader, cueing, lending emphasis, and guiding. The conductor uses both hands and moves his head and body, swaying and jabbing with the momentum, inviting and engaging different musicians. The musicians read his eyes, facial expressions, gestures, and movements. In lion taming too, it is easier and more effective to communicate with a group of lions using a long extension of your arm like the whip—they can all see and hear it.

Some lion tamers have demonstrated one of the secrets of lion taming by choosing to work without anything in their hands. One in particular was Professor George Keller, a college professor who fulfilled his dream of becoming a wild animal trainer in his fifties (and unfortunately died "with his boots on" of a heart attack in the ring in his sixties). In his act, called Keller's Jungle Killers, the professor guided the lions entirely with hand signals while wearing white gloves. The lesson here is that no matter what the lion tamer has in his hands, it has to already be there in his brain. Maybe it took a college professor to show us that!

Your understanding of the lion tamer's use of tools will shape your understanding of what lion tamers do in the arena and will influence your approach and strategies in the office. Most people assume that the lion tamer's behavior is reactive, even defensive. But if that were the case, there would be little contest.

Real Dangers

There are real dangers to lion taming, and they should not be minimized. People have been maimed or killed just by walking too close to the lion's cage or the arena. However, many things that seem like trouble to the audience are just part of the act. For example, when a lion charges or rushes, swipes the air and snarls from his pedestal, or reaches out from a lay-down to grab at the lion tamer's stick, he is exhibiting behaviors that are either practiced or are natural behaviors that the lion tamer has incorporated into the act. The lion tamer knows how far to get into the lion's personal space to elicit this response and how quickly to back away to prevent an attack.

Because everything with lions is bigger and more powerful—from roars to embraces—sometimes what the audience sees is how the lion tamer and the lion say hello before beginning a routine. It is no different than the way people shake hands firmly then back off. Some people even growl and snarl while doing that!

The lion tamer's objective is to get the lion to approach, then use their rapport and trust to communicate and work together. Therefore, the lion tamer's approach and the tools he or she uses are *primarily proactive*: looking, facilitating, urging, leading, reading the lion, guiding, cueing, signaling, listening, reminding, rewarding, paying attention, managing, and persevering.

This is doubly true with people. Every move and gesture—regardless of what the lion tamer is carrying in his hands—is linked to understanding what is going on inside the lion's skull. Lion taming is created from the same building blocks as any relationship, but in the workplace you have to do it with your bare hands! And this means using your brains, not brawn, to be a lion tamer.

Standing in the Lion Tamer's Shoes

> **Secrets of the Lion Tamers**
>
> *Patience is the key to lion taming. It requires many small steps and lots of time, and then it works beautifully.*

What constitutes the courage, the whip, and the chair in the workplace? What gives the lion tamers in the workplace the inner strength, motivation, and awareness they need to do their job?

Standing in the shoes of a lion tamer does not mean standing in the shoes of a daredevil or gladiator. The image of the lion tamer represents a deeper level of knowledge and preparedness. And as we will see, the whip and the chair, real or metaphorical, are merely extensions of the inner lion tamer.

> **Lessons of the Lion Tamers**
> **Preparation**
>
> The process of preparation is where most of the work is done. The lion tamer's influence in that process can be strong or even dominant. However, the lion's influence will be equally as strong if not stronger in determining the final performance. And, of course, especially with lions, you just never know what is really going to happen until you "get out there." Even in "blow-ups" or other emergencies, your pattern of cues and responses, your pattern of interactions, and your preconceived contingencies are all brought into play so that no event is completely unaffected by your preparation.

Courage

Yes, you need the lion tamer's courage in the workplace. It is the motivation, the "Pike's Peak or Bust" feeling, that propels real lion tamers into the cage. Courage is the magical spark that enables you to look in the mirror and see a lion tamer staring back. It is a reflection of how you see yourself, because as a lion tamer you:

- Approach situations proactively, not reactively
- Acknowledge your own independence and objectivity
- Balance the scales of a working relationship
- Think on your feet before standing your ground
- React to other situations constructively—not defensively
- Sharpen your awareness of yourself and the people and situations around you
- Confidently organize your mental and physical attention

The lion tamer's courage applied to the workplace is the confidence that *you* belong right in there in the job, meeting, or time and place. It is the opportunity to think on your feet and decide where to stand your ground. It is the opportunity to work proactively, and react in a constructive manner to steer the relationship back to where it needs to go. It is not simply the idea of dangers. In fact, in lion taming *things can go right in the same blink of an eye as they can go wrong*, and you have to be able to see just when to seize that opportunity. Here is an illustration of the struggle to keep an alliance alive between the managing executives of two businesses.

Holding Your Ground without Giving It Up

Two businesses with complementary expertise, skills, and resources agreed to work together on a project. One company had the dominant role of launching the project, and the other would bring it to completion.

> The executive with the "lion's share" of the project began to allege problems in the relationship—ones he suggested could stall the project. He was roaring to establish his territory—everything he could see and touch and then some—and he threatened to break the contract and find another partner. It all revolved around the lion's four senses: dominance, territory, standing, and survival.

What were his complaints? Essentially, communication, communication, communication:

- Not being kept in the loop
- Lack of communication between managers from each company
- Late reports and updates on projects, costs, and completions

The other executive had several choices: (a) Do nothing and ignore him, (b) Back out of the project, or (c) Strengthen communication, dialogue, and information flow.

The best answer was the last option. To fulfill this role as a lion tamer, he needed to remain focused and able to say that he was leading his company's effort to successfully complete the project. He overcame two perceptions—that he was subservient and that he was an opponent. He simultaneously met the demands and raised the standard of cooperation and communication. It was a chance for the smaller partner to show his stuff.

Intellectual Space inside the Steel Cage

> **Secrets of the Lion Tamers**
>
> ***Be respectful in tone and approach; everything works better when they are the lion.***

Courage is also the place where many other important things dwell in the mind of the lion tamer. In the workplace, this includes the inner consciousness or intellectual distance that everyone needs. It is your safety zone, the place in your brain where you can pause and collect your thoughts, gain your composure, assess the "optics" of the situation, review a catalog of experiences, retrieve knowledge or memories, and create your exit when necessary.

In some professions and disciplines, the goal is to minimize the intellectual distance between you and the subject so that you can better understand the subject. In books and film, the distance from the stories and the characters are fixed in the format; when it's over you close the book or leave the theater. In lion taming, there is no remove. You are already in the story, and something personal is always at stake for you and your boss. When you are working one-on-one or with a group of lions, your intellectual distance is your safety zone. It is the distance you need to maintain to understand the people and events around you, integrate information with experience, and bring knowledge to your fingertips.

Some people have the built-in radar, intuition, or ability to see everything more easily. Yet in lion taming it still takes extensive practice and experience. Your intuition may bring you in closer contact and interaction with the lions more quickly, but with that comes the responsibility to handle the actions and reactions more quickly and adroitly. Are you prepared for that? Almost everyone needs to maintain independence and objectivity as a participant observer no matter how close you get, and different lions will trigger different reactions in you.

Step back and create a living map in your mind of:

- The lions
- Their dominance, social standing, territory, and fear
- The political geography or lay of the land as it looks in the minds of the lions

> **Secrets of the Lion Tamers**
> *You need to prevent against lagging watchfulness. You need to know when to get out of the cage.*

Your objectivity will also enable you to gauge your staying power and manage the time that you spend together. From this vantage point, you must make independent observations, accurate judgments, and timely decisions in the blink of an eye. You must also be aware that you probably cannot outlast the lions. Real lion-taming acts are only about ten to fifteen minutes long: no one lets it go on for hours. The lions get overworked, and the lion tamer can lose his or her concentration or focus. Knowing that your nerve is slipping or that something you cannot control is developing requires courage as well—the courage to get out of the cage and recognize that staying in was riskier than getting out.

The warning signs you should be looking for are varied and may include anger, behavior, boredom, distractions, emotions, frustration, pain, being ignored, problems, and stress.

Exit...Stage Right!

Creating an exit strategy is how one "lion tamer," an executive in a large corporation, got out of his boss's office just in time. The executive had been reporting to a new boss whom he respected for his brilliance and tenacity, but who was quickly wearing him down. As a sign of respect, the executive would often sit in the boss's office for long periods of time, where the conversation would become dominated by the new boss.

One day the executive sensed that he was about to burst, possibly losing his temper in a fit of anger, which would have triggered a heated argument with untold consequences. Just as suddenly, the executive realized that he could step back. He told the boss that this was an interesting point, but he just remembered that he had another meeting he promised he would attend—and phew, got out of the office!

For the short run, the executive had created a legitimate exit strategy—avoid sacrificing his temper, face, or the boss's respect. For the long run he found a way to step back and if necessary end future meetings. Finding this strategy prevented the executive from losing his nerve and renewed the self-control, confidence, and flexibility he needed to do his job and work effectively with the lion.

The Invisible Whip and Chair

What is it like to handle an invisible whip and a chair? Most people do it unconsciously, unaware that every expression, gesture, and move is a "silent language" and that every inch of space is a "hidden dimension" of human actions and interactions that is full of meaning.

Whether you're in the steel-caged arena or the boss's office, you may be telegraphing your deepest feelings in the silent language of your facial expressions and your stance. You will communicate through your words, cues, and footwork. Your courage and strength will reflect your mental focus, physical stamina, and nerve. Ideally, everything culminates in an arc of understanding and communication that flows between the lion tamer and the lion. In all kinds of lion taming, you need to become aware and in control of yourself and these movements.

The invisible whip and the chair can be words and ideas that move someone in a particular direction. You can use them exactly how the lion tamers use it—to break the lion's concentration, switch the subject, or get things back on track. You have probably done it before. It can come from using humor, or getting onto a different subject, even temporarily—news, intelligence, gossip, information. And sometimes the best invisible chair to break the lion's train of thought or hard-charging style may be silence. If they believe you don't understand them, they are forced to rethink their plan and move in another direction.

Secrets of the Lion Tamers

Think of everything you are doing and its importance.

At the same time, you must be conscious and in control of your verbal and nonverbal behaviors and the signals you send. The people around you will react just like the lions in the center ring to what you do and say, even your tone of voice. Clyde Beatty, who handled twenty or more lions at once, noted that "I believe my voice irritates lions…so I whistle to them."

How aware are you of your nonverbal cues and signals, gestures and expressions, body movements, and sensitivity to personal space? One of the qualities that lions in the workplace share with real lions is an incredible perceptual sensitivity. They not only sense fear and weakness, some say they can "smell fear" and want nothing of it. Their radar is particularly alert to signs they interpret as having suspicious motivation. They will decide whether they want to deal with you or an issue, and you will not even know it happened. One CEO whose survival was increasingly in doubt stayed focused through constant meetings with his staff, but when an assistant entered the office with a worried frown on her face, the boss roared, "Wipe that look off your face if you are going to come in here!"

In another example, let's find out how one person learned that he was unwittingly triggering anger and negativity from his boss.

Giving the Boss the Evil Eyebrow

A vice president considered himself a patient listener in the face of a strong-willed and brilliant boss. The vice president considered among his strengths the ability to sit for long periods of time, calmly, nonjudgmental, and professional. Yet the boss seemed to fly off the handle as he explained his new plans and ideas to the vice president. What was going on? Every meeting was becoming a struggle and their relationship was worsening.

The vice president finally came out of a meeting so worried that he called a meeting of his staff to get some feedback. The staff glanced around the table at one another, and then one employee spoke up: "He's very sensitive, you're not doing that eyebrow thing, are you?" The vice president looked surprised. "What eyebrow thing?" The staff then told him that he often raised his right eyebrow as they talked, which they interpreted as an expression of doubt or skepticism.

The vice president was completely unaware of his eyebrow, but he quickly realized that he was triggering the very same feeling and reaction in his own boss, who reacted with bluster, anger, and distrust. As the vice president later realized, "I even have to control my face!"

Lions in Public and Private

There are two other particularly important dimensions to be aware of as a lion tamer in the office—public and private language. The *public language*—firm handshakes, deadly stares, or quick moves and charges—is often tied to establishing dominance, territory, or standing as a lion. It is meant to be up front so others can see it and make a social decision for themselves. The *private language*, however, relates to individual relationships. Part of a one-to-one relationship, this language is meant to convey a specific meaning that either you do not want to articulate or subconsciously do not even know that you are "saying."

The world of gestures and expressions is two-way. You must also think about what each individual lion is telling you with her expressions and gestures—and combine it with information and knowledge you have about her and her habits. Sometimes it is not as overt as a distinct growl or a roar.

A Smile That Means "Stop!"

For several years I was fortunate to have worked for a United States Senator who was comfortable in his role. He was easy to communicate with in private and just as accessible to others as a true American hero in public. He listened calmly and showed respect to his staff. He was one of the good lions—confident in his power and position, and interested in what you had to say. He wasn't like some of the more feared personalities on Capitol Hill that are perhaps stereotyped beyond Washington, but nevertheless do exist. One that comes to mind liked to roar in various ways, including telling people, "I don't get headaches, I give them. What do you think of that?"

As I learned over the course of time, whether you are working as an advisor or right-hand executive to leaders, it is up to you to determine the appropriate style of communication, and that includes how to listen. As I learned in this case, listening isn't always done with your ears.

I learned that the Senator's innate civility was an important strength in how others viewed him. But it was also how he communicated, or in some cases chose not to, because it was the polite thing to do. For example, when he wanted you to finish where you were headed in the conversation or to let him get on with his day, he might nod and say, "Thanks." Sometimes in the process of winding up the discussion he would just smile appreciatively, a signal most people would interpret as "I'm really on a roll. He likes this, I'll keep going." However, as I quickly learned, while the smile was genuine, it was intended to convey a different message entirely: "Okay, I've got what I need, please stop."

While I would like to say that I was a quick learner, it took several meetings in different settings—some one-on-one, others in small groups, some in larger groups—to do so. On the one hand it was part of the adjustment agenda and learning to avoid the trap of "know your stuff and show your stuff" with bosses. Fortunately, I did learn the signal quickly enough to work effectively together when it counted in front of others.

The test of my understanding came in a high-level meeting with other members of Congress, federal agency heads, and several high-powered lobbyists. I was invited as the subject-matter expert on a request that was being made of the Senator. I knew that my job was not to persuade the Senator to say "no" to the requests being made at the meeting—that would have been inconsistent with his personality. My job was simply to make it possible for him not to say "yes."

Looking back, I used good lion-taming skills, positioning myself directly across from the Senator, with the others attendees on my right and left. The biggest lion in the room was always in front of me. When it was my turn, I was constructive and informative, firm but not antagonistic, and I was always watching the Senator's expression. He was reading the room as I was speaking, and while I was not through putting the "kibosh" on the request, I must have

> come quite close. My signal came in the midst of answering a question from a respected congresswoman. A smile appeared on the Senator's face. My response to the congresswoman had contained some hard-edged evidence, and the Senator's smile widened as he shifted a little in his chair. It was my signal to stop talking.
>
> He was right, not just polite. A few more words would have triggered a fight from others in the room, but just enough words shifted the control back to him. And it was only his authority as the lion that truly mattered. As I look back, it was a also good illustration of how the lion tamer's job is to "present the lion, not the other way around."

As I learned in this case, when you are dealing with lions, the good lions in particular, the better you understand each other and each other's roles, the easier it is to maintain that arc of communication. In the final analysis, your goal in using courage, the whip, and the chair as a lion tamer is not to control the lion, but to move and work in unison together. When it is the lion's turn to perform, it is the lion tamer's job to stand back and let them do it!

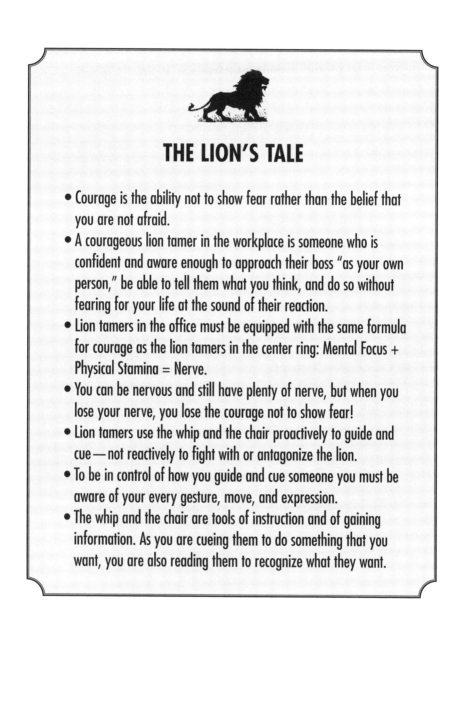

THE LION'S TALE

- Courage is the ability not to show fear rather than the belief that you are not afraid.
- A courageous lion tamer in the workplace is someone who is confident and aware enough to approach their boss "as your own person," be able to tell them what you think, and do so without fearing for your life at the sound of their reaction.
- Lion tamers in the office must be equipped with the same formula for courage as the lion tamers in the center ring: Mental Focus + Physical Stamina = Nerve.
- You can be nervous and still have plenty of nerve, but when you lose your nerve, you lose the courage not to show fear!
- Lion tamers use the whip and the chair proactively to guide and cue—not reactively to fight with or antagonize the lion.
- To be in control of how you guide and cue someone you must be aware of your every gesture, move, and expression.
- The whip and the chair are tools of instruction and of gaining information. As you are cueing them to do something that you want, you are also reading them to recognize what they want.

7

The Lion's Pedestal

> **Secrets of the Lion Tamers**
>
> *Lions always have your full attention but it is hard to keep their full attention.*

All lions in the workplace have a primal drive to be dominant and safe—and a need to be secure in their feeling of dominance. To work with them successfully requires recognizing and satisfying that need in order to achieve any next steps.

How is it possible to meet the lion's need for dominance without giving in entirely to its will? The technique that lion tamers depend on is something seen in every performance. In fact, it surprises most people to learn that this technique is a prerequisite and an invaluable secret to gaining and holding the lion's attention.

The answer is to *put the lion on a pedestal.* Lion tamers don't do this simply for the dramatic effect or to help the audience see the act better (although it helps). The lion tamers guide the lions to a place where they will feel dominant and secure in the feeling that they are dominant! The lion tamer uses his or her knowledge of the lion's primal needs to establish a safe and secure ground so that the lion has their own space from which to begin communicating and working together. That's the real goal.

As one lion tamer explained:

> To the cat, his seat is a security position. Other cats won't bother him there—he can't get in trouble for being there. The lion is rarely disciplined there unless he has just returned from a fight and is told that he is being bad.

As you may have noticed, the lions always return to the same pedestal after performing each part of an act. You can achieve that same effect in the workplace—establishing a routine through your own body movement, gestures, expressions, words, and experience to guide the lions in the workplace back to their pedestals.

Attention Getting and Attention Using

> **Secrets of the Lion Tamers**
>
> *If you don't get them to sit, you've got nothing.*

The *Lion's Pedestal* is the secret to minimizing *attention getting* while successfully maximizing *attention using.* As a mental reminder, visualize a real lion tamer in a steel-caged arena with a group of lions unwilling to stay on their pedestals—leaping on and off, fussing, fighting, and playing with the other lions around them. Until the lion tamer gets the lion's attention, he cannot use it. All of the lion tamer's attention, and likely the audience's, is on attention getting, not attention using. Again, that is why the one of the most valuable *Secrets of the Lion Tamers* is, "If you don't get them to sit, you've got nothing!"

Traditionally, lion tamers called this spot the *command pedestal.* It is the place where the trainer issues cues and commands, even though it seems like the spot from where the *lions* reign. Most trainers prefer using the word they call out to the lions—*seat!* After all, the lion tamers want the lions to go to their seat in order to communicate with them.

For our purposes, using the term "*lion's pedestal*" is a good compromise because every lion in the workplace has one—even if it must be created out of thin air. Bringing this technique to life requires two key steps, an equation that adds up to the kind of rapport and communication between two people that is easy to replicate in future meetings:

1. Determine the location of the lion's pedestal.
2. Pick the right position as the lion tamer in relationship to the lion—including whether you are sitting or standing, how much space is between the lion and you, eye-to-eye alignment, and more.

Being on the pedestal makes the lion feel safe, secure, and dominant. Where you sit or stand in relation to them also affects their feelings and may determine whether they speak to you and for how long.

In the workplace, the lion's pedestal might take several forms, from the concrete to the more abstract:

- Sitting at their desk
- Sitting or standing somewhere else in or near their office
- Another place in their office, a small conference table, or perhaps a separate conference room

- A place where they appear to be comfortable and relaxed, especially when they are outside of their own office or work environment
- An idea, perspective, or point of view

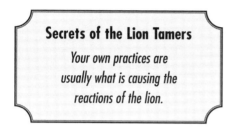

Secrets of the Lion Tamers

Your own practices are usually what is causing the reactions of the lion.

Whether it is a specific place or a frame of reference, your job is to find where the lion feels safe, secure, and dominant. Sometimes you create a place that signifies where they want to reign from and what they may wish to reign over. Take them back there as a beginning point and you will find that you have made it possible to pick up where you left off or leap to something new. Here is an example.

The Lion's Pedestal: The United States Senator

A United States Senator I worked for had a large office. The room was divided into two areas. There was a comfortable sitting area with tall-back chairs and couches on one side. The Senator's own working area was on the other side, consisting of his desk and chair, which faced two smaller chairs.

When the Senator received larger groups of people, he used the sitting area, but for meetings with one or two staff members he chose to sit at the desk facing two chairs. So if you were a staff member, which chair would you sit in? It may sound like a simple question, but it turned out that the choice could make or break a meeting. I learned through trial and error, and by taking some risks that proved worthwhile.

I learned that sitting in the first of the two chairs in front of his desk, although it was closest to the office door and the "first seat in the room," was actually the wrong choice. How could that be? The chair seemed to be almost directly in front of the Senator when he sat at his desk, right where he would look up and expect you to sit down.

That was also the problem. As I experienced, he was there for another reason because it aligned him with his inbox on his right, his most important papers in front of him, and his line of sight connected straight to his office door.

As I learned, if you sat in the first chair in front of the Senator's desk, it was hard to hold his attention, even though you sat just a foot or so apart. His hands were still focused on the important papers and materials in his inbox and before him on his desk. His head and eyes were always prepared to shift to the door behind where I sat because his chief of staff or scheduler might walk through the door at any time.

It just did not feel right, though I probably could not have explained why. To my eye, I noticed all the barriers to getting and holding his attention, and in the next meeting chose a different seat.

Even though sliding into the second chair closer to the window gave the appearance that I was "settling in," it was the only seat that allowed me to use the technique of the lion's pedestal. As I scooted in, the Senator and I both moved our chairs a little to adjust, the Senator away from his paperwork and habitual line of sight and toward me. Together as we leaned toward each other a bit as we framed a new space with minimal distractions. In the future, I would always take that seat, and the Senator easily grew accustomed to the routine. He would adjust his seat a bit, and we would move ahead with the subject of our meeting. If anyone else entered, they were always welcomed to sit in the first chair and be included in the meeting, and that was fine with me.

The Lion's Need for Personal Space

Secrets of the Lion Tamers

Get them accustomed to you. Give them a definite place of their own.

A few insights from the lion tamers may save you some valuable time in determining the lion's pedestal, and avoiding some unnecessary wear and tear:

- Recognize the characteristics and factors that shape the lion's feelings and outlook.
- Use that knowledge to shape how you can act and speak to them to maintain momentum and build rapport, trust, and mutual respect.

It seems that at almost every turn, there is further evidence that the art of lion taming involves a key component: the lion's strong sense of personal and social space or distance. All animals, including people, have a flight distance and a fight distance:

- **Flight distance:** the amount of space lions need around them to feel that they can escape.
- **Fight distance:** the reaction to a lack of flight or escape distance. (Note: If you cannot get out of the fight distance quickly enough, you will be the one who cannot escape.)

These same strong senses of personal and social space exist in the lions we face at work. Some people truly reign while sitting at their desk. Like most lions that sit atop their pedestal, they are secure in the belief that no one will dislodge them from their seat. Most of us feel that way when we are sitting at our desks, and are probably more relaxed, focused, and confident at that time—or for that matter, sometimes when we are just sitting.

However, our first lesson of lion taming was to remember that we are dealing with a different species, and that lions have different sensitivities. The people who are the lions have special sensitivities and preferences about space, and sometimes exhibit a greater need to move quickly from one place to another. Here's why.

Scientists studying lions in the wild, as well as in circuses and zoos, have observed something worth keeping in mind. It is important in approaching any of the people who are the lions at work to be aware of their division of personal space. Lions may view one part of their territory as their home, another as their individual space (such as the pedestal), and a related area where they play, roam, or socialize. You need to recognize how and where the lions in the workplace divide up their own space. This includes determining whether the lions you work with care to share some of their own space with others, and, if so, which parts. It varies with different individuals, but it will tell you a great deal about where they feel comfortable working and speaking with others *in person.*

Lion Tamers Must Have "360" Vision

The space can even vary depending on the subject being discussed. Sometimes people organize themselves so well in their own offices that it makes it easy to recognize where specific activities or parts of their day will take place. Lion tamers must have a "360" view of the room, and read behavior as it is developing. Here is a good example.

The Executive Center Ring

A senior advertising executive divided his office into three different areas: Creative—Strategy—Business. Creative was anything involving pictures, and that work was done at a large round conference table with no chairs. Strategy was done at the white board. Business was done sitting at his desk.

While the places and symbols were fairly obvious, they were unspoken, and the executive did not even seem to be aware that he made the distinction. The other company's account managers, creative people, and assistants needed to recognize that if they wanted to talk about a topic, they would be greatly aided by the ability to guide the executive toward the right "pedestal" where the executive was most likely to respond.

A word of caution: Don't try to divide up the boss's office on your own. More than likely the boss will interpret that as a sign of interference and attempted manipulation—even if they appear to have every intention of ignoring whatever you have done to "help" them.

Why the Center Ring Is Not a Square!

Secrets of the Lion Tamers

You can approach a lion from any side to make him go where you want him to go; you can crowd him; even provoke him a little.

The steel-caged arenas that lion acts are performed in are circular for a reason, and that simple fact of geometry has a significant effect on the behavior of the lions and the trainers. Lions don't like to be cornered. In the ring, there are simply no corners for the lion to be cornered in, and although the lion tamer is still working with a wild animal in a confined space, it is easier to keep things moving.

With the exception of perhaps the Oval Office in the White House, the average workplace or office is fraught with real corners and other ways that people can feel cornered. People are animals that feel cornered in both physical and other spaces that have been established both innately and consciously. For people, there are spaces within spaces. Even the executive, boss, or client that enjoys a large office may view their own desk as their most private area—their home, their den, even their nest—and they are not comfortable with anyone hanging around that space. In their minds it is a protected space, the place where they can relax and concentrate on what they need to do. When someone trespasses on their space, they feel and act like a cornered lion even though they often cannot come up with the words to explain it. The president of one company put it bluntly: "Why are you standing in front of me at my desk? This is where I do my work, you are not going to get my attention here!"

This also illustrates the earlier points we made about the lion's dual reactions of either flight or fight, depending on their instinctive sense of their ability to escape. The people who fail to realize this inadvertently trigger a negative reaction, and those who persist in this behavior without recognizing what they are doing are simply training the lion to react negatively every time they approach them at their desk. Intrude on the lion's space, even by just stepping too close to their pedestal, and the lion will roar right back!

Bouncing the Lion

> **Secrets of the Lion Tamers**
>
> *It is not all one-way. The lions learn that the pedestal is where they have your attention as well.*

Sometimes, as we will see, all hope is not lost in such situations. As we have mentioned, lion tamers know how to use the reactions of lions to achieve a specific result. Lion tamers who want that "fighting style" in their lion acts simply use the lion's natural ability to react in such a manner, and build these moves into their act. They even know how to briefly intrude on the lion's sense of confinement, to engage the lion's attention and bring them toward the lion tamer. When they do this, it is really to move the lion toward another objective, at the same time backing up quickly enough so that the lion no longer feels confined but moves to a pedestal. The same technique can be used effectively at work.

Have you ever needed to "get a bounce" out of someone? Little did you realize that the art of lion taming, including the use of space to get a lion onto a pedestal, operates on many of the same dynamics. As we will see, whether it is the real lion on their pedestal or getting the attention of leaders, bosses, or other tough customers, the ability to "bounce the lion" depends on your knowledge, subtle use of space, and your footwork.

Here's some valuable insight and theory from real lion taming to explain why "bouncing the lion" and other related techniques work.

Lessons of the Lion Tamers

From Flight to Fight

Real lion tamers use their knowledge of space and distances to drive the lions away from them and to attract the lions toward them. They can even drive the lions to a very specific location, like a pedestal. By placing the pedestal between the lion and the lion tamer, it is possible for the lion tamer to move forward into the lion's space, bouncing the lion forward as the lion tamer backpedals with the pedestal in between. At the appropriate moment, when the lion is on the pedestal, the lion tamer has to be just far enough away that the lion does not pursue the lion tamer anymore and gets comfortable with the pedestal. As we will see, sometimes a very similar formula of steps and footwork are exactly what is necessary in the workplace.

Consider this story about early-morning meetings when I needed to engage the biggest lion in my organization—my own boss. Bouncing the lion became an effective way to communicate initially, and then led a much less obvious way of signaling to each other that we needed to speak to one another. At the outset though, I had to be willing to risk a few snarls from the lion.

Bouncing the Morning Lion

Like many successful and hardworking CEOs, the chief executive I worked for arrived at the office in the dark and drove home in the dark. I realized that in working closely together, I had to match his schedule, although it was never formally required or expected. Perhaps the greatest challenge was engaging him in the mornings, particularly because at such times between 6 A.M. and 6:30 A.M., he would be working at his desk, a place that he considered his private working area. Nonetheless, it was important to say hello and try to have a very brief discussion, free from the pressures of the day, about hot issues, intelligence, and what kind of day was ahead of him.

There is a fine line in such situations between being persistent and being disruptive. While I knew that he really preferred not to be bothered, this brief discussion each morning was more valuable than spending an hour together. It was a chance to begin the adjustment agenda, learn to get the lion to approach the lion tamer, and even figure out where his actual lion's pedestal was—which in this case was not at his desk. In the process, I was able to learn about the world he was operating in, troubleshoot problems in advance, provide intelligence, and even pick up some valuable assignments to make his job easier.

That said, it was clear from the moment I walked through the door at 6:20 A.M. (on a good day) that he preferred to be alone. I would say hello as an alert that I was in the room. Even though he continued working with his head down, he tilted it just enough to suggest that it was okay but not preferable to approach further. Most people might assume "leave the lion alone," but you will never gain the understanding and rapport you need if you wait for the lions at work to choose the time.

Even when I walked directly up to his desk, there was usually not a response for about a minute. As I leaned forward a little he would emit a crisp, "I'm busy, give me a second," which was still not an invitation to sit down. I found that speaking at that point produced more resistance. Standing there for a few seconds and then backing off was about right.

Then after a minute or so he would sit back in his chair or stand up and stretch for a minute. He would ask in a serious tone, "What's up?" and we would engage in conversation for about two to three minutes, accomplishing something important. We soon merged these short conversations into a regular part of how we communicated, and in the future simply cued one another by saying "I need you for a minute." This may seem natural enough, but in fact if we had not actually established the routine with each other it might not have ever been something we could repeat. Over time I could simply make eye contact with him, raise my right hand and index finger as if saying "one minute," and he would nod me into his office for a quick chat. It was not a far cry at all from what Mabel Stark, the legendary big cat trainer, described as her technique: "I can get just as good a 'bounce' from a cat just by raising my hand. Just my voice and the positions I take is enough to start them bouncing!"

The Lion's Flight Zone and Fight Zone

Valuable lessons are provided by what is going on in the minds of real lion tamers as they bounce the lion. The lion tamer's knowledge is similar to visualizing the lion inside of two concentric circles. The outer circle is the lion's flight or comfort zone. If the lion tamer crosses into this area, the lion may begin to move away or flee. The inner circle is the lion's personal space, and it is said that even if the lion knows and likes the trainer, stepping into this circle will provoke an attack in earnest. If you have ever been around horses, deer, or even pet dogs, you may recognize these reactions. A strong step forward and they react with surprise and quickly flee; then they stop some distance away to look at you, returning to a state of rest. That's their flight reaction. Lion tamers use this to drive the lions away from them to a particular point or position in the ring.

When the Lion Shifts from Flight to Fight

However, as with all animals and people, if you cut off their flight distance, corner them, or just "get in their face," you will provoke an attack. And what makes both real lion taming and lion taming at work so dangerous is that in most cases you want to draw the lion *toward* you. Doing this releases the lion's fight reaction, and instead of having room to flee they must push against your intrusion to create the space they desire. The result is that they will move quickly toward you—even right at you—to push you away and enlarge the distance to where they are comfortable. They are shifting from flight to fight. In fact, if you fail to step back as the lion comes at you, the full effect of a fighting lion is exactly what you will feel. And if there is something that is already causing them to be afraid, then the fighting reaction may be released in a way that is faster, more unpredictable, and more difficult to manage.

However, it is important to realize that such reactions from flight to fight are the lion's way of handling a defensive emergency. In lion taming, it has been observed that a defensive or emergency attack is always aimed straight at the trainer. You can probably sense the result. Lions that perform in "fighting acts" are trained to produce just this kind of performance—sometimes propelling the lion halfway across the arena!

How can these distances and reactions be used proactively? Some have suggested that lion tamers can move the lions forward and backward with a precision "within centimeters." However, let's face it, whether you are working with real lions in the steel-caged arena or the boss in their office, centimeters may be all you have to work with! Not all lion tamers are convinced of the precision, since like working with people you are dealing with individuals, feelings, and many different variables—from mood to environment.

It is perhaps less science than art, but the general idea of viewing real lions or the people we encounter at work as being inside two concentric circles seems right. If you think of everyone having an outer circle that is their sense of a secure distance, and of everyone having an inner circle where you can expect a different reaction, you can enter the inner circle to create a stronger reaction and get their attention. However, you must quickly back out of that distance to stop the attack. The attack stops not because the lion is not angry any longer, but because you have *removed the motive for the lion attacking*. The result is that the lion remains on the pedestal and calms down.

Here is an example that reflects the parallel sensitivity of the lions in the workplace to their sense of space, flight, and fight—and in this case there was an extra twist.

The Lion's Pedestal: The Perilous Partner

How would you feel if your boss wouldn't let you into his office and wouldn't come into your office? Probably the same as the people working at this professional firm—completely mystified.

Anyone who walked into the boss's office received a defensive and aggressive reaction. People who tried to ask him something in passing were rebuffed. You might say that the only alternative was telephone or email, yet he liked sorting things out with his staff in person. But how?

The answer unfolded by surprise when a confused and frustrated employee was trying to figure him out—and was ready to quit. Asked if anything made sense in the boss's movements, he realized that there was a pattern. Sometimes the employee stuck his head into the boss's office and said, "Dave, I need to speak with you sometime," and then left. Later the boss would come back to the employee's door and say, "Bob, let's talk." Then they would invariably move to one spot in the hallway near the partner's office.

It seemed so odd that the employee had chalked it up to another bizarre character trait. In fact, he soon realized that the spot in the hallway *was* the lion's pedestal. To cue him to go there, all he had to do was stick his head in the boss's doorway and let him know they needed to talk, and then wait for the boss to appear in his own doorway. This pattern was so strong that even if the two saw each other in a meeting or in the hall in between doorway communications, they said nothing about getting together.

These steps needed to be precise. They did more than just provide an ability to communicate more effectively; they relieved a major source of stress. The employee no longer had to worry about when and where the boss might want to talk to him, and he knew exactly how to get the boss to approach him, especially when he needed him to.

Getting the Lion to Approach You

> **Secrets of the Lion Tamers**
>
> *You cannot dash and bob around haphazardly without thoroughly confusing the lion.*

Sometimes the question, as one executive with a few battle scars wisely asked, is, "How do you get the lion to approach you without attacking you?" Whether you're working with people or real lions, the stakes are high. You probably know from your own experience that some relationships seem like a one-way street. Lion tamers face that reality every day, and in most cases successfully work toward a mutual understanding and rapport.

Where you position yourself in relationship to the lion in the workplace is critically important. In addition to assessing how the lions feel in particular places and spaces, your ability to have an arc of communication between you depends on many factors, most that you will have to juggle intuitively:

- If you get too close, they will feel uncomfortable.
- If you are standing while they are sitting, they may never tell you what you need to know.
- If you fail to sit at the place that has been established for the person in this position or title, you will not be able to communicate effectively.
- Everything matters, including your posture, leaning or stepping forward or backward, tone of voice, and facial expressions.

You must become more sensitive to the place and to the space between yourself and the other person. It is a part of the lion tamer's job that begins by just standing still. You can best appreciate it by looking to other fields where basic forms of contrast are also essential to sharpen perspective, context, and meaning. For example, composers have remarked that there would be no music without silence. For artists "the space between" the painting or sculpture and the viewer is said to be as important as the object itself. One well-known artist planning for the exhibition of his works in a New York gallery not only believed that the lighting and spacing for his paintings was crucial, he also redesigned the walls of the gallery with a special color and texture of paint to help create the right "interior landscape."

It is important to note that this, too, is an area where you can have influence, though perhaps not complete control. The lion's pedestal is a two-dimensional technique; the arrangement, location, space, and distance involved must allow you, the lion tamer, to do your best. So if you feel cornered, uncomfortable, or disadvantaged, you need to change your position and posture, and if necessary move the pedestal to a location of mutual comfort.

The Feng Shui of Power

Perhaps you are familiar with related strategies about where people sit or position themselves in meetings. There has been plenty written on the subject in the context of negotiations, sales, and other venues. Some stories are legendary about presidents, CEOs, and others playing various forms of "furniture chess" to ensure that whoever walked into their office felt overpowered. President Lyndon Johnson is said to have preferred having his chair always a little higher, and that he even arranged to have this arrangement in his office aboard Air Force One. A prominent New York CEO who otherwise had a quiet demeanor became a forceful executive when he occupied his French antique desk and chair, which were both elevated and perched under a visibly important and valuable oil painting. The closest seating facing the desk was a gleaming white couch about ten feet away. Virtually everyone who worked for him felt that they were speaking to someone "on high," and it became important to avoid crucial conversations in his office because they were always, as one executive phrased it, "a one-way street."

To demonstrate how attuned you have to be to the lion's personal feelings about space and distance in establishing a lion's pedestal, let's look at some sharp differences between successive CEOs in a single organization—even when they occupied the same exact office.

"Move the Door So I Can See Everything"

In one company, there were three chief executives who succeeded one another over the course of a twenty-year period. All had the same exact office but perceived it very differently in terms of their personal space and style of management and communication:

- The first executive had a traditional and predictable arrangement with his desk to the left of his doorway and not visible from the hallway. There was a conference table to the right as you entered. That is where he would hold most of his meetings.
- The second executive, who had come up through the ranks of the company, felt secluded in the office and also wanted people to know that he was "keeping an eye on everything." He not only moved his desk, but told the office manager on his first day of work to "move the doorway to the office so I can see everything." In came the carpenters and painters. The original doorway was sealed off, and a new doorway was created with interior windows on each side. Now, with a view right down the main hallway, the executive moved his desk front and center. He felt on top of the organization and was equally visible to others. It brought more traffic directly to his desk, and that's how he liked it.

- The third top executive arrived on the job and avoided the desk altogether. When the office manager and others heard him complaining that he couldn't get any work done in his office, they realized something might be wrong. Here was a lion who felt that his desk was his personal space, and he did not want everyone watching his every move. He wanted privacy. So, the desk was moved back to its original location, and the conference area was restored. But curiously, his own office was not this lion's pedestal. Instead, as people learned, he liked to meet with people in the office of whomever the top executive was in each of the departments. So when he wanted to talk "admin," he hung out in the HR director's office. When he wanted to talk marketing or sales, he met with people in the office of the vice president of sales and marketing. Even the executives got used to sharing their own office with the chief executive, and it turned out to be a good management strategy for everyone.

These examples and others like them reinforce the tendency of many lions in the workplace to create their own pedestal. It may save the lion tamers in the workplace a step, or at least provide a beginning point for you to guide them—that is, if they do not guide you there first.

The Lion Tamer's Position in the Arena

The lion's dominant position is meaningful, but maybe not in a way you were expecting.

The lion's-pedestal technique works only if it results in a more effective rapport and communication between the lion and the lion tamer. If the lion's chosen pedestal makes you feel uncomfortable, cornered, or unable to be yourself, then you need to create an alternative. This is something you have influence over, and may in fact be just how you get the lion to begin approaching you.

However, if you are becoming more adept at reading the lion's behavior, then the pedestal and the distance between you are probably working. Perhaps it is a good distance to respect. It marks the boundaries between the lion's flight distance and fight distance. If you cannot move quickly enough when their fight distance is triggered, you may find yourself in trouble.

What is the best test to use in practical situations in the office? As one long-time top executive determined, the real question you must answer is whether you and the lion are positioned "Where the lion hears what you are saying."

The Lion's Pedestal: The CEO

A CEO had an enormous office, big even by CEO standards. Finding the lion's pedestal took some thinking and experimenting. The entrance was at one end of the office, and the CEO's desk was all the way at the other end. The entrance was so far away that a button was installed behind the CEO's desk to electronically close the door for privacy. To the right of the entrance was a sitting area in front of a fireplace, with two sofas facing each other across a coffee table, and two small arm chairs just above the sofas. At the other end of the room there were two chairs in front of the CEO's desk, and one off to the side against the inside wall.

Where was the lion's pedestal? Where should the lion tamer be positioned? There were many choices—too many, it seemed.

Answering this question required returning to the lion's own needs and characteristics. In this case, the CEO was the kind of person who treated his desk as his private workplace. It was his home. Of course, he would never say that, but it was observable, if you looked. It was clear from every reaction: "Even though everyone can see me sitting at my desk, hear my telephone conversations, see what I am working on—I want some privacy." He showed it whenever someone approached, keeping his head down, elbows flared outward.

He kept people away from his home by getting up quickly whenever a meeting was going to take place and moving to a different location, steering people away from his desk. You could interpret this as flight, or you could sense that he had another place to talk from, or needed one.

However, some people continued to hover before him at his desk while he kept his head down working, never getting the message. They were usually the same people who would keep asking, "How do you talk to the CEO? I can't figure him out!"

When pressed on an issue while sitting behind his desk, the CEO tended to act more defensively, as if he were cornered. It was the classic example of people thinking only of approaching the lion, not thinking or working to get the lion to approach them.

For this CEO, the lesson was to recognize these traits and reactions. Getting him away from his desk would free up his mind and attention, and reduce the feeling of being cornered. The couches by the fireplace were too informal, leaving only a pair of small armchairs in the middle of the room. To many people, the armchairs seemed too small, too unassuming to guide the CEO to. Yet when he did move there, for a moment it allowed him the chance to sit in the middle of the room, free to move and reign over the room.

It was also a smart move on his part. He either recognized or determined that other people's behavior changed

> toward him when he moved away from his desk. It worked perfectly, particularly with the added step of moving the chairs closer together after the CEO sat down. The CEO, a very quick learner, especially of things that worked well, adopted this routine easily. The attention-getting routine was set by finding the lion's pedestal, and as a result the attention-using always began almost immediately.

You may already be thinking about the people you work with and where their "lion's pedestal" is located. Although they may share some common characteristics, it is important to remember that each lion has his or her own style. But no matter how different the lions are, this kind of lion taming allows you to create time and space that did not exist before. The lion's pedestal works because the lion tamer and the lion are discovering the path of least resistance, something that like individuals cannot always see themselves.

THE LION'S TALE

- The lion tamer's goal is not to get the people who are the lions to simply sit. Your objective is to find and use a path of least resistance to communicate together by meeting the lion's need to feel dominant and safe, and to be secure in those feelings. It is then that they will turn their attention to what others may want and need of them
- Study their use of space—their personal sensitivities, how they divide up their office mentally and physically—determining where they are most comfortable with other people and discussing specific subjects.
- Identify the natural pedestal where their need for dominance and security can be met and where they are certain no one will dislodge them from.
- Recognize that some people feel that their desk is a private area, or feel cornered there, and would prefer to have conversations and a pedestal somewhere else. If that is the case, then the lion's pedestal is usually in a location that must be the opposite of somewhere they feel cornered—an open area. These can include standing by their window, standing or sitting on chairs in the middle of the room, a designated sitting or meeting area, or even outside their own office in the hall or someone else's office.
- Natural lion's pedestals often exist in formal meeting rooms, such as executive conference rooms. However, it is important to remember

(continued)

that such settings can also change the dynamic of the way you are with each other from a private one-to-one discussion to a public setting. In private you can often confront and challenge the lion's views in a more open discussion, but in public the same discussion will be seen as competing with them or challenging them.

- To bounce the lion remember this: When it appears that you may be infringing on the lion's space and you have engaged them sufficiently, make sure that you are backing up at the same time to achieve the distance needed to remove their motivation for attacking you. Remember that the motivation is not anything you said, it is the simple fact that you are in their space. In fact you will probably have to repeat what you said once both the lion and the lion tamer adjust the space between them.

8

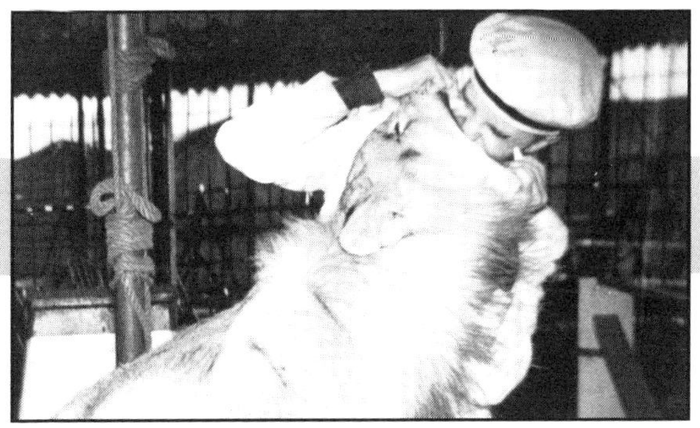

Sticking Your Head in the Lion's Mouth

Secrets of the Lion Tamers

The animal's dignity has to be respected.

One of the most vivid images associated with lion taming unfolds when the music stops and the lion tamer walks empty-handed toward a group of lions poised on a pyramid of pedestals. From outside the arena, the ringmaster barks, "The only man in the world to place his head in the mouth of a five-hundred-fifty-pound African lion!" Learning the details from the lion tamer's own mouth provides a truly close-up experience. Sometimes too close, even for lion tamers like "The Professor" George Keller, who strove for authenticity. And, he got it!

Lessons of the Lion Tamers
The Big Fangs

"I discovered that at least some of the few other trainers who performed this trick were much less thorough. They merely pulled the lion's jaws apart, quickly inserted and withdrew their faces. I actually wedged my head inside Leo's jaws, so that his fangs locked me in. I used to keep my head in there for ten seconds—I counted to ten slowly—and then I'd tap him under the chin with my knuckles. That was the cue for him to release me."

On most days the chasm of danger opened, closed, and reopened without harm. But then one day the lion tamer was not so fortunate.

"Just as I began to put my head in his mouth, rain began to fall. It came in a sudden downpour. I felt Leo become suddenly tense; he had never performed in the rain before…and he evidently resented the experience. But my head was in now, and the big fangs had come down behind my ears. I counted to ten, slowly—perhaps not as slowly as usual—and then gave him the cue by releasing my hold on his jaws and tapping him under the chin. There was no response at all. The jaws were clamped on my head and I could feel no movement in the muscles; Leo's mouth might have been steel."

Several minutes later, Keller came to, squirming and mistaking the oxygen mask attached to his face for the lion's head. The medic by his side explained what happened, "You had your head in the lion's mouth and he wouldn't release you so you suffocated.…As soon as you became limp he dropped you—the way a cat drops a mouse when it's exhausted. You fell on the ground and we went in and picked you up.…I don't want to scare you, but for nearly three minutes you had no heart beat and no respiration."

"How It's Done and Why It Shouldn't Be"

> **Secrets of the Lion Tamers**
>
> *Present the abilities of the cats rather than your own machismo.*

Despite the popularity and the danger of the trick, not all lion tamers believe that sticking your head in the lion's mouth is a feat worth attempting. In fact, some object strongly. As we will see, their reluctance provides several valuable lessons for the workplace.

Clyde Beatty addressed the subject as "The Head-in-the-Lion's-Mouth Trick—How It's Done and Why It Shouldn't Be." He may have saved many a future lion tamer the need to discover the apparent truths about "lion's breath." He believed strongly that nothing is so important—not even getting a roar from the audience—that you should put yourself in a totally defenseless position. For Gunther Gebel-Williams, the choice was simple: "I do not do anything ridiculous to show off, such as putting my head into a tiger's or lion's mouth."

Others pointed to a bigger picture, believing that people who stick their heads in the lion's mouth are risking more than their own neck.

> **Lessons of the Lion Tamers**
>
> **R-E-S-P-E-C-T**
>
> Lion tamer Pat Anthony achieved fame as the only person to study lion taming under the GI bill. Succinctly capturing what is most real and important, he offers a plainspoken philosophy that applies whether you studied lion taming or received an MBA:
>
> "The main reason I don't stick my head in the lion's mouth is because it's a display of stupidity. It belittles the wild animal and knocks down the standard of the act. You tell the public that you're working chickens, you take away the anxiety from the act!"

Anthony's words should be engraved on a plaque and hung in every office—including the boss's. His philosophy reflects a showman's wisdom that transcends "giving the audience what they want." If the lion doesn't look good, you don't look good. Similarly, if your boss doesn't look good, you don't look good.

There is always a triangle of perception between the lion, the lion tamer, and the audience (not to mention the other lions). Anthony recognized that he was never truly alone in the cage with the lions. Who is watching the interaction? What lessons do they draw from the experience?

In the workplace, the triangle exists between employees, managers, and executives. In the office, everyone observes the interactions of others, hearing about events they did not actually see, casting judgment, reaching conclusions, and acting accordingly. They decide who is strong and who is weak, who is smart, who is a leader, and who is dangerous.

We may cringe at the image of the lion tamer sticking his head in the lion's jaws, yet the workplace is rife with such examples each and every day. Sometimes it seems to be a function of individual personalities and attitudes; other times it plays out in power struggles and personal agendas—the stuff of office drama.

Head in the Lion's Jaws—Corporate Style

Consider the new Senior Vice President for Operations at the New York headquarters of a large international company. It became clear to everyone from the very first department meeting what they were really watching. There might as well have been a ringmaster announcing the thrills and chills to follow:

1. *Now, before your very eyes, I will stick my head in the lion's powerful jaws!* The new executive announces to everyone assembled, "I didn't come here to be head of operations, I came here to become CEO."
2. *Opening the lion's jaws.* He meets with the CEO and all major executives, telling them he is there, reminding them why he was hired, and—despite the fact that he does not generate revenue for the business—says just how invaluable a role he will play.
3. *Sticking his head directly inside the lion's mouth.* He follows up weekly with his own department's managers and staff, who refer to the meetings as "ego-bending" and shudder as their new boss criticizes each of the company's leaders, makes jokes about their traits, and even imitates them.
4. *The lion chomps down.* Less than a year goes by—fast for large organizations to evaluate senior-level hires—and the senior vice president is fired. Ten years later, the CEO was still on the job.

Not surprisingly, the most common reason that anyone can find to explain why such situations develop—regardless of their title, position, industry, or occupation—is ego. Their dedication to success and advancement appears so self-focused that is ingrained whether they are trying to claw their way to the top, keep from being banished from the pride, or merely hold on for the sake of survival.

How does Pat Anthony's plainspoken philosophy apply to this situation?

- In this case, the department executives and staff reacted to their new boss's behavior as a "display of stupidity," or at least foolishness. Everyone else already knew who had the power in the company, and it wasn't their new boss. Why didn't he see that?

- Instead, his behavior "belittled" the company's leaders by suggesting that they were going to be easy to control or manipulate.
- He "knocked down the standard of the act" and weakened the image of his own department—a group that suddenly everyone else in the company wanted to avoid because of their boss's conduct. After all, the danger such people create spreads by association to others with whom they work closely.
- Finally, by criticizing and belittling the top leadership of the company, the senior vice president removed "all the anxiety"—the aura of respect or fear that people have for top people in the company—because of the way that he repeatedly trivialized and treated them.

The bottom line is that in business, the leaders, bosses, and other tough customers are an investment. If you do anything to diminish their value, you will pay for the loss as much as they will, perhaps more.

No doubt you have your own experiences and observations to add to a list of behaviors to avoid. How about the people who plant themselves next to the boss at every meeting like an appendage, or others who finish the boss's sentences with "What she meant to say was..." or "What I think we can all take away from this is..."? Sometimes it is intentional; sometimes, inadvertent. Most of us have experienced it in one form or another. Have you ever helped to prepare a boss or client behind closed doors for a more public meeting or event, sensing that they were intensely interested in the information and observations you had to share, but as soon as the scene changed you were expected to melt into thin air?

Don't forget that they are lions. You can do plenty of one-on-one to help them, but the minute you are in public together you are seen as a challenger to their reign, standing between them and a bigger kingdom.

One boss I worked for was so sensitive about this that I was tempted to buy him a button to pin on his suit that said, "Steve Who?" But even that would have been too much. Be bold, be funny, but above all else, you must always be respectful.

Depending on your own perspective, position, and experience, you may think you have heard it all. Yet everyone is always surprised when people who seem to have so much at stake—regardless of their level or title in the organization—stick their head in the lion's mouth. A right-hand executive to top-level leaders and corporate executives had this comment:

> You come in as a hotshot chief of staff or senior aide to the CEO or VP—that official does not want competition or for you to be the hotshot. They want you to ensure that they continue at their job and that you will make them a great big lion!

Secrets of the Lion Tamers

A display of temper paves a sure road to an early grave.

The list of possible ways that people stick their heads in the lion's mouth at work reads like a coroner's statement of the hasty lion tamer's "cause of death." Whether it is a leader, boss, or other tough customer, any of the following is the equivalent of sticking your head in the lion's mouth:

- Bruising their ego
- Challenging them gratuitously
- Competing with them
- Condescending or patronizing
- Controlling them

- Embarrassing, humiliating, or insulting them
- Lying
- Losing your temper
- Making them do something they cannot do
- Manipulating them for your benefit
- Micromanaging them
- Over-promising and under-delivering
- Positioning yourself too closely to them in public
- Pushing them to do something they fear
- Representing them as dependent on you
- Revealing secrets, confidences, or "inside information"
- Sitting next to them without being asked or told to do so
- Taking credit (even if you believe you deserve it)
- Talking behind their back
- Teasing or laughing at them
- Telling them everything (e.g., compliments you have received from others at their level)
- Upstaging them
- Wasting their time

Who's the Real Lion?

Executives interacting with one another often stick their heads in the lion's mouth. Their biggest weakness is failing to sense—instinctively, intuitively, or by just reading the sign on the door—when to assume the role of the lion tamer instead of the lion. The best can switch roles in the blink of an eye, but many miss it routinely. They forget that there is always a bigger lion, and instinctively go to war before using diplomacy. Here is an example that occurred at the very top of the food chain.

The President and the CEO

The CEO of a large company held Monday-morning meetings of the executive team attended by the company's president, the chief financial officer, and three executive vice presidents. The nice surroundings aside, it was an increasingly uncomfortable environment. The company president was argumentative, challenging virtually every idea the CEO offered. The only mystery was how vocal he would be about each point. Yet he wondered why no one else around the table ever agreed with him, even when he sensed they believed him?

As the board-of-directors meeting approached, the CEO invited a couple of friendly board members to attend the Monday "exec" for a dry run of the corporate vision and strategy for the upcoming year. Even though there were high-level visitors, the president continued in his usual display. If anything, he was more intense, getting into one-sided arguments as the CEO patiently listened and moved through the presentation.

After the meeting, the CEO, president, and the board members were taking a break before having lunch together. One of the board members asked the president if he could have a friendly word. "You may not realize how strongly you come off, but it looks bad. It looks like you have no respect for Jim," he said.

The company president looked surprised: "I'm just trying to do my job, I wasn't hired to be a yes man."

"There is a big difference between providing constructive criticism and tearing somebody else down," the board member said. "It weakens the CEO's leadership, but I don't think that is what you are trying to do, are you? It looks like neither you nor Jim is taking advantage of your ability to sit down together in advance. I am going to recommend at lunch that you meet weekly to hash out the agenda for the 'exec,' give yourselves a chance to do your reacting in private, and prove to others that you are a team. Who knows, you might even come up with a few good ideas!"

It dawned on the president that perhaps the board members were actually invited by the CEO to provide feedback on *him*, not the presentation. He learned a long time

> ago that some of the best advice he ever received was given when he did not expect it, often in informal exchanges on the way to a meeting, in the hallway, or catching a flight with a boss or another executive. He always took it as genuine, and did this time too.
>
> The CEO and president agreed at lunch to meet weekly—at a private "pre-exec." That meant hearing each other out in private and talking about their perceptions, strategies, and objectives; learning how to agree to disagree, but disagree without being disagreeable. Finally it meant ending one-upmanship and power struggles, and coming up with their own cues, such as, "Jim, let's sit down and talk this further," or asking others in the room to provide some additional ideas to them both.

It is hard for a lion to realize when they need to act more like a lion tamer. They are on "autopilot," controlled by the *Lion's Four Senses* of dominance, territory, social standing, and survival. They are used to displaying the behavior, often aggressively, that lions use to size each other up, determine their place in the hierarchy, and demonstrate up-front strength and agility. Most problematic is how their behavior impacts everyone around them. Most surprising is how easy it would have been to use the advantages of their status and position to work cooperatively with their boss rather than challenging them outright. As we will see, sometimes this can be remedied; other times it is simply too late.

These situations happen in the corporate world and anywhere there is a hierarchy, and perhaps no organization is more hierarchical than the military. Consider the next example.

The Three-Star General and the Two-Star General

Even in the military, where the first thing people are taught is to salute, there are those who confuse responsibility with command authority, even among those who should understand it most clearly.

One of those who should have understood this reality was a two-star Air Force general who mistakenly took ownership of a major restructuring process—seeing it as his career ladder to climb, rather than the command responsibility of his boss, a three-star general. After spending months directing his own personal staff to prepare his plan of action, he arranged for a meeting with the three-star general, naturally bringing along his troop of admirers. He proceeded to tell the general how he and his team would lead the restructuring.

It was another classic case of sticking your head in the lion's mouth, and had virtually all the elements we have discussed, including a tragic ending, at least for the two-star general. He failed to respect the dignity of the three-star general, treated him as someone who could be controlled, tried to show others how the three-star general was dependent upon him, and lowered the perception or aura of respect that others had for the general. The two-star general left himself completely defenseless, learning shortly after the meeting that the three-star general killed the proposal and established his own planning process and team. Not long after that, the two-star general wound up retiring without ever achieving another promotion in rank.

Once again, we are dealing with a high-ranking executive who cannot recognize the bigger lion, even when it is staring him right in the face. How should the two-star general have approached the situation? Even a two-star general can be a lion tamer to a three-star general, facilitating and helping the superior officer be successful in ways that reflect well on the entire leadership. The subject of restructuring was obviously public, yet how the general was dealing with it was best explored in private. He could have let the three-star general know that he had an interest in helping, and created a working group chaired by the three-star general to come up with a plan, conduct outreach, and establish a base of knowledge, action, and implementation. A public meeting with the three-star general, the two-star general, and any necessary staff would be designed to preserve the leadership of the three-star general and launch the effort. There is an old adage about "working the boss's problems for him," but it has to be done in such a way that the boss retains ownership of the solution.

Mid-level managers face some of the most difficult challenges, supervising some people and also being supervised by other executives. As we learn in this case, communication and establishing the proper expectations are important. Subtle omissions and the desire to please can be interpreted by bosses as lying, which weakens trust and mutual respect. How is trust established with the boss? In one sense, it happens quickly or not at all.

The Manager and the Partner

A law-firm partner and her paralegal were a well-known team at a large firm. They were two women, one who made it as partner in the days when the men dominated the profession, the other starting as a typist and ultimately becoming as valuable as any lawyer. When the paralegal decided to retire, the partner knew it would be hard to replace her, but left it up to the human resources director to get it done. The HR director was new, and interpreted the partner's professionalism as a signal to rely on his own expertise to find someone new. He quickly assigned someone who was tried and true as a legal secretary. "Is she really good?" asked the partner. "Excellent, very strong," the HR director replied.

After just two weeks, the partner was fuming, angry that she had to take more time to communicate and train the new paralegal, realizing that the combination of energy, knowledge, and personal rapport was missing.

Confronting the HR director, she said accusingly, "You lied to me, you lied straight to my face! I asked if this person was strong, and you said 'Yes, excellent.' But it is not true."

What should the HR manager have done? He should have been honest about the process, told the partner that initially someone temporary would staff her, backed up by a more experienced paralegal. Then he could interview the former paralegal to get the profile for the partner; interview the partner to identify what she needed—even things the former paralegal couldn't do; provide a timeframe to accomplish this; and always have an open door about problems.

What can he do to regain the trust and respect needed to make the necessary changes? Face it head on, and let the lion know he made a mistake. Find her the person she needs.

As we move across the organizational food chain, the pressure points for blow-ups, misunderstanding, and miscommunication often increase. Sometimes it is because executive assistants, confidential assistants, or secretaries are expected to be virtually telepathic. The boss assumes that they possess x-ray vision or a sixth sense. From the assistant's standpoint, the intimidation factor is lessened because they see them so often, while the frustration curve increases sharply. As one long-time executive assistant put it, "You know the person, you know how they will act, you can't do anything about it, and it drives you crazy." The problem is, you also cannot show it without getting your head bitten off!

The Executive Assistant and Vice President

While top executives may have their very own executive assistants or support staff, it is not an uncommon experience—particularly in the age of information technology and personal computers—for other groups of executives to share support staff. It can lead to multiple obligations and expectations, and when things pile up, there can be a lack of time to get everything done.

In the case of one particularly busy office, a vice president asked one of the executive assistants assigned to his division about the status of a report that she was responsible for assembling and sending to an important customer.

Exasperated and feeling pressured, the executive assistant decided to just level with her boss: "I haven't started yet."

The vice president was startled. He turned on her, asking: "What do you mean you haven't started yet, I asked you to take care of this last week. I am having lunch with the customer tomorrow!"

The executive assistant shot back, "It wasn't a priority, I couldn't get to it." For this employee, the rest was history.

What should have happened? The responsibility of course is on both parties. The executive didn't take the time to ensure that the person whose help he needed was available to do it in the necessary time frame. It was also the executive assistant's fault for not informing the vice president that the report was not going to be ready. And yelling back at your boss is never a recommended alternative.

The Head-in-Mouth Trick in Private and Public

Where does the head-in-mouth trick usually occur? It can happen in a one-on-one meeting, a small group, or in public. Your ability to demonstrate the same degree of awareness, sensitivity, and respect in all settings is critical. While mistakes and accidents can happen, if you have successfully established the rapport, mutual trust, and respect you need to work with someone, then the risks are significantly minimized. In reality, however, what makes it so difficult is the constant shifting back and forth between private and public discussions and interactions, and remembering that when you are in public it is the equivalent of the stage lights going up, and a bright silent flashing sign reading "On the Air!" "On the Air!" "On the Air!"

From the standpoint of leaders, bosses, and other tough customers—just like with real lions—once they are out in public, everything changes. Their radar is on and they are acutely sensitive to how every breath, glance, gesture, and word impacts upon how people might perceive them. As a result, things that were not an issue, a challenge, or a threat in a one-to-one meeting can become huge problems. Meetings and conversations, public events, or even just talking with a customer require that as a lion tamer you have to change gears mentally and have eyes in the back of your head. Your radar needs to be operating at 360 degrees and picking up signals as fast or faster than the lion is. What's your best tool? It is remembering the *Lion's Four Senses.* Imprint it on your brain like a radar screen and you will begin to sense the issues that may affect their dominance, territory, social standing, and survival. However, you must be alert and prepared to step into the lion tamer's shoes almost anywhere—in the car, on a plane, or at a dinner.

The E-Tamer

How creative does your thinking need to be? In today's world, technology puts you in an electronic center ring without the benefit of your senses, where you aren't eye to eye with the lion. You might call it being an "electronic lion tamer."

Can you imagine a real lion tamer trying to perform his or her job by transmitting words, sounds, or even pictures electronically to lions on their pedestals? In the e-ring, the entire dynamic is changed. *Lion taming is deeply rooted in a personal relationship that grows one encounter at a time.* You cannot simply send a message that says "trust me" to a lion. However, you can easily send one that sends the lion spinning out of control! The real problem is that your intuitions, built-in radar, and instincts are rendered inoperative when you are not communicating face-to-face.

"SEND": The Most Dangerous Four-Letter Word for a Lion Tamer

In the workplace, a telephone conversation, voicemail, or email can instantly put you in the arena with the lion from wherever you are. It is another irony of lion taming in the workplace that while most of the world is gaining opportunities from electronic communication, it creates significant risks to the lion tamer.

You must be alert to these problems, even if your boss, client, or others insist that you carry a cell phone, laptop, or wireless communication. Whether it is an email from inside the office or a cellular phone call from anywhere, it can cause a "blow up" that you will not be present to control or influence. The most dangerous four-letter word for the lion tamer in today's workplace is: SEND.

You are off guard; the context is not the safety of where you are writing this from but the context where it is received.

You must think to yourself: What if I was saying this while I was standing in front of my boss or client? Would I say it?

What are the most common risks in communicating electronically with the lions?

- Giving up privacy and confidentiality
- Being unable to look and see how the recipient is really feeling and acting
- Creating a false sense of familiarity, involvement, and security because you are communicating one-to-one
- Mistakenly sending a confidential message or sensitive message to the wrong person
- Representing to others that you have the full picture from someone with whom you are simply trading emails or voicemails
- Not knowing who else is listening, reading your email, or interacting and influencing the lion
- Getting too comfortable with distance and technology
- Relaxing and putting your guard down because the lion is not directly in front of you
- Forgetting that their behavior and reactions will influence everyone around them
- Saying things you would never say in person
- Giving people more than they want or need
- Using technology to avoid one-to-one meetings
- Ignoring the signals that certain people dislike technology and find it impersonal

Today's electronic world poses many new risks and potential embarrassments. It is one thing to experience them with friends, but they can become very serious on the job when you're dealing with leaders, bosses, and other tough customers. Which risks are the most significant? It depends on whom you are working with.

Take, for example, the CEO who had recently moved from Atlanta to take over a New York company, and who liked to stress the importance of his personal "down home" touch with the most highly visible customers: "Kill 'em with kindness!" He always felt compelled to email the senior sales vice president whenever he returned from these meetings. After several months of always responding with a complimentary, if over-the-top email response, the senior vice president felt that the CEO could handle a slightly more humorous pat on the back.

The CEO emailed her to say that a client meeting went very well, because he successfully condensed an hour into the customer's less-than-twenty minutes. "I think we'll win the new contract!" The senior vice president wrote back: "Congratulations Bob, I always knew you were the fastest mouth in the South!" The CEO shot back this message, in bold: "Watch it, Suzanne!" Again, be bold, be brave, be funny, but be respectful.

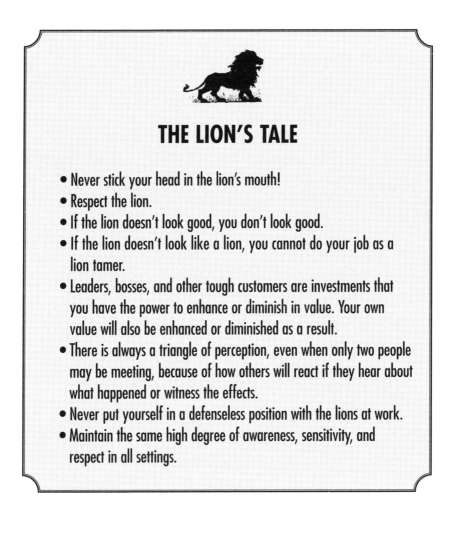

THE LION'S TALE

- Never stick your head in the lion's mouth!
- Respect the lion.
- If the lion doesn't look good, you don't look good.
- If the lion doesn't look like a lion, you cannot do your job as a lion tamer.
- Leaders, bosses, and other tough customers are investments that you have the power to enhance or diminish in value. Your own value will also be enhanced or diminished as a result.
- There is always a triangle of perception, even when only two people may be meeting, because of how others will react if they hear about what happened or witness the effects.
- Never put yourself in a defenseless position with the lions at work.
- Maintain the same high degree of awareness, sensitivity, and respect in all settings.

9

Lion Taming in Action

Let's step back and see how the wisdom of lion taming can be used in a workplace situation. The following story describes a scenario that applies the understanding and techniques we have looked at so far:

- Treat the lions in the workplace as a different species.
- Approach the lion so that the lion approaches you.
- Overcome the lion's experience with other lion tamers who left a bad taste by sticking their heads in the lion's mouth.
- Give the lion room to become adjusted to the lion tamer.
- Find and use the lion's pedestal.
- Build rapport, trust, and mutual respect.
- Reach a common goal by working together.
- Stand back.
- Let the lion leap through the hoop of fire.

I Am Lion, Hear Me Roar!

The president and faculty of a large university have been in hard-fought salary negotiations. The discussions are deadlocked, and the school year is ending with the two sides barely speaking to each other. The faculty representatives have publicized their frustration, giving numerous interviews to student and local newspapers that blame the university president for the deadlock. Both sides are about to have their summer plans disrupted. The president may have to decline a prestigious summer teaching post at Oxford if things are not resolved soon.

The campus is quiet and the crowds of students have gone. The president and the faculty agree to meet. The room has the feel of a practice arena for the lion and the lion tamer, but everything about it is very real.

The president comes into the room but won't sit down—his jaw is tense, he's ready to dominate. But he immediately sees that something has changed. A new professor is stepping forward as the faculty's team leader. The president greets the faculty gruffly, reacting loudly that he wasn't informed of a change in the participants. He's not starting over just to educate someone new—roaring about Oxford, and snarling about the consequences for the faculty.

The new faculty leader recognizes that the university president is a lion, so she must be the lion tamer. Lion taming handled correctly will calm the lion down, get him to work productively with the lion tamer, and leap through the hoop of fire—that is, signing a mutually satisfactory and timely contract. The president will get to be the lion king of the university; he can then roar all over campus if he wants—including at Oxford over the summer. The faculty will sign the contract they want and need. Everyone can see the hoop of fire, but before it can be lit, there's a lot of lion taming to do.

The lion tamer has prepared for the meeting by talking to her colleagues and reading up on the negotiations. She even has a rough schedule in mind, using the first meeting to get acquainted and then dealing with details in subsequent meetings. Now she's in the middle of the arena where the lion is sizing her up and she must think on her feet. There's not much that can be accomplished with an angry lion, and no amount of screaming or whip cracking can solve the problem. Let's watch as it unfolds!

Stand Your Ground

The lion tamer quickly begins to work out in her mind what she is dealing with—an angry lion that needs to be calmed down and become more trusting of the lion tamer. She must not cause the lion to flee, bluster, or attack. So, her first steps follow the basic laws of lion taming:

- Stand your ground.
- Maintain visual contact with the lion at all times.
- Keep a positive attitude and a firm tone of voice.
- Stand back; give the lion room physically and verbally.
- Let the lion roar—after all, he's a lion.

The professor greets the university president and retraces her steps backward while remaining directly in front of him. Even as he is complaining and acting belligerent, the lion tamer stays calm, smiling, and "killing him with kindness." She's respectful, a nod in response without backing down, letting him know that she regrets how things have turned out, and emphasizing and repeating, "We'll get it done, I have confidence. Your leadership will help make a difference."

The Lion Knows That He's the Lion

In the minutes and seconds that have ticked by, the lion tamer is making progress. Together with how she acts and what she says, the lion tamer works to establish trust with the lion. Building a rapport with the lion is a continuous part of lion taming. Initially, however, it is part of the sizing up—it happens quickly or not at all.

The lion knows he is the lion, and so does the lion tamer. How does the lion tamer communicate this to the lion? She does so by reflecting back to him that he is the lion and calming him down at the same time. Call it verbal stroking and an arc of words and emotion—the equivalent of how real lion tamers use a stick as an extension of their arms to work with the lions. So here, the lion tamer says how much the university president's leadership means to the university, listing several well-known accomplishments. Then she personalizes her comment by saying that his leadership influenced her decision to come there and teach. This signals that she's a stakeholder in what he's there to do and is part of his team to make it happen. Together they'll get through the hoop of fire. Lion taming is really lion teaming!

"Read" the Lion

To figure out her next steps and ensure her survival, she asks herself an obvious question: Why is this lion roaring with his fangs bared and claws swiping the air? Her answer lies in some valuable lion-taming wisdom: "There's no such thing as a bad lion, only a bad lion tamer." True or not, the previous faculty negotiators broke every rule of lion taming—not a recommended approach since lions are survivors at the top of the food chain. Here's what they did wrong:

- Even college professors are capable of *using brawn instead of brains* as they did by constantly trying to dominate the lion.

- They *gave up the lion tamer's ultimate leverage over the lion*: recognizing the president's primal drive to be the lion of the university. Instead of using that leverage, they tried to stop him from being a lion entirely.
- When the lion roared by disagreeing or failing to accept their offer, the faculty *tried to hurt the lion back* or mobilize public opposition to the president by publicizing their differences in the press. This only hurt the lion and angered him more.
- The faculty *got into the lion's face* at every opportunity, backing him into a corner.

The faculty created a dangerous situation by sticking their head in the lion's mouth, making the lion look bad in front of many others whose respect he needs. Now the lion tamer must reverse that to achieve progress. She has to remove the bad taste in the lion's mouth left there by her faculty colleagues. Is there any wonder why this lion won't let anyone near him?

The Lion's Pedestal

The lion tamer's challenge is to meet the lion's need to be the lion while preventing him from darting around the ring. She wants him to focus on the task at hand, as opposed to dominating the environment. The lion tamer also has to be able to develop a rapport with the lion—communicate, set expectations, and work toward the hoop of fire. Fortunately, the technique she needs is at hand. Lion tamers have been doing it forever. She must identify or create a lion's pedestal and get the lion accustomed to go to it.

The negotiations are being held in a neutral room, so, as is often the case, it is unclear what the lion's natural pedestal might be. So the lion tamer simply gives the lion a little distance and asks, "Would you like to sit down?" It's not always that easy to accomplish. The lion tamer has two choices: 1) draw the lion to a pedestal between yourself and the lion, or 2) guide the lion to the pedestal, hoping that they see the obvious attraction.

- The first option is more dangerous than it sounds, since to engage the lion to move forward you must cross into their personal space, prompting the lion to come at you! To keep them on the pedestal you must quickly back off, otherwise they will keep coming at you in earnest.
- The second option is more desirable. The lion tamer can read the lion well enough to know when sufficient trust has been established to gain the lion's cooperation.

In this case, the lion tamer begins moving to a chair at the table and motions the president to the head of a table. It's a good pedestal. The lion will think he is in the top place, and the lion tamer will find her own seat and adjust her distance in order to facilitate dialogue. Assuming that the lion is comfortable with the position and the distance, it will be crucial for the lion tamer to return to those same seats and positions as the discussions continue.

The lion's pedestal is also crucial to setting the expectations and environment for the negotiations, and allows her to reach her goal for that day. It has only taken a short meeting for the lion tamer and lion to become acquainted, assess each other, decrease the lion's anger, build trust, and introduce techniques that can be repeated and built upon in subsequent meetings. The day started with a roar and has ended on a deep rumbling purr.

Through the Hoop of Fire

Like many things in life, the journey is everything. In lion taming, the painstaking work and patience that goes into establishing the trust, respect, rapport, and understanding between the lion tamer and the lion will determine the result. In this case, it proves particularly important to work with the lion to build and maintain his trust, set and meet expectations, and ensure that he does not feel threatened, flee, bluster, or attack.

The lion tamer has given the lion the room he needs, and the feeling that she is trying to help him become the lion, not compete with or defeat him. She has also used the lion tamer's leverage; she has made clear that the consequence of not reaching a satisfactory agreement is that he will not be the lion king. The hoop of fire is placed before the lion. Can he jump? How high? Is he afraid of fire? Can he do it *NOW*? In the end, the lion jumps through the hoop of fire on his own initiative by signing the contract. Although many are surprised that the president became willing to sign, for the lion tamer the result was natural. Lions in the office want to jump through hoops of fire, they just don't want it to appear that someone made them do it!

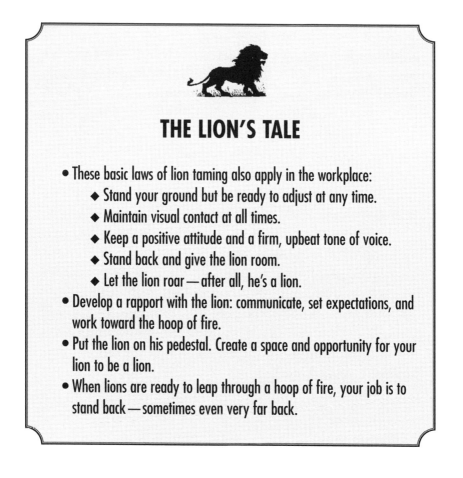

THE LION'S TALE

- These basic laws of lion taming also apply in the workplace:
    - Stand your ground but be ready to adjust at any time.
    - Maintain visual contact at all times.
    - Keep a positive attitude and a firm, upbeat tone of voice.
    - Stand back and give the lion room.
    - Let the lion roar—after all, he's a lion.
- Develop a rapport with the lion: communicate, set expectations, and work toward the hoop of fire.
- Put the lion on his pedestal. Create a space and opportunity for your lion to be a lion.
- When lions are ready to leap through a hoop of fire, your job is to stand back—sometimes even very far back.

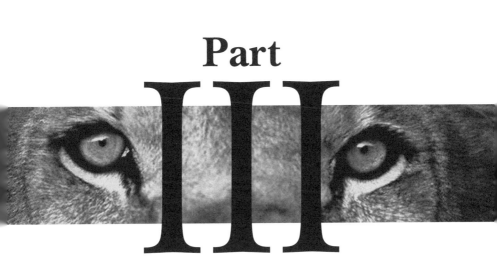

Part III

Lion Taming Is Really Lion Teaming

10

Lion Taming Is Really Lion Teaming

> **Secrets of the Lion Tamers**
> *Dependence on others is what makes lions different.*

Lion taming is full of ironies. Nowhere is this as subtle—yet so crucial to grasp—as in the way lion tamers and lions work together to achieve something that neither could achieve alone. Is it really the lion tamer's purpose to portray *man versus beast* in an intense yet productive standoff? Would this be an effective strategy to achieve success in your job?

Behind the mystique of the lion tamer that is projected onto the screen of life lies another reality altogether. Lion taming is not merely a coexistence of individuals in the ring.

What is the secret? It is the golden nugget of lion-taming wisdom. ***Lion taming is really lion teaming!***

It is the basis for the one-to-one relationship between the lion tamer and each of the lions. At the same time, it is the concept that connects the lions and everyone that surrounds them in the larger environment. While taking quite seriously the matter of establishing his or her own presence, credibility, and reputation with the lions, the lion tamer works with a positive attitude to foster rapport, trust, and mutual respect. Behind every performance are hours of long training and a sorting of roles between the lion tamer and the lion, and also others around them. It is the building of the lion team.

> **Secrets of the Lion Tamers**
>
> *When lions leap through hoops of fire, they don't want it to look like someone made them do it.*

The same ironies that underlie the difference between mystique and reality in real lion taming also exist in the office environment, and make it equally important to consider how lion teaming applies to your job. Step back and consider your own experiences. Where do new ideas come from? How are problems identified and solutions developed? Who identifies the strengths and talent needed to achieve objectives? What is the role of the lions and how do others play a part? Is there a time when everyone checks their titles and expertise at the door in order to put their minds together, after which they don their titles, talents, and capabilities to implement and perform?

Hoops of Fire

The purpose of any team is to work toward a set of goals—hoops of fire, you might say. Executives, bosses, clients, and customers need to jump through hoops of fire. These are not only identifiable goals, but often the very reasons that bring people in contact with the lions that they work with every day.

Four kinds of hoops of fire—leadership, management, communications, and relationships—are good examples, and you may have others to add to the list.

Leadership hoops of fire include:

- Creating momentum and energy
- Providing vision
- Achieving goals
- Making crucial decisions, large and small, that enable others to do their jobs

Management hoops of fire include:

- Hiring and firing the right people
- Handling a crisis effectively
- Addressing specific needs related to operations, people, policy, markets, finance, or technology

Communications hoops of fire include:

- Developing the right message
- Saying it to the right people at the right time
- Connecting to a larger public
- Setting expectations
- Satisfying the need for accuracy, accountability, and transparency

Relationship hoops of fire include:

- Maintaining old relationships
- Establishing new relationships
- Clarifying relationships and status

The hoops of fire may also be related to short-term decision making, direction setting, policy-making resource allocation, or delegation of authority—the hoops of fire that are always visible when you think of the reasons why you are walking into the boss's office.

How does it all get accomplished? The same persistent irony that lion tamers must confront in the steel-caged arena exists in the office. Despite the appearance of strength and self-sufficiency—not to mention the scary glances and off-putting indifference to others—lions in the office can and will work with others to see goals, develop the process for reaching the goals, and execute individually and as part of a team. However, never forget that they are still lions. As one observer noted, "When lions leap through hoops of fire, they don't want it to look like someone made them do it!"

A Place in the Pride

> **Secrets of the Lion Tamers**
>
> *Many things are not what they seem.*

There is another nugget of lion-taming wisdom that explains how and why the lions in the wild and in the office *can* team with others individually and as part of larger group. It is that lions are hardwired to be dominant, but they are also hardwired as "pride" animals. Lions in the wild and in the workplace are social animals, and to survive as lions they must operate in two parallel worlds—the hierarchy and the pride or group. There are specific qualities to their lives in both the social hierarchy and social groups or organizations that reflect how the lions in the wild and in the workplace are hardwired for teaming.

In the workplace, on the one hand, that translates into the power structure of titles, rank, and position. On the other hand, it means the surrounding worlds of nations, communities, companies, organizations, groups, networks, and the individuals in society that give meaning, purpose, and support to the lion's place in the hierarchy. After all, social dominance is meaningless without social context. These worlds are not merely complementary; they are necessary to the lion's survival. As part of a group, even the leader has a specific and useful role that has countervailing limitations. There are things that lions cannot do no matter how powerful they are. Hierarchy and the existence of a larger group work together as a catalyst for important roles and responsibilities for everyone, *including the lion.*

Most people don't consider the role they could play in teaming with their boss, or consider whether their boss has everything he or she needs to get the job done. When lions enter the arena, everyone's attention is focused on *the lion's* every breath, move, and look! It's true whether it is a CEO at the podium, a school principal addressing an assembly, or a foreman on the production line. We don't figure that they need the help of others, and most would not advertise it. Yet all good performances begin behind the scenes, working together and in a disciplined manner to learn, train, and prepare.

Why do we have a tendency to assume that the lions in the workplace do not need to team? Simply put, we are convinced by their image of dominance that they can take on all comers and need no one. Sometimes we want to be convinced of this because we want our lions to be strong, charismatic, and ready to pounce. The imagery and the visible battles for position and status convince us.

As a result, the lion's mystique continues to rule the day. We mistake the lion's image in the hierarchy for his or her specific purpose and role. However, in almost all cases, the functional purpose and abilities of the lions in the workplace are far less defined than their status or title, and that is in part why they need others around them.

A Field Guide to Lion Teaming

> **Secrets of the Lion Tamers**
>
> *Remember that they are wild animals...always be on your guard. And, most important of all, learn to know them well!*

To change the way we look and act toward the lions and work in the context of teaming together, we must look more closely at how the lions behave in their own world. Leaders, bosses, and the other lions around us often appear to command and traverse a large area of the world. However, much of their time and energy is devoted to marking specific parts of the larger environment that are essential to meet their needs and serve their interests. They establish networks of personal contacts, places, movements, routes, relationships, resources, and events. These networks are essential because they ensure the boss's rank and position, ability to succeed, and very survival.

These needs and patterns constitute an identifiable physical and social geography, revealing a forceful reality in the lives of leaders and bosses—one that we often overlook. Despite appearances, these lions, like lions in the wild, do not spend their days enjoying the total freedom of where and when they go and with whom. On the contrary, the lions in the workplace are compelled to:

- Establish defined patterns of movements and relationships that symbolize and sustain their rank and position, obtain resources for their needs, and allocate resources to help others.
- Remain focused and concentrated on doing their job, adapt to changing conditions around them, and successfully face challenges that may arise from any direction.
- See how their rank, position, title, and responsibilities

inherently limit their movements and relationships.

- Recognize the potential value and role of others whose rank and position allow them to be less conspicuous and to enjoy greater freedom of movement and relationships inside and outside the organization.

The lions we encounter at work create their own territory, social order, and resources. It is something that is inside of them. Leaders and bosses want to do it, and they are expected to do it. Their job is not defined by the four corners of their desk, but by the four corners of the Earth! Lions are proactive—creative in ways that are self-fulfilling and can benefit others—by establishing territory and paths to people and resources inside and outside the office. Understanding how the lions establish these patterns is vital to building a lion team.

Lions Work in Patterns

If we step back and look at the leaders and bosses we have encountered, we can often see well-defined and sometimes confined patterns of movement and relationships, well-worn routes, and specific zones for particular activities. The lions of the workplace have a very vivid sense of their own domain. The topography is embedded in their minds. You need to watch them, absorb the information as a secret map, and have it ready at the forefront of your mind as you approach them.

> **Secrets of the Lion Tamers**
>
> *Lions have their own sense of where they want to go and when, including where they don't want to go.*

Where can we see these patterns of movement and relationships most visibly? Do we have to embark on an office safari to find out? Many patterns develop inside the office, while others are a system of trails connecting the lions in the workplace to the outside world—personally and professionally, and with varying degrees of overlap.

Think about how your boss organizes his or her office. I know a CEO who divides up his work area like this: "talking business" at his desk, "planning strategy" at the whiteboard, and "new ideas" by the window. An executive vice president "problem solved" at her desk, but preferred to handle any "relationship" discussions sitting in a couch and chairs around a coffee table. She further divided meetings into their own separate purposes:

- One-to-one dynamics between her and other managers or employees
- Organizational or cultural issues, politics, or patterns
- Relationship-building, such as meeting with visitors to her office

Capitol Hill in Washington, D.C., where five hundred thirty-five lions in Congress make their home, provides a virtual island laboratory to observe the movements and relationships of leaders. Despite the wide hallways and open spaces, the lions in Congress stick to specific paths and trails that take them where they need to go, places where they go to have contact only with other lions, such as the House and Senate chambers or the "cloakrooms" of their respective political parties "off the floor" of the House or Senate.

These lions have their own "Members Only" elevators and sections on the underground subway cars that transport them to the Capitol and back for votes. They have their own personal offices, sometimes with private entryways. Interestingly, the staff members who occupy adjacent offices may go days without laying eyes on their boss. Some may only rarely, if ever, set foot on the staff side of the office. It is usually easier for Hill staffers to glimpse their boss on

C-Span than to see him or her in person in the office.

Patterns Emerge and Expand

Patterns emerge, expanding out into the workplace, involving particular people meeting at specific places. It is not uncommon to see patterns formed based on whoever the boss considers to be the "go-to" person for different components related to the workplace: for specialized knowledge, institutional history and understanding, strategic thinking, or "just in time" know-how.

While some leaders and bosses prefer to rely on people who are close by, others know what they want and where to find it, and will make every effort to get it. Preexisting relationships and experiences can be an important factor. A lion who came up through the ranks may have formed early patterns to obtain information and perspective, and may go right back to those sources "to get the real pulse of the organization."

Patterns of Socializing

External movements and relationships form another set of important patterns in the lions' domain in the workplace. *People count.* Individuals, experts, and colleagues, as well as others who share similar titles, positions, or aspirations, are important to the lion. *Places or organizations count, too.* Memberships in private clubs and exclusive associations, golf, tennis, charities, special events, and other "lion societies" are where lions can avoid isolation by being around other people like themselves.

Sometimes, for example, a senior executive who is weighing an invitation to a meeting or outside event asks "Who else is invited?" What he means is, What other lions will be there? Some lions might not attend if other lions aren't going to be present, either because they don't think it's worth their time or because there isn't a chance to be with other lions.

Remember that they have a biological need to know where they stand by testing the hierarchy.

Yet also remember that there are times when the right answer is that no one else at their level will be at a meeting or event. Lions sometimes want to be the only lion or the biggest lion in the room, and may see this as an important leadership opportunity. If you pay attention to the lion's cues, you can determine how to structure a team so that the lion is enticed to participate.

Covering the Territory

Some leaders and bosses do not want to travel far and wide, even within their organization. They may be isolated and need help learning how and with whom to network and establish their position and territory. Others, by comparison, are so active that they require two full staffs: one to help them network internally and another to help them move and shake externally.

Some leaders and bosses—whether isolated, just busy, or completely "out there"—know that they need help. Others are surprised and resentful when they discover that they cannot say and do whatever they want, whenever they want to. Others still will just forge ahead. However, even if they do succeed in doing what they want to do in their own way (who is going to stop them?), it doesn't mean it is a good idea. Everything that works is not useful.

Have you ever encountered people at the top who have:

- Bypassed, ignored, or weakened an executive or manager just to get information or assign a project?
- Caused extra or unnecessary work for someone who was already focused on meeting other internal or external demands and deadlines?
- Reinvented the wheel or added costs because they

wanted something immediately?
- Created a climate of crisis where a crisis did not exist, and then didn't provide a solution?

A lion roaming wild, without clear destinations and purposes in his or her patterns of movement and relationships, can cause confusion and contribute to their ineffectiveness across their territory. This is why it is so important to help the lions create a support structure to help rule their kingdom.

Movements and Relationships Define the Lion's Domain

The way lions in the workplace move around, the people they interact with, and the places where they go begin to explain how and why the lions in the workplace define their territory the way they do. They also underscore their behavior as well as their view of the world and the people who inhabit it, including what often appears to be selective, even exclusive, attitudes about people and places.

> **Secrets of the Lion Tamers**
>
> *Lions memorize their terrain and map out their steps, even when others suggest where to go.*

By studying this world, territory, and domain, you can obtain the same vivid sense that the lions in the workplace possess. Map it for yourself and you will begin to understand a great deal about them: who they talk to, where they go, and how they understand the role of others around them—including their perception of you!

It is natural to attribute the styles of different leaders and bosses to personalities and individual traits. The fact is, though, that whether people are reserved or extroverted, cautious or risk-takers, some of these limitations arise by the very nature of power and authority. It is not personal; it has to do with position and rank.

In the office, we assume that all meetings with the boss must be in the boss's office or somewhere in their domain. Why? It must be because they are the boss, right? However, this reflects the inherent limitations of movements and relationships lions have in their own organizations or companies because of their prominence and position. *They cannot camouflage their presence.* They are celebrities. They have a significant impact just by showing up. This is not to suggest that the boss doesn't have a need for physical presence. There must be a presence and it must be effective. But as we will see, it cannot be a pervasive presence.

Wild Kingdom

Real lions in the wild provide the best illustration of what happens in the workplace and why. The male lion that leads the pride, displaying a full mane and powerful musculature, confines his daily movements to a small part of the territory. Others, though, especially the lionesses, are responsible for hunting and killing prey, providing the food for the pride. Why aren't the big powerful males out there helping? What would happen if they did? Well, suppose the boss began showing up at every meeting trying to pitch in?

The male lion's physical features are designed to help him fulfill his role. His job *is* to be masculine, win battles of dominance, wear the leadership mantle of the pride, fight to preserve his role, and produce as many offspring as possible in his own image. His thick mane exudes power and masculinity, attracting the lionesses and intimidating other males. Studies have shown that the bigger the mane, the more healthy, robust, and attractive the lions are to the lionesses. Such manes may in fact be a barometer of the male lion's overall health. The manes may also serve a practical purpose to protect the carotid artery on the back of their necks during ferocious fights.

But these features also limit these lions. The lion cannot easily camouflage himself. The lavish mantle around his neck and shoulders that shields him against slashing claws and ripping teeth is also a walking advertisement of dominance, strength, and virility. Since lionesses do not have a mane, every member of the pride, including the powerful males with the biggest manes, depend on the lionesses' hidden strength of being less visible—"bellies low, every muscle and hair and nerve magnetized"—toward their prey as they spring unforeseen from the savanna floor. When the large males are around, every other inhabitant of the animal kingdom knows it. "Male lions on the hunt look like large haystacks moving through the grass," a naturalist observed.

It is no different in the office, where the boss cannot begin showing up to every meeting. Imagine the chaos this would cause. Sooner of later, it will look like the filming of *Wild Kingdom,* complete with leaping gazelles and zigzagging impalas, forlorn looks from those who want to be left alone, and others frozen in sheer fright. Tension. Distraction. Stress. Uncertainty. Worse, the boss's presence can trigger behaviors from showing off to aggression, especially in people who have been looking for an opportunity to tell the boss what they really think! All of these limitations of power are the immutable laws of the corporate jungle. If the boss's presence became too pervasive, nothing would ever get done.

Observe the reactions of employees the next time the CEO or other top executives eat lunch in the cafeteria or appear at a favorite watering hole. Look around. A still smile appears on people's faces while they quietly ask their nearest colleague, "What's *he* doing here?" Chairs start to rustle, people stop their conversations and look up from their tables. The natural state of rest, relaxation, and harmony quickly disappears.

Freedom and Responsibility

What does this insight into the behavior of bosses tell us? Something that you may already recognize from your own experience and observations: ***You can live and operate in the lion's world, but they usually cannot operate in yours.*** This inherent limitation of movement and relationships creates a need, a role, and responsibilities for others that can move more freely. Without the help of other people at all levels, the leaders and bosses often lack the context, information, and timely intelligence about the world they command, even if they do personally traverse every square mile, floor, office, and cubicle. Some leaders and bosses are aware of this, and others are not. Some wouldn't want to admit; others understand it fully and create effective strategies to make it work for them.

If you work for and are directly identified with the boss, you may very well send your own ripple effect through the room. But you can also enjoy greater freedom of movement, observation, and contact. You have the direct ability to learn from many others because you can be less obtrusive than your boss.

More generally, a very important role for others exists as part of the lion's team through their ability to operate in the world that the lions cannot easily roam. It is part of your role and it means that you have a responsibility—but not an unlimited license—that must be taken seriously and neither breached nor abused. It is a freedom, trust, and responsibility that the boss has no choice but to delegate to others on the team.

That's why it's so important to understand the style and needs of the people you work for, decide on your own interpretation and approach, and still be able to achieve the objectives. It doesn't mean that you have permission to lord over people as if you are the boss or throw the weight of their power and position around. Because the presence of leaders and bosses can sometimes have unintended consequences, part of your job as a lion tamer is to determine how to help present and portray their presence in the office so that it is productive.

It is the lion's responsibility to see that the lion tamer is respected for his or her unique role. Together they must ensure that the role is viewed as authentic, instead of creating situations where the lion tamer is acting as a surrogate lion. Nothing is perceived by employees and others as phonier, and ultimately is seen as the sign of a very weak boss. What if a circus portrayed a lion-taming act that only contained the lion tamer? Even a mime would be more convincing!

How does this understanding affect, clarify, and implicitly enhance your role? What freedom do you have that can be better exercised as a responsibility? When I asked one top-level executive what he thought he could do most effectively for the leaders and bosses he worked for, he said, "I work their problems for them, preferably before they become the boss's problem." So long as it also furthers the boss's objectives, your role can enable you to do many things, including:

- Gathering information and intelligence
- Strengthening relationships
- Managing projects
- Discussing problems and helping find solutions
- Being reactive and proactive
- Identifying roles and opportunities for leaders and bosses to use their position
- Preserving the exercise of their power so it can be most effective
- Preventing the exercise of power when it will cause harm, including to the leaders and bosses

In fact, you need to use these experiences and intelligence to support the insight, advice, feedback, or opinions that you offer. You need to be able to present the total picture so that when the lions in the workplace apply their own senses and instincts to a problem, they can make a good decision. They not only need information from someone who can help deepen their knowledge and understanding, they depend on it.

Hardwired for Teaming

Secrets of the Lion Tamers

Lions are hardwired as pride animals.

As we have emphasized, even though the lions in the wild and the workplace are riddled with hierarchical hang-ups, they are also hardwired as pride animals. And, as a result, two separate yet complementary social structures—the hierarchy and the pride or social group—are essential to their existence, define their identifies and roles, and create relationships with others around them.

On first impression, it would seem that the role of lions in either the hierarchy or the larger group sets them apart from everyone else. However, they are not statues. Social dominance in any form, but particularly in the work environment, is meaningless without a social context. Hierarchy and prides, groups, or organizations are social in nature and combine to serve as a catalyst for many people, including the lions, in creating important interrelationships, roles, and responsibilities for everyone.

What does the hierarchy do? Visualize how this might operate where you work. The hierarchy establishes rank and controls competition among the lions themselves, while establishing visible and identifiable leaders in the eyes of others—inside and outside the pride, social group, or organization.

What is the purpose of the pride, group, or organization? Hierarchy tells the lions who they are, but a larger social setting or organization is necessary to inform others, provide context, and bring it all to life. It is the pride or organization that supports the lion in the rank or position they have fought to attain and creates a social framework and organization for others to live, work, and survive in.

When we say that lions are hardwired as pride animals, that also means that the lions accept that there has to be a leader, which may or may not be them—at least at that point in time. Recognizing their role and how they need to be treated as part of the hierarchy is different than how they need to be treated as a team member. The lions need a role in relationship to others. They need to know what that is, even as they doing everything else. This can result in a series of different roles for the lions on the team. Leaders and bosses can often accept that for a specific project to be successful, someone else must take the lead. It always helps if they have their role assigned to them.

Even the head lion in the pride has a specific role—to lead, protect, defend, or expand, and to create future generations. The other lions and lionesses play different and essential roles in relation to each other as individuals and as members of a group. And often, as in hunting and stalking prey, lions are recognized as unique among the big cats for the way they work—in teams. You can help the lions determine their personal role as part of the team by drawing their attention to the capabilities that are available to them, and going with their lead.

As the lions in the workplace live on an everchanging landscape of independence, interdependence, and dependence, it is perhaps not surprising that the closest lion parallel in human society—which everyone, including leaders and bosses, understands—is the team. It is needed to support them in being a lion and to create a foundation on which the lion's position, qualities, and strengths can perform. That is how the role of the lion tamer in workplace becomes such an important one. You never really tame a lion. Lion taming is really lion teaming.

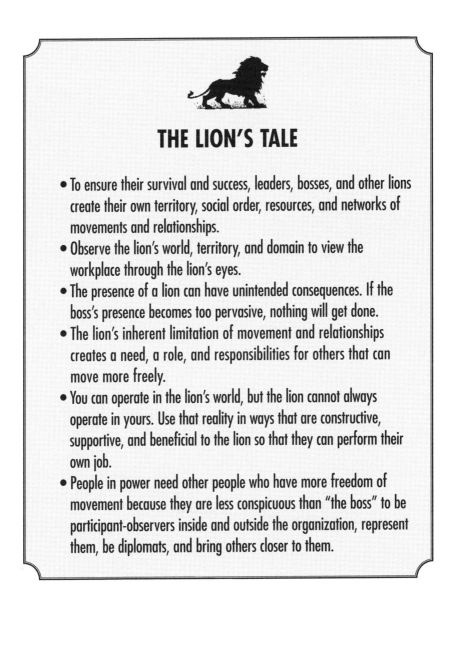

THE LION'S TALE

- To ensure their survival and success, leaders, bosses, and other lions create their own territory, social order, resources, and networks of movements and relationships.
- Observe the lion's world, territory, and domain to view the workplace through the lion's eyes.
- The presence of a lion can have unintended consequences. If the boss's presence becomes too pervasive, nothing will get done.
- The lion's inherent limitation of movement and relationships creates a need, a role, and responsibilities for others that can move more freely.
- You can operate in the lion's world, but the lion cannot always operate in yours. Use that reality in ways that are constructive, supportive, and beneficial to the lion so that they can perform their own job.
- People in power need other people who have more freedom of movement because they are less conspicuous than "the boss" to be participant-observers inside and outside the organization, represent them, be diplomats, and bring others closer to them.

11

Bringing Out the Lion *Teamer* in You!

> **Secrets of the Lion Tamers**
>
> *It is self-confidence in your mastery of the traits and behavior that you need, not self-confidence that you can control the lion.*

By now you may be convinced that lions in the workplace are dependent on others in ways that are best served through an attitude of teaming together. You may legitimately ask, though: Can the lions at the office really work as a team? Every one of them is an individual who is their own person. Each is a king who reigns from wherever he or she stands. As leaders, bosses, or lions they are presumed to be self-sufficient—possessing rank, resources, and all the power anyone could ask for. Still, the answer is *"Yes!"*

So what about frequently heard suggestions and theories that people should learn to "partner" with bosses and clients, or, *gulp*, try to "manage" them? Perhaps. There is probably no single approach that will work in all situations. However, if you are already beginning to see a lion tamer staring back at you when you look in the mirror, you may have also sensed the answer: When you work with lions, there is no parity, no equality—only rank. Manage the lion? I'll tell you what, you go first!

Teamwork Complements the Lion's Natural Thinking

Teamwork may sound ironic in the context of leaders, bosses, and other tough customers, but it leads to more effective roles and relationships because it complements their natural thinking and behavior in ways that managing your boss or "managing up" does not.

What is the secret? It is to recognize the complementary yet distinctly different worlds of the hierarchy and the pride that lions live in simultaneously. If a lion perceives you as competing with them to operate in the hierarchy of lions, he will resist you and may try to eliminate you altogether. You may be the most capable, expert person to do what they need done, but if they view you or your approach as furthering your own importance, not theirs, you'll be up to your neck in teeth!

However, by approaching the lions in the workplace with an attitude of teaming, where the issue of status and roles is undisputed and the focus is on what needs to be done, you can be helpful, influential, and effective. As you will find, you can even be an expert in your role and it won't bother the lion one bit. Just make sure you're not trying to be the expert lion, but the expert lion teamer! The good lions never see this as a problem. They recognize such expertise as something they need, but can leverage through you and others.

You can help the lions achieve something important to

their job, succeed in new ways that they had not envisioned, and obtain something that you and others need to get your job done. And one of the most important distinctions of working as a lion tamer is that even though you may step in and out of the role, it is not merely a transactional or situational approach that you call to mind when you need the boss to do something. You are stepping in and out of a relationship that is based on a foundation of rapport, trust, and mutual respect that always hangs in the balance. The lions must always know where you stand in relation to them, that your intentions are consistent with their objectives, and that they can achieve something by working together that they could not achieve alone. In fact, the people who are the lions are counting on you to be able to do that!

Contrast: The Lion Tamer's Advantage

> **Secrets of the Lion Tamers**
> *There are forty of them, weighing nearly 20,000 pounds…*
> *Me, I weigh 145 pounds.*

There is a sheer contrast in "size" that you may at first assume separates you from the lions. In fact, this works to the lion tamer's advantage as a positive differentiating factor. It serves a basic, existential purpose that signals to lions that you are reflecting and not challenging their strength, power, capability, and talent. It provides the dramatic contrast they need to communicate more effectively with others.

In real lion taming, a fundamental ingredient of the drama is not the looming danger that hangs heavily in the air, but the dramatic and contrasting presence of the lion tamer in the cage with the lions. Whether sauntering into the ring, perched on a pedestal, or springing upwards through a hoop of fire, the lions may look big enough. However, the lion tamers, who spend many more hours practicing and training with the lions, know just how big and powerful the lions really are. Indeed, if you have ever had a chance to see a lion stretch itself upwards from the arena floor—vertically unfolding its entire body into a tower of muscle, then resting its front paws well above the cage door—you realize just how significant the contrast really is! It is the real-life David and Goliath drama between the lion tamer and the lion that pulls the spectators from their seats by their hearts and minds, into the arena. The contrast puts the audience in the lion tamer's shoes, albeit vicariously, and makes the event more personal.

There is also an art to the way the lion tamer provides contrasts. Experts in the finer points of lion taming note that from the standpoint of performance, the lion tamers who are shorter—and who can also demonstrate speed, agility, and footwork—may provide the most dramatic contrast to the audience. Clyde Beatty, who was five-foot six, did the math in a newspaper interview, emphasizing that when he enters the ring, "There are forty of them, weighing nearly 20,000 pounds....Me, I weigh 145 pounds." Joe Arcaris was five-foot three and was awarded the Carnegie Award in 1940 for leaping into "the lion's pit" and saving the life of a man attacked by five lions. Gunther Gebel-Williams—with his trademark wave of blond hair, bare chest, gold-embroidered vest, and gleaming white smile—remains recognized worldwide for his rapport, skill, and versatility with dangerous big cats. Gunther was a giant in animal training at five-foot six.

While this observation seems like common sense, people are surprised at the enormous difference in size between the lion tamers and the lions—surprised in a way that confirms their anxiety on the other side of the steel bars. The same ingredients are needed in the workplace. At a minimum, the lions need other people to provide the contrast and context to reflect the lion's role and actions. They need someone to project them onto the screen of life, make them bigger, clearer, and more intelligible to others.

The lions themselves may be indifferent to such efforts, despite this need. They expect that their persona is sufficient to ensure a steady supply of "natural light" to illuminate who they are. Don't let that stop you. For leaders, bosses, and others to achieve their most effective level of visibility, credibility, and functionality, they must be seen as authentically connected to and actively operating in a rich, multidimensional, and dynamic environment. Power inspires awe, but it needs to be seen *and* understood. It must be deeply engaged and connected to such an environment by something greater than reputation, rank, or position. That requires a variety of other people, in particular those who are sensitive to the need to "de-isolate" the lions in the workplace, to take the lions off their level and become focused, connected, and moving in concert with others in the organization. As one experienced executive observed, "Other executives need this just to keep pace with what is going on."

People in the role of the lion tamer can also help project and translate the lion's policies, procedures, goals, and objectives to the four corners of the organization and beyond. That is very hard for the lions in the workplace to do on their own, and creates a role for others—one of the fundamental realities about lion teaming.

Take with you these three lessons about power and contrast, which show invaluable roles you must play and why the lions in the workplace cannot do it alone:

- ***Power needs contrast and context:*** to shape and present the lion's power—helping even the lion to recognize his or her own power.
- ***Power needs communicators:*** conduits for inbound and outbound information to organize, describe,

condition, and project—but not necessarily to speak for them. Communicators help lions project and have an appropriate, though not pervasive, presence.

- ***Power needs other people who have more freedom of movement*** because they are less conspicuous than "the boss." These people can represent them, be participant-observers inside and outside the organization, be diplomats…and bring others closer to them.

Contrast creates perspective, context, and meaning. Just as in real lion-taming acts, it is the lion tamer's role in the workplace to enter the arena with the lion and bring others closer to the lion.

Lion Tamers Do Not Feel Alone in the Cage

Secrets of the Lion Tamers

I don't notice whether there are five or five thousand people watching.

You may be thinking, "Well, contrast I can probably handle, but do lion tamers really feel comfortable working with lions?" In fact, one of the most helpful insights and underlying ironies gleaned from real lion tamers is how they perceive themselves in relationship to the lions.

Yes, the lion tamer stands poised in a cage full of lions with nothing but a slender whip and a kitchen chair, or just a thin stick for cueing. Yet contrary to what spectators see, lion tamers do not perceive themselves as standing alone among the lions—not even for a minute.

Lessons of the Lion Tamers
"I Prefer Lions, Thank you!"

British lion tamer Patricia Bourne described her feelings: "The fact remains that still today I fear people more than wild animals. I would rather walk into a cage packed with lions than into a room full of people….I think I prefer lions, they are always glad to see me."

Bourne also carefully explained working with lions as if writing a personal advice column for lion tamers: "You must like them, have a great understanding of their feelings, see things as they do, and remember each is a character on his own, having different ways, likes, and dislikes as we have; so don't put lions in uniform because they are frightfully independent people."

Others who have entered the lion's cage do not seem to make the distinction between people and lions that we might expect. Alex Kerr, another British big-cat trainer who began his career in the lion's cage, once recalled: "Now that their eyes expressed awareness of me the lionesses altered from the beasts that I had seen so often from outside the cage into real vivid human beings."

Yet another trainer, Joseph Arcaris, who worked with lions for more than fifty years and lived well into his nineties, was remembered because, "He treated them like human beings….He even gave them aspirin when he thought they had a headache."

Admittedly, when you hear a lion tamer describing a lion like this: "He did not like affection—he preferred life on his own terms" or "Like most individual characters, he was very quickly bored," they could be describing almost every leader, CEO, or boss. However, for most lion tamers relating *mammal to mammal* makes for perfectly fine company in the cage. And never forget, as one lion tamer reminds us, "They are wild animals…always be on your guard. And most important, learn to know them well."

The same rule of thumb applies to office life, where many of the very same contrasting perceptions, feelings, and stark realities of working with the lions prevail. You've probably had many experiences that fit into this category, juggling the ups and downs of daily office life, ultimately deciding your own style of effectiveness. A colleague wishes you "good luck" when she hears that you are going to meet with the boss or are presenting a big project to the senior executives. To her you are headed into the lion's den alone, with nothing but a slender pen and a notepad in your hands. It is with a mixture of confidence and curiosity that you may respond with a nod of thanks. On the one hand you know what she means, and for a moment you may even fear that she knows something that you don't.

You will find out. Just as in real lion taming, everything is not as others see it. Something inside your own mind guides your thinking in a different direction. After all, you cannot get inside the minds of leaders, bosses, and other tough customers if you fail to get in to see them in the first place. It doesn't matter whether your goal is to assist, influence, help them do their job, or help yourself and others to do your job more easily. *Your degree of contact must be intensified in order to be accepted as part of their world.*

Lion Tamers in the Office Do Not Feel Alone Either

Secrets of the Lion Tamers

Once you go through the cage door you are completely absorbed.

Just like real lion tamers, you will not feel alone. Motivated? Captivated? Energized? Stimulated? Rewarded? Confident? Yes. As one lion tamer commented: "I felt no nervousness, only a tingling of excitement and a longing to be in the ring." Another remarked at his reaction when the lions enter the arena: "Maybe it's the rush of adrenaline. You just get bigger."

Proportions and dimensions do change, and so do inner strengths. Fear translates into heightened awareness, not flight, and your courage is a measure of your ability to manage fear. It is reflected by something that you can clearly feel and others can keenly sense: steady, cool nerve.

When you stand your ground with your boss, you don't do it to further the mystique of man versus beast or to engage in a battle between adversaries. Nor is it the time to freeze or to dig in aggressively. You stand your ground with nonverbal language to identify a fixed point or to create a recognizable intersection in the lion's day. It is a point from which something new and meaningful will progress—something you believe that the corporate lion needs to learn about. It will focus and use her attention, and is itself an act of working together as a team. The next idea or the next move may be yours or it may be hers; nonetheless, you are on your way.

Something in the minds of the lion tamers connects emotionally and intellectually with the lions. You are compelled into the ring, closer to the lions, not further away. You have a preference to be in there. Yes, you know that rapport, trust, and mutual respect must develop. Yes, you also know that you must be highly aware, the signals from the lion have to be right, and you have to read them correctly.

Still, it is not with mere compliance to a command that you enter the boss or client's office, but with a bigger vision. You have a sense that there are issues, needs, problems, and opportunities that come to life when you are together—sometimes even more so than when others are involved. What is happening?

You intuitively look beyond the individual, beyond the species, to the world that the lion can reach. It is the sense that you provide focus and opportunities for their instincts, connect their strengths with their thinking, identify the hoops of fire, and as a result often help them succeed in new ways. In the workplace, that translates into achieving something together as a team, seeing the goals, sharing values, and determining each other's roles and responsibilities.

What kind of team is it? People pull together, backing each other up, coordinating and working together toward common goals and objectives. Talent blends with roles and responsibilities. Skills are executed in steps; first in training, then in performance. Focus, discipline, and consistency are required. Training is repetitive. Communication becomes compressed into looks, signals, and gestures. Pace and speed, coupled with deliberateness, are important. Resiliency, adaptability, and improvisation go hand in hand. You compete to win without competing against each other. A tense but palpable *esprit de corps* holds people together, focused, keeping the momentum going.

You will no longer be simply another creature that appears on the horizon, visible beyond the edge of the boss's desk. Your view of yourself will change and strengthen as well, adapting to the new environment as you become part of something new—a teaming relationship.

The Lion Tamer in the Mirror

> **Secrets of the Lion Tamers**
>
> *Lion tamers are schooled to meet their danger calmly.*

Are you ready to take the step and work as a lion tamer, engaging leaders, bosses, and other tough customers through lion teaming? It is likely that several of the signs that point the way are realizations that have entered your mind before. Little did you know that these were the same intrinsic forces pulling you again and again toward the steel-caged arena in the workplace. Here are the driving forces of lion teaming in the workplace:

- As a general rule, nothing ever gets accomplished entirely by one person.
- Even the most powerful people need others to help them focus and leverage their position, strengths, and performance.
- Interdependent needs and relationships allow you to help make leaders, bosses, and clients more effective.
- You are reliant on the lion in the office to leverage his or her power, but it is often up to you and others to help find the ways and opportunities to do so.
- Helping leaders and bosses to be effective at their job sets the stage for you and others to perform more easily and effectively.
- You cannot work solo as a lion tamer. Others share the same environment, come in contact with the boss or client, and possess valuable information and experience. They are part of a larger team.

Do you want to check one more time and confirm that you are the right person, that you have it in you? Okay. There are a few more specific and more telling personal qualities that may only be visible to you, traits that are already an important part of your own constitution.

Treating your instincts as if they matter is the most important first step. Recognize how these traits not only differentiate you, but perhaps qualify you to be a lion tamer in the office in the first place. However, don't wear these traits on your lapel or list them on your resume. They are personal driving forces—tested by your ability to help others become successful in new ways even as it helps you do your job better. Do you have, or want to acquire, the following traits?

- Feeling a kinship to the lions in the workplace—not so much as individual people, but as individuals in the context of their position.
- Preferring to work with leaders, bosses, and other tough customers—you like it and you feel that you belong at their level too, albeit in a different role than the "lion king."
- Valuing, even enjoying, getting to know people in their own environment.
- Visualizing and conveying a sense of teaming to the people at the top.
- Seeing a bigger picture and dynamics beyond the individual or the "species."
- Respectfully recognizing that the lions usually cannot operate in your world but you can operate in their world!

When you look in the mirror, you really do see a lion tamer staring back at you! And seeing yourself as a lion *teamer* is a defining part of your role as a lion tamer in the office. Teaming means working together in ways that help lions achieve results every day. You must sometimes take several extra steps to assure the lions in the workplace that they have nothing to fear, and indeed have something to gain, from relying on you.

Teaming also means engaging them. But you cannot rely on intermittent contact or recognition—and neither can they. You want a stronger reaction, evidence that they know what you can do and have literally chewed on something you gave them! That's when you've crossed the threshold to building the rapport, trust, and mutual respect for them to rely on you, for you to learn and understand what you need to know to work together, and to determine what they are really thinking and feeling.

Lion teaming is like all teams. You train together, compete but not against one another, and prepare for your different roles. No two players on any team play the exact same role. Ultimately, the lion's job is to perform, and your job is to stand back. Give the lion room! Lion taming rises to an art when the lion's performance is seen as a natural extension of the lion's own ability and stature. That is when it also looks instinctive, up-front, and credible. Nothing strengthens the reliance, trust, and confidence in the lion tamer faster than helping it all look and feel easy to the lion—a great speech, executing a strategy, or a management decision or action. The lions in the workplace will want more.

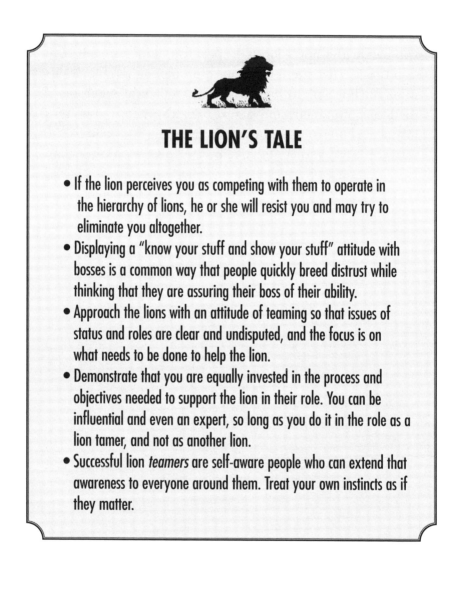

THE LION'S TALE

- If the lion perceives you as competing with them to operate in the hierarchy of lions, he or she will resist you and may try to eliminate you altogether.
- Displaying a "know your stuff and show your stuff" attitude with bosses is a common way that people quickly breed distrust while thinking that they are assuring their boss of their ability.
- Approach the lions with an attitude of teaming so that issues of status and roles are clear and undisputed, and the focus is on what needs to be done to help the lion.
- Demonstrate that you are equally invested in the process and objectives needed to support the lion in their role. You can be influential and even an expert, so long as you do it in the role as a lion tamer, and not as another lion.
- Successful lion *teamers* are self-aware people who can extend that awareness to everyone around them. Treat your own instincts as if they matter.

12

Performing in the Center Ring

> **Secrets of the Lion Tamers**
>
> *There is nothing they sense more quickly than fear and uncertainty in the trainer.*

As in any relationship, the purpose of establishing rapport, trust, and mutual respect is not simply for two individuals to coexist. The ultimate secret of lion taming is that neither the lions nor the lion tamers can meet their needs or accomplish their goals alone. Just as the decision to assume the inner identity, self-image, and self-control of a lion tamer is your own—something that you can undertake without telling anyone—it also is up to you to begin to visualize *lion teaming* in your own mind. However, thinking about it will only take you so far. You need to become genuinely engaged with someone you are teaming with to bring it all to life. At some point, the lion tamer in the mirror must carry that image into the center ring with the lions!

You must have confidence to succeed. You must have the will to succeed! After all, as it has been said for centuries, "There is nothing that the lions sense more quickly than fear and uncertainty in the trainer." Informal studies have even been conducted to ascertain if lions can actually "smell fear." At least one practitioner concluded after years of experience and participant observation with lions that "animals cannot smell fear" and that "fear is not something tangible." However, he explained, "Animals can sense fear, but I think they get it through the tone of a person's voice and from his actions." So what enables you to have the confidence to get off on the right foot?

Sparking a Positive Chemistry with the Lion

Secrets of the Lion Tamers

When I enter the cage I do so with no morbid thoughts in my head....If a trainer is afraid of tackling his animals he had better keep away from them, for sooner or later they will do him in.

For many, the idea of working with lions arouses a sense of danger and doom. However, others repeatedly demonstrate in both real and corporate lion taming that the ability to spark a positive chemistry has a contagious effect on others around you. Try these techniques:

- Acknowledge that you have a preference and an ability to work with the lions around you.
- Treat your instincts as if they matter.
- Recognize that that these capabilities genuinely reflect your style of effectiveness.

You will find that you implicitly communicate this to the people who are the lions. In fact, lions look for and recognize these qualities in the people they work with. It is part of what brings you together as a team in the first place, and is an essential part of the chemistry that keeps you together.

You must change your mind-set. Perhaps the best way to describe this mind-set is that it is one of *awareness, consciousness, and attitude.* This includes recognizing that the opportunity you need is not the well-defined kind delivered to you on a silver platter, but the chance to work with someone who sets the course and the pace of your organization. You may find that you do not need new strengths or skills so much as the opportunity, focus, stamina, and patience to begin putting what is inside of you to work.

However, like real lion tamers, you have to be strong. You are not in the arena as an appendage, but to see possibilities for becoming successful in new ways. Just because the lions do not recognize the course of things does not mean the goals can't be accomplished. The relationship and focus that develops is a creative experience. In fact, part of your responsibility is to be creative about goals, strategies, division of responsibilities, schedules, and the desired results. It is the vision of the lion ultimately leaping through the hoop of fire that keeps the lion tamer working patiently "from scratch" toward a capability or event that did not exist before—even though the lion's power, strength, smarts, talent, and aptitude existed all along!

How Should the Lions Respond to You?

How should you expect the lions in the office to respond to your role? After all, you are no longer just another creature way out on the horizon beyond the edge of their desk.

Sometimes the response can be overt, as when the boss publicly assigns or articulates your responsibility because he or she wants everyone to know it. Other times it can be quite subtle. Perhaps an otherwise neutral or even negative sense of your relevance or importance is replaced by a new and positive significance. It is not that the lions are more relaxed *per se,* but are more focused, intent, and engaged. They are headed somewhere, and you are going along. They have resolved the *Lion's Four Senses* of dominance, territory, social standing, and survival favorably with you—even if guardedly and tentatively—and are moving ahead.

The lion gives you a change of signal, a plus sign instead of a question mark or a minus. The shift may be signaled through a combination of body language and actual words. Remember what those signals are and what they mean, because these are the successful signs of approaching the lion so the lion approaches you. They are personal signals based on individual experience. No one else may have even seen them, and if they did they may not have interpreted them the same way. You may see it in the hallway, in a meeting, perhaps even in the way something is assigned to you.

As one top executive recalled after rising through the ranks over the course of many years of working with project heads, mid-level managers, top executives, and leaders:

> I look for something that does not seem very scientific, but is very human. It is when you build enough trust with the person that they begin to act normally around you, and it's a signal for others they work closely with to do the same. It's just that the "normal behavior" occurs in short bursts. It's their way of reaching out, but you've got to have your eyes open.

Their behavior may also have much to do with the kind of person they are and the level on which they believe they are connecting with you. They will show it in their personal style or professional demeanor—friendly, brusque, introverted, or extroverted. What it means is more important than how it comes across. Don't take it personally. Just remember that they are not focused on you in the same way that you are focused on them.

In many ways these are the subtle signs that are already keeping your eyes open and ears perked. Sometimes, for example, what the boss is looking for is not so much the substance or brilliance of an idea but the fact that you got it to them first. Explaining this simply in terms of "office protocol" does not even begin to tell the story!

Leaders, bosses, and other tough customers need to know that you are equally invested in their leadership objectives and process. Loyalty in this sense is equated by your ability to create new opportunities for their instinctive strengths and leadership. Many dimensions to the concept of lion teaming involve recognizing the hidden ability and needs of boss and executives to work more effectively with others than is commonly perceived, and the many opportunities, needs, and challenges that are created as a result.

However, the concept is not intended to suggest that you become the equivalent of the athletic director in the boss's office. Nor should you rename the softball team for the CEO! But when it comes time to accomplish something that takes the shape of a team, and the lion is involved, it's time to put your lion-teaming skills to use and show just how you are invested in the lion's leadership. You need to ensure that the team reflects the boss's leadership, that the boss recognizes the team as a reflection of himself or herself, while at the same time reassuring him or her that your supporting role will be ongoing.

Here is an illustration of some high-level lion teaming at work, and why the obvious next step is not always obvious to the lions around us!

Whose Team Is It Anyway?

A new CEO took over an organization of several thousand employees during the technology boom. He was hired in large part because he was an expert at linking information systems and the performance of companies and their employees. In other words, he was an expert at transforming organizations into successful modern enterprises.

Immediately putting his stamp on the organization meant conducting a full-scale technology review of the organization as a whole, built from analyses of every office and department. The CEO assigned the job to the Vice President for Operations, who was part of his executive suite but oversaw all the in-house IT functions and staff.

While others saw this assignment as a big deal, the vice president tempered his own view with the knowledge that success depended on the CEO's role as the driving force. Organizations are like people; if something isn't important at the highest levels of priority, it won't get done. Therefore, the vice president's solution was a natural one: create a CEO-led working group of the top executives, aligned with the functions, personnel, and resources, to prepare an in-depth review, report, and recommendations.

Yet every time the vice president raised the idea of having a working group take the lead, the CEO balked. Finally, it dawned on the vice president that the CEO was not hearing him right. Every time he mentioned the "working group," the CEO assumed that the vice president was trying to use the CEO's offices to create the vice president's own working group.

Two weeks quickly passed, and the CEO wanted to know whether the technology review was ready to roll out. This time the vice president was prepared. He handed the CEO a small folder with a title page that read *CEO* Technology Working Group, with just three pages attached.

Here was VP's checklist for the folder:

CEO's Technology Working Group

- ❏ Organizational chart for project
- ❏ CEO in a big box at the top
- ❏ VP and all the other appropriate executives and supporting staff and functions aligned in boxes below
- ❏ Detailed calendar and schedule of responsibilities with the VP's office in a project-management role.
- ❏ Draft memo from the CEO to the entire company announcing the review, its purpose, the executive team, and the personnel.

The CEO smiled and said, "This looks good. Get this on everyone's agenda for the executive committee meeting in the morning."

What did the vice president do so quickly that was so right in the eyes of the CEO? He recognized that the CEO knew who the lion was and wanted others to know this, including the vice president. The memo served to mirror back to the CEO and everyone else in the kingdom who the lion was, and created a process that the CEO could own to address the problems he perceived across the company. That meant that in the end, the CEO would also own the solution.

Inner Lion Taming

Secrets of the Lion Tamers

There is an emotional link—you must be willing to put yourself into it.

The core dimension to the concept that "lion taming is really lion teaming" is of course the one-to-one relationship between the lion tamer and the lion. In the center, you'll find what is unique between you and another person. It is a teaming relationship intertwined in personal dynamics that cannot always be explained. It becomes part of the instinctive and intuitive thinking and behavior between two living things, and it cannot be precisely replicated in others.

The one-to-one relationship involves highly personal stakes for both the lion and the lion tamer, in relationship to one another. From the outset we have emphasized, respectfully, that the lions in life frequently interpret things personally. Being a lion in the workplace and in life *is* personal. It is usually visible in their personality, psychology, emotions, and desires, and is brought to life through their specific position and responsibilities. They got to where they are in life by putting themselves on the line. Assessing the world from their personal standpoint is essential to their *modus operandi* and to their survival.

As we have said, the lions in the workplace are not focused on you in the same way that you are focused on them. While you are looking to determine the best distance to approach them from, primarily to work more closely and effectively together, they instinctively measure their relationship to others along a spectrum of independence, interdependence, and dependence. As you may have experienced, it can cause them to react with fluctuations quickly, wildly, and without explanation.

We have also stressed that there are times when the lion tamer must share certain qualities with the lion. This includes being acutely aware of everything going on around them, holding more in reserve than they may be showing up front, and being able to think and act instinctively and intuitively.

Being a Lion Tamer Is Personal, Too

Secrets of the Lion Tamers

With lions, sometimes you just never know.

As a lion tamer, your own personal stakes may be what attracts you to the equivalent of the center ring in the first place. Making a difference by doing things right at a high level? Being close to power? Working with someone whom others are afraid to approach? Training for the day when you might become the lion instead of the lion tamer? This is what can make it exciting, productive, enervating, and challenging! *Being a lion tamer in the center ring and in the workplace is personal too—personal in your role as the lion tamer, not in trying to be the lion!*

From the risks and the rewards to everything in between, lion taming, especially in the office, takes on a heightened personal dimension as you step forward—just like the apprentice lion tamer who graduates from "shadowing" the boss—to assist, guide, or facilitate someone more powerful. The job is personal because you:

- Are investing time and energy in the relationship and the specific purpose, projects, or goals that are being pursued
- Operate by your own instincts
- Must know yourself and demonstrate self-control to a greater degree than you can ever hope to control the lions
- Are upholding your own reputation, pride, and sense of standards and satisfaction for a job well done—even though you may never receive credit

One result is having a greater sense of ownership about the job you are performing. When successful—when the lion tamer-to-lion relationship is a functioning, productive, and positive working relationship—your preference and affinity for working with leaders and bosses gets a big boost. You also are motivated to do your best and give it all you've got, often accomplishing more than others and being accountable in ways that transcend any typical or formal performance measurement.

These qualities are all a strength and a necessity to the one-to-one relationship at the core of being a lion tamer. Such people are essential ingredients to the success of any lion team! However, the potential specialization and exclusivity of the rapport can also create limitations, challenges, and even career decisions that you should be prepared to address.

How could something that you have worked so hard to establish, maintain, and preserve become problematic? It is a reality of dealing with the lions in the workplace. As we have said, they view themselves in relationship to others on a sliding scale of independence, interdependence, and dependence—and they are not always focused on you the way you are focused on them. If we hearken back to what we learned about the instinctive behavior and thinking of lions in the workplace, then it makes sense that they feed their own instinctive appetite for opportunities. In fact, it is part of their self-fulfilling mandate to show that they are still the lion, capable of instinctive, fast, and powerful moves, including showing that they can change the state of things in the blink of an eye.

The best evidence of this is that even after long-established relationships, leaders or bosses may decide that they want to move in a new direction. That means changing the mix of people around them. When this happens, most people in the role of office lion tamer react the same way real lion tamers would about suddenly adding another person to the act: "It could blow the act." It's like adding another lion; the lions have to get readjusted and reestablish, sometimes fighting out who is the dominant lion—and so do the people around them.

In the workplace, however, it is not usually up to the lion tamer how and when such changes might occur. As sacred as you believe the relationship you have with the lion is, you also recognize that the lions in the workplace are naturally curious. They are focused on many things at once, including an intangible something that they feel may be missing and only comes into sharper view when they meet someone who can help them make it happen.

The lions in the workplace possess an agility of reserve that is more worrisome than what they are doing at the moment. The prerogative to change the dynamic at the core of your relationship is one of them. It's often triggered by the lion's instinctive sense of opportunities and using people to explore and make them their own. Things can change very quickly, and your leverage and influence in such situations can sometimes be quite minimal, even after many years of working together. Here is how it was experienced by one long-time right-hand executive who was also a very effective lion tamer in the CEO's office.

"I Didn't Know We Were Looking."

A CEO and his right-hand executive had worked together for almost a decade, growing a small and relatively unknown company into an economic success story and a leader in its industry and community. Perfectly in step, the CEO handled the outside world and the vice president "ran the place." Yet after years of success, growth, and expansion into numerous new areas, the CEO casually mentioned over lunch one day, "I've found someone great to handle strategy and communications for us."

The vice president was surprised: "I didn't know we were looking." Ignoring the response, the CEO continued, "Oh yeah, she's great, a friend of.…I really need your help bringing her up to speed. Don't worry. It will take some of the weight off your shoulders."

The vice president tried several times to gain a better understanding of what the CEO needed and why someone new was necessary to do it. In the process, he realized how much he liked his solo interaction with the CEO, and that a big part of it was being relied on as the principal strategic advisor. However, he knew the CEO well. His sights had shifted. To what and where were problems for the new person to figure out.

Deciding to leave the company and parting with the CEO on friendly terms, the vice president later explained, "We had our act down! Why would I want someone else involved at the top?"

While it may seem short-sighted on the part of this lion tamer, it nevertheless reflected his knowledge of his own limits, or rather the ingredients necessary for making his teaming relationship work with his boss. The result of a change like this will not be the end of the road in every case. But it points to something important about lion taming and lion teaming that is crucial to understand. While lion taming is a think-on-your-feet job, the secret is that you must be prepared and in control of yourself and your faculties to succeed at it, and that means having your act down.

Learning to Say "No"

> **Secrets of the Lion Tamers**
>
> *It is a patient process in which the trainer, if he is a good one, grits his teeth to hold his temper; and smiles many and many a time when he would like to swear.*

Lions and lion tamers share another important quality in their relationship. It's what makes lion taming in the office the ultimate think-on-your-feet job. Everyone's primal senses and survival instincts are operating simultaneously—this is one relationship that is truly *live!*

Lion taming uses all of your faculties—*visual, physical, emotional, intellectual, and psychological.* These are the ingredients of how people interact and communicate, the forces that trigger emotions and behavior in each other. The lions in the workplace have all their faculties operating at once. Yours need to be operating just as fully, but not always as visibly. As the lion tamer, you need to demonstrate a greater degree of awareness and self-control to be effective and keep up, even to stay ahead when you can! It may ultimately be the true test of your ability.

At the same time, however, you must also judge when to let your own gut feelings show. When should you demonstrate a visceral speed and agility? Treat your instincts as if they matter, but only when you need to and when it is useful.

As Alex Kerr, a big-cat trainer from Great Britain, explained:

> With a fierce lion, it is not so much a question of gaining his confidence as of instilling into him the knowledge that I am as confident as he and that, although I shall never attack him, I shall be quick to answer any challenge he may make.

When do lion tamers in the ring and office feel that it is useful to answer a challenge in a way that the lion recognizes? When it is imperative to stop something from happening that pushes the relationship too far, or when there is no other way to stop something that you feel is headed in a dangerous direction. You must react even though you also realize that you do not truly have the power or authority to stop the lion if he wants to go ahead. It may seem like nothing more than an effective bluff on the lion tamer's part. Yet to the lion tamer, out-bluffing the lion is serious business, and as you already recognize, the alternative could be disastrous. One lion tamer said it best: "Those fractions of a second, when only the speed of reflex counts, can mean the difference between safety and disaster."

Here is an illustration of just what he meant.

Lessons of the Lion Tamers

'Now' Is the Moment

Great Britain's Alex Kerr had to deal with a lion named Rajah that Kerr knew was a careful plotter and "the most unpredictable lion I have ever met. He struts, swivel-hipped, for all the world like a tough gangster." Here's how the action unfolded.

"Rajah came straight across the cage with his mouth open and his tail rigid behind him like a bar: a lion stiffens his tail as a rudder to steer him in a charge. I answered his challenge at once. As he came, I bellowed to make more noise than he....I sprang forward to meet him. He stopped in his tracks amazed, about a paw's reach away from the chair and stood there."

Kerr's need for awareness, timing, and speed was demonstrated again in response to another lion with similar intentions:

"Nero was another planner, like Rajah....As he came away from the center of the cage on his way out one night I noticed that, instead of being about five feet away from me, he had come inwards about three inches—just enough for me to see the difference....I just watched and smiled to myself and was

(Continued)

determined not to let him know that I realized what he was up to. A couple of shows after that he came nearer and again the next night just that fraction closer.

"With each performance he came that tiny bit nearer until he had boiled down his original five feet of distance from me down to two feet, and now he only needed to stick out a paw to be able to hook my legs as he passed. I judged it best to interfere. All I did was jump at him. It was a swift jump when he was about two feet away from me, and he rocked back in his tracks and veered away.

"These sorts of attacks must be answered at exactly the right moment....It is when you see that he has made up his mind—'Now' is the moment —that you take the moment away from him and it must be exactly then, for a second later his mind and body would have gathered impetus and it would be too late."

Such situations are not uncommon between lion tamers and the lions in the workplace. It prevails everywhere from the executive suite to the factory floor!

"NO" Is the Moment!

A situation arose between the managing partner of a law firm and an important client whose success in business was in no small part attributable to "aggressive business practices." It had become routine for the client to deal with his attorney in the same way. Discussions would focus on a problem, and the client would always describe what he wanted to accomplish and how the lawyer was going to help him do it. The attorney would patiently ask questions, shedding light on the risks and benefits. If the discussion grew too intense, the attorney would find a way to stop the conversation, even if it meant creating a reason to take a break and then call him back.

However, in one case the client was particularly demanding. He insisted that the only way to "make the deal" was to write a contract that very blatantly favored his own interests. The lawyer knew that it was an unfair approach. He didn't want his firm to be perceived as finding it necessary to use such guile, and as an advisor to his client felt that such practices tarnished him as well. The client pushed and pushed, as if he were dictating the draft of the agreement to the attorney, and then finally screamed into the phone, "You will do it this way and I want a draft! Close of business!"

The attorney shot up out of his seat, phone in hand, shouting right back: "NO! We won't do it and don't ever push us that far! Bill, I told you clearly, this is a bad approach for everyone, including you!"

The client was silent, sensing that the attorney was serious. Then he simply said, "Okay, let's see a draft."

Lions Need to Know You're Authentic

Secrets of the Lion Tamers

Those fractions of a second, when only the speed of reflex counts, can mean the difference between safety and disaster.

So, there you stand in the office, at your job, in a meeting, or on the phone with a boss, client, or colleague, and you need to say no. Such confrontations are, hopefully, not the norm. And as we have said, some of the most exciting lion taming performances to watch are not ones you want to recreate in the office. However, sometimes the scales of power and strength seem as unbalanced as if you were in a cage full of real lions.

If you need to stand up to the lion, you need to do it in the right way, and at the right time. What are the strengths and strategies that the lion in the workplace will recognize and respect in this situation?

1. The *authenticity* of your reaction.
2. The lion's *realization* that his own actions might

jeopardize a valuable and beneficial relationship upon which he or she relies.

3. The lion's perception that you have a capability—including knowledge or relationships—that they cannot pinpoint and do not wish to trigger.

The strength of your reaction alone will not suffice. It is the authenticity, timing, speed, and proper context of your reaction combined with the appropriate strength that gives the lion in the office pause. There are plenty of people—from assistants in many occupations to chiefs of staff and even other executives—who have found their careers cut short or their span of influence curtailed because they simply tried to roar at the lion.

Ironically, when it is their turn to react to your response, the leaders, bosses, and other lions in the workplace do not focus on whether you were right or not. They have realized that something more is now at stake; that you are drawing a line and if they cross it there could be consequences for a relationship that they value and need. In addition, there is always the recognition and fear, not unlike the lion in the ring, that the lion tamer might just have some power or ability in reserve that the lion has not discerned. In the workplace, that includes the risk to reputation.

Secrets of the Lion Tamers

Had I been the "take it easy" sort, I would never have mastered the lions, because it is energy and keeping on the move that compels them to work.

It is surprising to people to realize the extent to which their own persona, behavior, and energy level can motivate the people of power and influence that they work with. Yet your own pace and tempo, and your awareness of using it to help achieve goals when working with others, is as crucial to success as the style of the lions themselves. It is not that you are trying to overpower or control how they will behave, but rather that they need to see in very visible and behavioral terms the energy, dedication, and focus that you bring to the task at hand before going along with it. In fact, it is often because people freeze in their tracks in dealing with the lions that the lions jump into things in an overpowering but not always useful way. The people who are aware of the strength that this gives them and when to use it are the most effective in their jobs. And as we are about to see in the final chapter of the book, "Building the Lion Team," such awareness and self-control is the foundation you need to build the lion team, and make it work for the lion, yourself, and others around you!

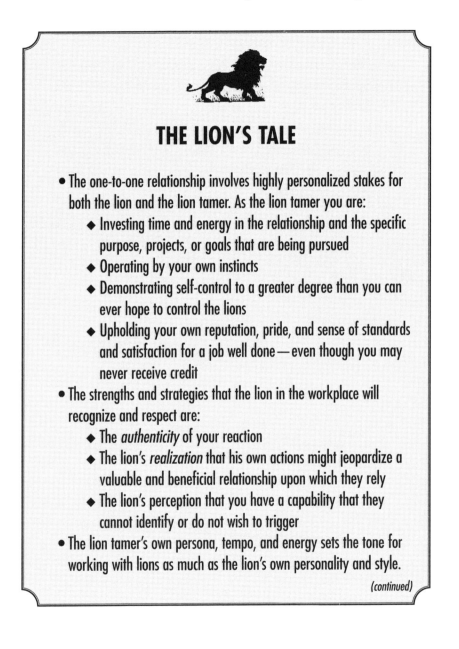

THE LION'S TALE

- The one-to-one relationship involves highly personalized stakes for both the lion and the lion tamer. As the lion tamer you are:
    - Investing time and energy in the relationship and the specific purpose, projects, or goals that are being pursued
    - Operating by your own instincts
    - Demonstrating self-control to a greater degree than you can ever hope to control the lions
    - Upholding your own reputation, pride, and sense of standards and satisfaction for a job well done—even though you may never receive credit
- The strengths and strategies that the lion in the workplace will recognize and respect are:
    - The *authenticity* of your reaction
    - The lion's *realization* that his own actions might jeopardize a valuable and beneficial relationship upon which they rely
    - The lion's perception that you have a capability that they cannot identify or do not wish to trigger
- The lion tamer's own persona, tempo, and energy sets the tone for working with lions as much as the lion's own personality and style.

(continued)

- The lions need to see this in visible and behavior terms. They need to see the energy, dedication, and focus that you bring to the task at hand before going along with it.
- It is often because people freeze in their tracks in dealing with the lions—and the lions don't see the energy and behavior that they are looking for—that the lions jump into things in an overpowering but not always useful way.

13

Building the Lion Team

> **Secrets of the Lion Tamers**
>
> *Celebrate little victories as training and understanding, not as performance.*

In the "old days," the climax of the three-ring circus performance came when all three rings simultaneously featured "big cat" or "wild animal" acts. In New York City, the venue of choice was Madison Square Garden. There, a capacity crowd of eighteen thousand people could watch, as was reported of a typical show in 1941, when the "three rings contained a total of sixty animals (including lions, tigers, spotted and black jaguars, snow leopards, black panthers, pumas, Great Dane dogs, polar bears, Himalayan bears, leopards, and ocelots.)"

Opening night for one big show at the Garden brought the audience more thrills than even the customary circus hyperbole promised. The center ring featured a famous bear act, and in each of the other two rings stood a large steel-caged arena with bars on the sides and the tops enclosed by a tent of stiff netting. The lion tamer in one cage displayed a rip-roaring "fighting style" with a mixed act of lions and tigers.

Meanwhile, the lion tamer in the cage at the opposite end commanded the audience's attention by the way he commanded the attention of the animals surrounding him. A parade of big cats sauntered into the ring: lions, cougars, tigers, a black panther, and a cheetah. The lion tamer wore a look of intense confidence, yet showed no signs of being a safari-clad "subduer of jungle beasts." He bore no whip, no chair, no pistol and holster, and certainly no pith helmet. Instead he wore a white suit with matching gold and black stripes on the shoulders and pants legs, and a black shirt and white tie. To top it off, he wore a trademark white captain's hat with a gold braid and a shiny black brim that he turned backwards when it came time to fit his head between the lion's jaws. His hands were empty but for a pair of white gloves he wore to cue and guide the animals through their steps and leaps, as if he were conducting an orchestra.

As if three rings of wild animal acts were not enough to hold the attention of the spectators and curiosity seekers, a chaotic scene unfolded. Yet only one of the three wild animal trainers—the man who did not have either a whip or a chair in his hands—maintained sufficient composure and focus among his cohorts in the cage to report what unfolded next.

Lessons of the Lion Tamers

When the Bars Broke

"I was facing the center ring at the moment and, looking beyond it to the furthest arena, I could see that a lion had leaped from his pedestal and hit the side of the arena. As I watched, the bars broke and the lion came through. He jumped an eight-foot partition and ran toward the hall. People were trying to find a place to hide, except for one newspaper photographer who was directly

(continued)

in the lion's path. I could see him in the glare of sudden flashlights, and he was standing absolutely still. The lion passed within three feet of him, up and over the ramp and down into the back hall where, I heard afterward, he was captured in a phone booth.

"Meanwhile, the bears in the center ring had taken fright at the sight of the lion. They were running out of the ring when the owner of the act ran in and tried to hold them by their leashes. The panic had gone too far, however, and the act broke up completely."

What can we learn from this lesson? Sometimes it is just this challenging to deal with the people at your job. Compared to real lion taming, the subtleties of the workplace and the complexity of human personalities pose different, if not greater, challenges. Certainly not everything that you need to know and see at work is always so public or accessible. Perhaps even greater vigilance may be required of you. However, it is more than a heightened awareness that you need to be most effective. Knowledge, information, and history are all part of it, but it is only meaningful and valuable if you obtain it first-hand from where the lions can smell and reach you!

How did the one lion tamer hold the act together? As we will see, the answer had much to do with what he did well before he entered the ring that night. Equanimity of the sort that he demonstrated is only possible because of the rapport, trust, and mutual respect that is first established. Yet even those prerequisites are based on something that must be at the forefront of a lion tamer's mind before, during, and after the act.

Visualizing Lion Teaming

> **Secrets of the Lion Tamers**
>
> *The process of preparation is where most of the work is done.*

Visualization—the hybrid of imagination and the way things really are. This is the tool you need to work smarter and more strategically in collaborative relationships with others around you. It is the ability you need to be more effective in the arena of workplace relationships, to have a mental framework that expands and adjusts with each new piece of information you collect on the job. It is the ability to experiment with ideas in your mind so that even when *you* are operating by instinct to gauge the next right step, you do it intelligently.

Meanwhile, the evolving picture is always in the forefront of your mind. Remember, lion taming is a think-on-your-feet job, and that means thinking before, during, and after you go in and out of the office of any leader, boss, or other tough customer.

How to Visualize

What are the steps? You prepare by visualizing an arena just as in the previous story, steel bars and all. Include the relationships, dynamics, and perceptions that are born of the lion team you are working within.

Even real lion tamers have found it helpful to visualize and practice step-by-step what they will say and do before bringing the lions into the cage. As one lion tamer asked in preparing for his very first public performance with lions: "How do I go about learning it all on my own? There are no books on lion training!"

Here is how he approached it. The lion tamer engaged in some brief training as the lion tamer's shadow, literally. Standing behind the lion tamer and holding on to his belt, he followed and learned every move, word, and gesture.

However, before he took on the challenge of entering the ring alone with the lions, he wanted to make sure he had prepared in his own mind.

Lessons of the Lion Tamers

Props, No Animals

"On my first solo in the arena, I used only props, no animals, going through the cues repeatedly, practicing footwork, bodily movements, verbal commands, and cracks of the whip. While I must have looked rather silly, gyrating and talking to the animals that weren't there, it was worthwhile, for soon I had all the details of the act in mind, ready to carry them out reflexively."

The first step in lion teaming isn't creating the team; it's seeing it. No matter where you work—whether you have been there a long time, or are just coming on to the scene—there are almost always existing relationships, dynamics, and perceptions that are embedded in a broader and deeper culture. It may not yet include everyone you consider the most important, nor will it necessarily exclude others you do not see as either very helpful or very effective.

Your first review needs to see things as they really are, not what you think or want them to be. How would you visualize working with the people, relationships, dynamics, and perceptions around you? Imagine yourself moving between pedestals and unlit hoops of fire. How do you begin to fill in the rest of the picture in your mind before entering the arena?

The Lion and You

If the lion tamer's dressing room had a chalkboard on the wall, Figure 1 is the picture we would first draw. You can begin to visualize lion teaming using two concentric circles. It looks simple, but there is a lot going on in that inner circle. Just think what it might be like with more than one lion!

Figure 1 **Lion Teaming**

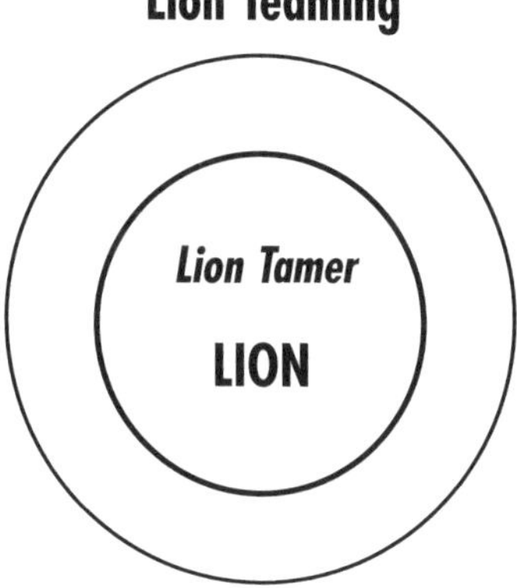

Rapport, Trust, and Respect

In theory, the inner circle represents a physical place: the steel-caged arena for the real lion tamers, the boss or client's office for the rest of us. Most important, the inner circle symbolizes the *one-to-one relationship*, the personal and individual teaming relationship between you and the lions at work.

> **Secrets of the Lion Tamers**
> *Nothing can be achieved unless mutual trust and respect are established.*

You might be the one person, as in the story when the lion broke through the bars of the cage, who could foster focus, provide feedback, reinforce consistency, and still keep a watchful eye on the larger environment. Yet the lion tamer's secret in this case is something they have worked hard to earn and, with a little luck on the side of interpersonal chemistry, is also the underpinning of their successful teamwork with the lions.

Rapport, trust, and mutual respect increase the self-confidence of the lions, both in the center ring and the boss's office. As a result, the lions amplify their confidence in you. It enables you to create time and space that did not seem to exist before. Combining forces more frequently and over longer periods of time is what it is all about. One consistent and valuable indicator that trust is increasing is when your boss sees that you can help him succeed in new ways that he could not have achieved by himself, even if it simply involves opening his eyes to new realities.

People are surprised when they learn how the formula for establishing such rapport, trust, and mutual respect is revealed, particularly at upper levels of hierarchies and organizations. It is not necessarily found among the people or accomplishments that get the most attention. The person who lands the million-dollar deal may win the boss's admiration and even a great bonus, but then it is back to the reality of "What have you done for me today?"

Indeed, the experience of many top-level executives who have also spent years working alongside leaders and chief executives is offered in these observations:

> Trust comes from the belief that you can help them do things they have never done before. Trust is given to an employee when they enable the person or people they work for to experience success in new ways.

You build trust and confidence when you help leaders and bosses persevere in the context of their own past experiences and existing abilities. It is often the basis for how lion tamers and lions in the office are first brought together. However, helping them become successful in new ways has an almost magical effect. It may ultimately be the test of whether the lions in the workplace continue to look to you, even though their confidence has been firmly established and remains strong.

Here are some of the most valuable ways to help leaders, bosses, and other tough customers experience success in new ways:

- Overcoming a crisis
- Strategic or new thinking

- Accurately anticipating or predicting
- Pairing problems with solutions
- Gaining access and visibility within new worlds of people
- Demonstrating candor and honesty where and how the lion can respect it
- Diffusing action that will hurt them, including their own behavior
- Placing problems and risks in the context of how it will affect them personally (by using the *Lion's Four Senses* of dominance, territory, social standing, and survival)
- Providing them with organized, digested information in a timely way that is relevant to the day's activity
- Your consistent good works

Tough Times

What are some of the most difficult yet unavoidable situations that you also may find yourself in? As we have said, in lion taming, things can go right in the same blink of an eye that things can go wrong. As a lion tamer, you have to become adept at looking at situations that are about to go wrong as an opportunity to make them go right. As a result, some of the hardest things to address as a lion tamer in the office also stand as tests of the trust and confidence that has been established.

Here are the situations and scenarios that may be the true test of your patience and ability. Address these directly, because if you don't the impact on the boss's standing as a lion can jeopardize for you both even more than the problem itself:

- When the lion needs to hear bad news, tell them how to save their skin, even if he or she doesn't want to hear it.

- When the lion is justifiably angry, yet their responses and reactions could result in unwanted harm or damage, you must let them know.
- When the lion thinks that you have hurt him or her, sit down and have an honest exchange with the mutual intent to reconcile the different perspectives.
- Recognize that no matter how closely you work together, the lions understand that they are responsible and accountable for their own behavior and actions; it is not someone else's responsibility.
- Even when the lion you work for doesn't want to hear it, tell them the potential consequences of his or her ideas or behavior, including ones that they don't want to be reminded of.

The Right Moves

If you want the lion to turn to you, give you access, and offer you the opportunity to be influential, effective, and successful, you must step back into the shoes of the lion tamer. Lions will accept you as a lion tamer if you do three things:

- Help them succeed in new ways
- Tacitly acknowledge that you can help them in ways they cannot accomplish alone
- Don't be afraid to say no, alert them to consequences, and keep them out of trouble

Regardless of how they respond, don't take it personally. Stay with them. Realize that a genuine roar or a snarl may mean you have engaged their interest and involvement as much as if they were smiling. As one corporate lion tamer commented, "I didn't realize I was a lion tamer until I said no to the lion!" And as another executive reflected from his own experiences:

> Candor—honest but not judgmental. That may seem difficult to combine when you have to say something critical, but if you have to say it, the lion must know that it is for the perpetuation of his dominance.

It is not uncommon to suddenly find yourself in such situations, caused by factors beyond your control, though not necessarily outside your realm of knowledge. Performing in the role of a lion tamer in the workplace means that you will deal with a wide range of moods, reactions, and fixations. While it is inherently a risky and rewarding job, how you handle yourself can make the difference in producing more rewards than risk. It is made especially difficult because many of the people who are the lions at work have a certain feeling of invulnerability. They assume that whatever the problem is, they can handle it. And if they can't handle it, why would they tell you? It is the value of rapport, trust, and mutual respect that will lead them to either tell you the problem or let you talk about potential solutions.

We've also noted the importance of how lion tamers carry themselves, act, and communicate in the cage. You must be acutely aware of where you stand or sit and the space between yourself and the lions in the workplace. Is there a tone and demeanor that will help you achieve this style of effectiveness? Can it help you hold your ground in tense and challenging circumstances? As one lion tamer put it succinctly:

> The steps you take and the movements you make actually provide many of the cues. You cannot dash and bob around haphazardly without thoroughly confusing the animals.

You may have already anticipated the answer in the lesson of "When the Bars Broke," related to us by the one lion tamer whose act was not disrupted by leaping lions and unleashed bears. The steps you take and the movements you make not only provide cues of direction but also provide the cues of your own confidence and comfort with the role you are in—to do what you have to do. Are you comfortable inside your own skin?

The key is your equanimity. Your equanimity is calming to the lion. It enables her to remember that she is working on a team, collaboratively, rather than focusing on her own feelings and fears that could trigger resistance.

Equanimity is not only a matter of your personality and interpersonal skills, or just your self-confidence and sense of security around the lions. It is based on your ability to balance the internal and external environment in the context of how the world looks and feels to the lions.

The Lion's Team

> **Secrets of the Lion Tamers**
>
> *Everyone has to work as a team, all with the same goal and not competing against one another.*

It's clear that lions in the workplace need others and benefit from working in teams. As the lion tamer, you cannot afford to think of yourself as working solo. Typically, such boundaries are firmest only in people's minds. In reality, the boundaries where the lion tamer and the lions work are permeable. But the real worry may not be about lions escaping through the bars, but rather about the influences that can flow in.

In the workplace, for every relationship and contact between people and lions, there is a dynamic of influence and a myriad of perceptions. Before you decide how you reach out beyond the individual lion to a broader helpful team, there are many factors about which you must become acutely aware. This includes the people who are critical to and who influence the boss—even if they are never in the spotlight.

Most people approach the boss from their own personal standpoint. It is the "know your stuff and show your stuff" school of executive training. It is "managing up" for the sake of getting something you need without regard for anything larger. In other words, there is no art to it at all.

But visualizing it puts your needs and world aside and focuses you on the dynamics and relationships as perceived by the lions. For our purposes, while the first circle will always be the core arena in which the lion tamer and the lion operate, all the concentric circles or "arenas" that you visualize are dotted lines, just like the steel bars that surround the real lion's arena. In the office, the lion's world is also permeable to sights, sounds, and man-made influences—some that may not even be in the room!

The view that you need to worry about begins from the inner circle but extends outward to a second circle (and perhaps a third and a fourth) that encompasses other people whose lives, work, and responsibility touch the lion. You may divide people up by function, location, expertise, professionalism, or personal connection, as long as you identify them in terms of their value and significance. As one right-hand executive expressed, "You need to know the social geography of the world the lion lives in so that when he or she talks about something, you are familiar with the context. Even when the phone rings, you need to be able to guess who might be on the other end."

Figure 2 **Mapping the Lion Team**

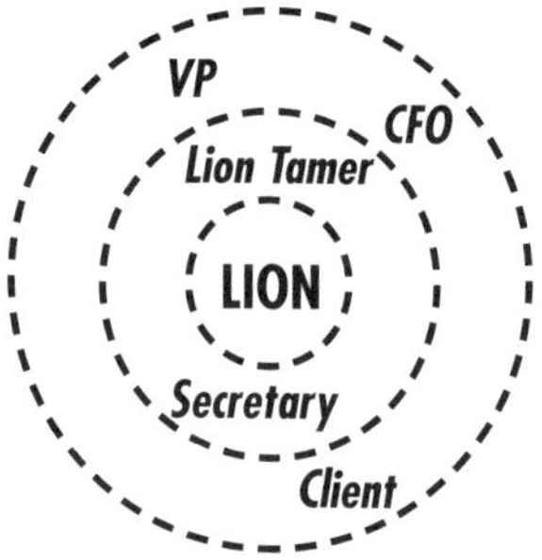

Beyond the inner circle of your drawing lies an important zone of activity, influence, knowledge, and power. However, it is important to remember that *you are not drawing a hierarchy; you are drawing a web or perhaps a constellation.* Who is in it? Anyone who has contact with the leader, boss, or client—a secretary, executive and confidential assistants, the chief of staff, other executives and professionals, perhaps outside contacts and associates.

These people are not limited to those who you ordinarily decide are important to include in your network, constellation, or empire. Don't measure their importance by their relationship to you. If you do, you risk minimizing the importance of people who could play a key role, even though they aren't in your personal circle of colleagues or if you simply don't like them. *You are conducting an environmental analysis requiring the utmost objectivity.*

What are some examples of who the lion's team includes? For the CEO, there are several teams, such as:

- The CEO's office of executive assistants, plus an executive suite of top-level executives and professionals in the organization.
- An array of other internal business specialists in areas such as management, operations, finance, legal, sales, marketing, products, or services.
- A variety of external resources, including financial, legal, and regulatory. Consumers and customers or clients may form their own circle.

Another example would be public or elected leaders for which there are also several distinct teams of people for the lions:

- Internal political leadership or navigators
- External fundraisers, pollsters, campaign specialists, and party officials
- Internal advisors related to policy, law, legislation, or regulations-related responsibilities
- Constituents, campaign contributors, the media, and a variety of other outside influences

You are, essentially, mapping the lion's own team. Depending on your own status, you may or may not find yourself on it. If the latter is true, there is no greater motivation for beginning to apply the concept that lion taming is really lion teaming. For many people, the exercise of drawing the connections between the lions and others in the workplace is a cumulative exercise that is already taking place in their minds. The speed with which you have perhaps asked yourself whether or not this is true in your own job may reflect this.

Assistant Lion Tamers

> **Secrets of the Lion Tamers**
>
> *The assistant lion tamer is also a lion tamer. Just not the one with spangles.*

Having begun to visualize the larger environment and people in it, you can begin to identify the people who form your own lion team. Despite the appearance that real lion tamers are operating solo in the ring, few would ever go into the ring without assistants close by.

Lessons of the Lion Tamers

"Invisible to the Audience but Not to the Cat"

Lion tamers have assistants—"grooms" and cage hands—who lay eyes on the lion just as much, if not more, than the lion tamers. They handle the care and feeding when the lions are not training or performing in the center ring, and when the lions are at work they are just outside the ring. Together with the lion tamer, they form a team. And importantly, as one lion tamer described: "The assistants are on the outside. But they are really only a few inches away. The cats can see them, hear them, and smell them. The assistants are nearly invisible to the audience, but not to the cat."

The same is true in the workplace. There are many different people who play different roles in relationship to the lions. To be effective, everyone in contact with the lions at work, regardless of their function and role, needs to reflect the underlying attitude that makes it possible to succeed at lion teaming:

- Overcoming the perception and sensitivities about rank
- Having something to offer that makes you authentic in the lion's eyes, serves their objectives, and makes them successful in new ways
- Working in a style that is collaborative, supportive, and even enabling

Generally speaking, in the same way that this approach has a positive effect on the lions, there will be a collaborative effect with others, including others who would like to replicate your success but don't know how. In some cases, it may be your access, influence, and capability to work effectively with the boss that will be noticed. Some will find it a threat or competition, but others will wander into your office to seek your advice, ask how you did something, and begin to share information and ideas. In part, that is how your lion team develops, by working hard to build rapport, trust, and mutual respect at other levels of the organization as well.

One executive who has been a natural at lion teaming described the way it has worked at all stages of his career, especially as part of the executive suite in several companies:

> You know that you are teaming well when everyone checks his or her expertise at the door. Your goal is to communicate and strategize together toward the common goals and issues involving the lions at work, finding ways to include them if they have not found you already, and then resume your functional expertise and individual roles to execute the next steps. It is also important to remember that not everyone on the team will have a next step, or at least not in unison. Some are invaluable to developing the approach and remain a valuable team member throughout. The people who are the lions may be in every meeting, but their actual role requires more preparation by everyone else. Nonetheless, they need to be part of things at an early stage.

If you map your own team of assistant lion tamers, it may look like this.

Figure 3

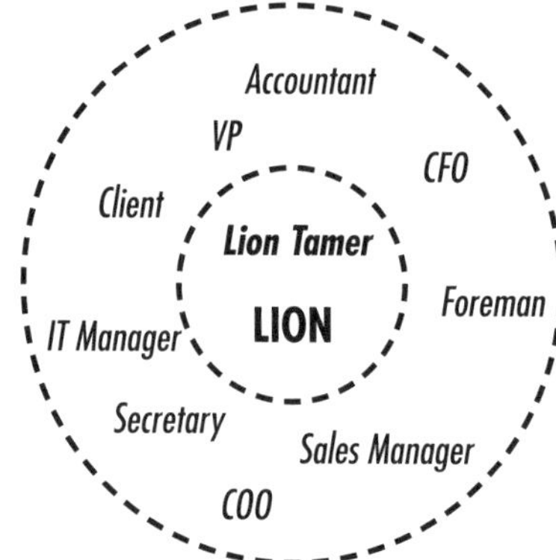

What are you looking for in others who might be members of your lion team? Often they are the people who:

- Possess valuable information, relevant experience, or expertise
- Have responsibilities that intersect with your duties or goals
- Represent a natural team that should be operating together in certain ways, instead of each as a solo lion taming/teaming act.

Perhaps the best answer is that you want to make sure that they are also very good lion tamers. The question is not whether they know everything you have learned in reading this book, but whether they have the talent or ability for it. One indication is their interest and ability in recognizing that there is more to it than going by the seat of their pants. It is whether you sense that they share some of the intrinsic qualities that lion taming builds upon—and importantly is reflected in their existing or potential role and relationship on the larger lion team with the boss.

As you look back on what you have read in this book, would they grasp many of the fundamentals we have discussed? From learning to approach the lion so that the lion will approach you to recognizing when and how people stick their heads in the lion's mouth; from the *Lion's Four Senses* to grasping that the lions need hierarchies but need others around them to get things done; and most importantly, understanding the importance of rapport, trust, and mutual respect? When they look into the mirror, do you think that they see a lion tamer looking back at them? I have always found that there are many people who can fit this role, and who make excellent people to be lion teaming with. But it is also important to be selective, and if you find that you have made a mistake, act quickly to correct it.

Secrets of the Lion Tamers

I would never enter the cage without knowing what kind of a day the lion is having.

Good assistant lion tamers make themselves known in several ways. For example, real lion tamers need to know the lion's mood before entering the cage, and so do you. Just outside the office of one top-level executive, his personal secretary sat in a reception area, and on the edge of her desk hung a interchangeable sign for everyone to see:

The Boss Is in a _____ Mood.

Most of the time the sign read, "Good mood," but not always. It was essential to be prepared. The boss also knew about the sign and it did not bother him a bit. In fact, he felt that people were better off knowing what they were walking into on any given day. It also helped him be more self-aware at times. In another organization, a top advisor to an important public figure found that the most informed person about the actual timing and schedule of the boss was the boss's driver.

There are many valuable assistant lion tamers, if not truly co-lion tamers, with whom you may form a more effective lion team. Who are they where you work? Expect this group to be smaller but deeper—and quite wide-ranging in their jobs, titles, or positions. And no matter how you perceive them or yourself along the food chain, organization chart, or hierarchy, don't assume that important information exists only at certain levels of the organization. Your job is to be exceptionally knowledgeable and well informed, not to be the membership director for an exclusive club.

Finally, in recognizing the role of others, remember that you are probably not the only lion tamer on the scene. You might assume that you spend the most time with the boss or client. You might assume that you are involved in some of the most important discussions or decisions. You may even have the impression that you are relied up more than others. That still does not make you the only person who has a lion-taming relationship.

When others draw their maps, you will be on the perimeter, in the outside circle. You must not only respect this, but also learn to recognize this when you happen to be in meetings together. Realize what's at stake for everyone in the room—and potentially how confusing this might be for the lion! When is it someone else's turn? How can you be helpful to *them*—provide information, be observant, and assist them? This may even be the ultimate test of your strength as a lion tamer, by working as a team member with others who must perform as lion tamers and enable the lions to look good and perform at his or her best.

Pyramids of Lions in the Cage

More than one lion tamer in history has gained fame by presenting larger and larger groups of lions. At the turn of the last century, Teddy Roosevelt watched at the Pan American Exhibit as Captain Jack Bonavita presented twenty-seven lions in one act. Over time, the ante was upped. Meeting the challenge of adding more and more animals to the ring became a trademark of lion tamers like Terrell Jacobs, billed as "The Lion King Presenting the World's Most Sensational Group of Jungle-Bred Performers," who handled "fifty males lions all at once" perched on pyramids of pedestals reaching to the top of the steel-caged arena!

Secrets of the Lion Tamers

Lions have few inhibitions about showing their strength at close quarters.

In the workplace, bringing together groups of lions is also uniquely challenging. From the lion's standpoint, it is also equally challenging, if not more so. It is seen from weekly meetings of managers and executives to groups of "big lions" such as boards of directors, committees in the United States Senate or House of Representatives, CEO roundtables, teams of brilliant scientists or engineers, the president's Cabinet, and many others.

Even some of the best corporate lion tamers are nervous about entering the equivalent of the steel-caged arena. Sometimes it blows up, just like a real lion-taming act can result in a "blow up" when uncontrollable fights break out.

As we have said, in lion taming things can go right in the same blink of an eye that things can go wrong. However, the lion tamers who overreact because they assume that things are going to go wrong, and therefore must be controlled, have an unfortunate way of turning battles upon themselves. Where are the answers to be found? Often by looking to the lions themselves.

For subtle reasons known best to the lions, even the most powerful groups of lions are often capable of working out the lines of power and authority in relationship to the business at hand. Lions often seek each other to be around other lions. In the lion society that *they* live in, there are many unwritten signals, codes, and rules that can come into play, including when the lions need to be constructive with one another. That does not mean that the room will not be without the kind of rocking and shaking that roars, battles, and posturing can trigger. So how do they stay focused on something bigger and more important as a collective goal rather than an individual performance?

That may be your job to figure out. When it is, there are rules that help us understand and anticipate what the lions will do. This is something that is useful for anyone dealing with groups of lions, whether you are organizing the meeting, preparing one or more lions to attend, or simply observing. Here are some of the rules and realities from the standpoint of the lions at work. These apply whether the people involved are mid-level managers, a group of sales executives, CEOs, boards of directors, members of Congress, or military officers:

- ***Lions are hardwired as fight animals and as pride animals.*** The capacity for more passive group dynamics does not mean that the lions will refrain from fierce fights. But just as lions are hardwired for fighting, they are also hardwired as pride animals. They not only know where and when to pick their battles, but they know that lions need other lions around them, and that not every one of them will be the lion king.
- ***Lions don't learn from other lions.*** When real lions are trained for an act, each must be trained individually, not as a group. The lion tamer does not bring them into the ring and say, "Okay, today we're all going to jump through the hoop of fire to my right." The same is true in working with groups of lions in the office. The lion tamer must worry about the adjustment process involving everyone; be focused on whether each individual lion's needs have been met regarding dominance, territory, social standing, and fears about survival; and still be prepared, if necessary, to provide explanations that are compatible with each lion's frame of reference. While this may be an exaggeration to some point, consider the work that goes into passing anything before a board of directors or other voting body.
- ***Lions have social egos.*** While most people would attribute such behavior to the egos of individuals, lions are social animals, and they have a social ego. How important something is to their standing in lion society is what

counts. For example, the opportunity to rub shoulders with noteworthy members of lion society that they normally do not have contact with may be socially significant in lion society.

- ***The opportunity or particular activity may itself be a "bigger lion."*** From an exclusive meeting to an important project or opportunity, the activity itself may be distinct and large enough to signify that everyone is a bigger and more important lion simply because they are involved in it.
- ***Not every lion always wants to be the leader***—at least not as much as being included, recognized, and respected (and sometimes also feared) as a lion. It may be more crucial to have the opportunity to be recognized as a leader or expert on something of personal importance to them, and only when they want the attention, responsibility, and visibility. But when they want it, they might just kill for it!

Finally, just as in any group, there are inherent differences of experience and character among individuals. Some of the people in such a group are more naturally suited by temperament, maturity, reputation, or ability to be the lion over other lions. Some are more comfortable if they know the other lions or they have worked together already. Others are sensitive to the social pressure of a group and do not find it comfortable to be very involved.

Some lions are content to be "seat warmers." These lions are used to "populate the act," helping to create the critical mass and dramatic dimension of a large lion act, even though the particular lion may have no greater talents or ability to perform other than to sit peacefully on its pedestal, and, well, look like a lion. The corporate boardroom—and almost any board of trustees or directors—has its seat warmers too: the quiet members who are always there when it is important to "have the votes."

Secrets of the Lion Tamers

You need to prevent against lagging watchfulness. Know when to get out of the cage.

Building the lion team is the culmination of applying the secrets, strategies, skills, and insights that you have been gaining about being a lion tamer when working with leaders, bosses, and other tough customers. After all, the social dynamics of the workplace are what brings the lions to life around you. That is when the part of everyone's job that involves lion taming needs to be activated. Your skills as a participant-observer will be tested because you must exercise them about yourself, the lions at work, and everyone around them. Whether you are working with individual lions or with any size group, it is your chance to match your instincts and intuition, not to compete, but for purposes of working effectively as a team.

It does little good to realize that your job may at times make you feel like a lion tamer because of all the things you are unable to control, including your own desire to run for safety! If there is an underlying lesson to take away from reading this book, it is the same understanding that you now share with the real lion tamers. As Jason Peters, who deals with a dozen or more roaring lions in the center ring every day for Ringling Brothers and Barnum and Bailey Circus, has remarked about the similarity between his job and working with executives:

> I know that I am about to enter a cage full of lions, and I think carefully about it before, during, and after I go in.

THE LION'S TALE

- The lion team must reflect the lion's leadership, and the lion must see the team as a reflection of himself or herself.
- Neither the lion nor the lion tamer can accomplish their goal alone.
- You are not the only lion tamer in the office, and you must:
    - Have a team of assistant lion tamers around you when you take the lead
    - Identify the people that impact, influence, and contribute to the thinking and behavior of the lions you work with
    - Become an assistant lion tamer to help others when it is their turn to be in the center ring with leaders, bosses, and other tough customers
- Visualize and map the lion team even if you need several lion teams for different situations. Help others visualize and map the lion teams in order to work more effectively together.
- Lions achieve status on the team because they are the lion. Lion tamers achieve a position on the lion team because they earn the lion's trust, confidence, and respect by making the lion successful in new ways, including:
    - Accomplishments that the lion did not think possible
    - Handling a crisis
    - Telling them NO! in a respectful but candid way
    - Giving the lion bad news even when they do not want to hear it

(continued)

- **Even if you believe that the lion team is focused on something specific, the lion's minds continue to operate in a highly multidimensional way beyond the boundaries of the team and issues that everyone else is concentrating on.**

Conclusion

Take Your Bow

> **Secrets of the Lion Tamers**
>
> *Lion tamers are presenting the lion, not the other way around.*

As you take the image of a lion tamer in your mind and shape it around your own role and responsibilities in the workplace, there is an irony that applies equally to when you must also exit the center ring. The degree of nerve and concentration that is required is as essential for your own self-perception and self-control as it is for how others will see you. Lion taming is exciting because it is not a theory; it is a role that you step into and absorb as part of your responsibilities and as part of your persona. However, it should not be a role that is confused with power, especially the powers that others think you have. It will sometimes take all your calm, nerve, and concentration to hold your ground with others who expect that you can work wonders because you have the rapport, trust, and mutual respect that they lack with the leaders, bosses, and other tough customers. In fact, remaining focused on what you have earned and how you earned it is a guiding, if unconscious, measure of a lion tamer's own effectiveness.

As we have said, *in lion taming, things can go right in the same blink of an eye that they can go wrong.* This applies to how and when you step into the role of lion tamer, and how you take your bow. You do not need to have studied lion taming to recognize the danger in upstaging the lions around you, either at the beginning or at the end of a performance. So, especially in the workplace, how do you take your bow, and what are the rewards? As we said in the first page of this book: *You know the dangers, a growl if you throw them a compliment and a roar if you ever look for thanks.*

The lion tamer's thinking may be so ingrained in you that gaining public recognition makes you more visible than you may be comfortable being—especially in the eyes of the lion you work for. This would not be surprising, after all, as it has been said, "True art is to conceal the art."

Lion tamers who succeed are the ones who recognize satisfaction and reward on a personal level without always needing to be rewarded publicly. As one executive described, "I am right where I need to be. Recognition would ruin it." Another high-level advisor to numerous leaders on the national level reflected that: "You don't enjoy yourself until you know the magnitude of your own insignificance."

Is it a lion tamer's humility that is at work? There is an intense desire to learn, to go beyond the rapport, trust, and confidence that develops, and a drive to "get it right" in a highly dynamic environment with people whose instincts drive their thinking and their credibility. There is a bigger vision as well, to work with the lions in the workplace because they have the persona, position, and often the ability to make things happen that are bigger than life, and a commensurate impact on a scale from individuals to organizations and more.

Lion tamers are driven by a personal standard that they

can feel from deep within—a reality that translates very well into the workplace. It is as a senior partner and top executive knowingly described in revealing his path to a more focused and successful career—"I had to feel that I earned." To do that, you need to not only be focused on the objectives and goals of the people who are the lions you are working to help, but also establish your own standards. When those elements—your standards and methods, and the successful performance or accomplishments of the lions—come together in ways that you define as successful, then as a lion tamer you can also feel that you have earned it. And it is then that you can take your bow in your own mind.

References

Ames, Evelyn. *A Glimpse of Eden.* Boston. Houghton Mifflin Co. 1967.

Ballantine, Bill. *Wild Tigers and Tame Fleas.* New York. Rinehart & Company. 1958.

Baumann, Charly. *Tiger, Tiger, My 25 Years with the Big Cats.* Chicago, Illinois. Playboy Press. 1975.

Beatty, Clyde with Edward Anthony. *Facing the Big Cats, My World of Lions and Tigers.* New York. Doubleday & Company. 1965.

Benyus, Janine M. *Beastly Behaviors.* Reading, Massachusetts. Addison Wesley. 1992.

Bostock, Frank C. *The Training of Wild Animals.* New York. The Century Co. 1917.

Bourne, Patricia. *Thank you, I Prefer Lions.* London. William Kimber. 1956.

Brick, Hans. *The Nature of the Beast.* Crown Publishers. New York. 1962.

Conkin, George. *The Ways of the Circus. Being the Memories and Adventures of George Conklin Tamer of Lions.* New York. Harper & Brothers Publishers. 1921.

Cooper, Courtney Riley. *Lions 'N' Tigers 'N' Everything.* New York. Little Brown and Company. 1924.

Court, Alfred. *My Life with the Big Cats.* New York. Simon and Schuster. 1955.

Denis-Huot, Christine and Michel. *The Art of Being a Lion.* New York. Friedman/Fairfax Publishers. 2002.

Dhotre, Damoo and Taplinger, Richard. *Wild Animal Man.* Taplinger Publishing. New York. 1973.

Eder, Boris. *My Animal Friends.* Foreign Languages Publishing House. Moscow.

Emery, George. "The Only Little Girl Who Ever Ran Away From Home To Join The Circus and Became A Big Star." *Yankee Magazine.* June 1971. Illinois State University Archives.

Fulks, Danny. "Bainbridge Ohio's Cat Man, Clyde Raymond Beatty" *Timeline,* Volume 19/Number 4. July/August 2002. Ohio State Historical Society.

Gebel-Williams, Gunther. *Untamed.* New York. William Morrow and Company. 1991.

Hagenbeck, Carl. *Beasts and Men.* New York. Longmans, Green, and Co. 1909.

Hall, Edward T. *The Hidden Dimension.* New York. Doubleday and Company. 1966.

Hediger, Dr. H. *Studies of the Psychology and Behavior of Animals in Zoos and Circuses.* London. Butterworth Scientific Publications. 1955.

Hediger, Dr. H. *Wild Animals in Captivity.* London. Butterworth Scientific Publications. 1950.

Henderson, J.Y. *Circus Doctor.* Boston. Little Brown and Company. 1951.

Hoagland, Edward. *Cat Man.* New York. 1955. Arbor House.
Joys, Joanne Carol. *The Wild Animal Trainer in America.* Boulder, Colorado. Pruett Publishing. 1983.
Keller, George. *Here Keller Train This.* New York. Random House. 1961.
Kerr, Alex. *No Bars Between.* New York. Appleton-Century-Crofts Inc. 1957.
Kiley-Worthington, Dr. Marthe. *Animals in Zoos and Circuses.* London. Plaistow Press. 1990.
Martin, John G. *'Doc, My Tiger's Got an Itch'.* Indianapolis. Guild Press. 1996.
Morris, Erol. *Fast, Cheap & Out of Control.* Columbia-Tristar/Sony Pictures Classics. 1998.
Nelson, Bert. "*Lion Taming's the Bunk.*" *Saturday Evening Post.* March 30, 1935. pp. 67, 69.
Patton, Kevin T. "*Confessions of a Lion Tamer,*" *Cat Fancy.* October 1987. pp.62-66.
Pfening, Fred D., Jr. "*Masters of the Steel Arena,*" *Bandwagon.* May/June, 1972.
Proske, Roman. *Lions, Tigers, And Me.* New York. Henry Holt and Company. 1956.
Rendell, Sharon. *Living with Big Cats.* Naples, Florida. IZS Books. 1995.
Robeson, Dave. *Louis Roth Forty Years with Jungle Killers.* Caldwell, Idaho. Caxton Printers, Ltd. 1945.
Schaller, George B., *Serengeti A Kingdom of Predators.* New York. Alfred A. Knopf. 1972.
Schaller, George B. *The Serengeti Lion.* Chicago, Illinois. University of Chicago Press. 1972.
Seidensticker, Dr. John, and Lumpkin, Dr. Susan. *Great Cats.* Pennsylvania. Rodale Press. 1991.
Stark, Mabel and Orr, Gertrude. *Hold That Tiger.* Caldwell, Idaho. Caxton Printers, Ltd. 1938.

Notes

PART ONE

Chapter One: Lions are Never Tame

Photograph courtesy of Circus World Museum at Baraboo, Wisconsin. AN-N81-Lion-5, Lion photo. Image by photographer named Atwell who photographed the circus between the 1920-1940s. Photograph circa1935.

Secrets of the Lion Tamers

1 Kevin Patton, former lion and wild animal trainer. Interview with author.

3 Dr. H. Heidiger, *Wild Animals in Captivity.* London. Butterworth Scientific Publications. 1950. p. 107.

12 Alex Kerr. *No Bars Between.* New York. Appleton-Century-Crofts Inc. 1957. Foreword p. xv.

13 Hans Brick. *The Nature of the Beast.* Crown Publishers, New York. 1962. p. 23.

14 Kevin Patton in interview with author.

16 Frank C. Bostock, *The Training of Wild Animals.* New York. The Century Co. 1917.

20 Pat Anthony quoted in Bill Ballantine's *Wild Tigers and Tame Fleas.* New York. Rinehart & Company. 1958.

Chapter Two: Getting Inside the Lion's "Skull"

Photograph of Alfred Court courtesy of Circus World Museum at Baraboo, Wisconsin. WA-np-CrtA-14. Based on Court's outfit, it appears this was taken in 1940 while he was on the Ringling Brothers and Barnum and Bailey show.

Secrets of the Lion Tamers

25 Bill Ballantine. Wild Tigers and Tame Fleas. New York. Rinehart & Company. 1958. p.126 [See also Alex Kerr. *No Bars Between.* New York. Appleton-Century-Crofts Inc. 1957. Foreward p. xii. "To me, the art of training is to get inside the mind of the animal you are working with and to know its mind as well as it knows its own."]

28 Hans Brick. *The Nature of the Beast.* Crown Publishers, New York. 1962. p.2

33 Roman Proske. *Lions, Tigers, And Me.* New York. Henry Holt and Company. 1956.

34 Mabel Stark. *Hold That Tiger.* Caldwell, Idaho. Caxton Printers, Ltd. 1938. p.13

37 Dave Hoover quoted in the Erol Morris film *Fast, Cheap & Out of Control.* Columbia-Tristar/Sony Pictures Classics. 1998.

39 Boris Eder. *My Animal Friends.* Foreign Language Publishing House. Moscow. p. 56.

41 Boris Eder. *My Animal Friends*. Foreign Language Publishing House. Moscow. p. 45.
42 Patricia Bourne. *Thank you, I Prefer Lions*. London. William Kimber. 1956. p. 26.
43 Jorge Barreda in interview with author.

Chapter Three: The Top of the Food Chain

Photograph of Mabel Stark courtesy of Circus World Museum at Baraboo, Wisconsin. WA-np-StkM-73. Taken circa. 1938 while she worked on the Al G. Barnes & Sells-Floto Circus (which was owned by Ringling Brothers and Barnum & Bailey that year, and had a couple of variant titles).

Secrets of the Lion Tamers

56 Dave Hoover quoted in the Erol Morris film *Fast, Cheap & Out of Control.* Columbia-Tristar/Sony Pictures Classics. 1998.
57 Patricia Bourne. *Thank you, I Prefer Lions*. London. William Kimber. 1956. p. 37.
63 Kevin Patton. Interview with the author.

Chapter Four: Bringing Out the Lion Tamer in You

Photograph of Harriet Beatty courtesy of Circus World Museum at Baraboo, Wisconsin. WA-N81-BtyH-5-N. Taken circa. 1935 by Atwell.

Secrets of the Lion Tamers

71 Joys, Joanne Carol. *The Wild Animal Trainer in America*. Boulder, Colorado. Pruett Publishing. 1983. p. 250.
73 Alex Kerr. *No Bars Between*. New York. Appleton-Century-Crofts Inc. 1957.
75 Patricia Bourne. *Thank you, I Prefer Lions*. London. William Kimber. 1956. p. 109.
76 Roman Proske, *Lions, Tigers, And Me*. New York. Henry Holt and Company. 1956. p.135. ("The deafening roars and snarls, like the thunder of a tropical storm, is itself enough to unnerve a human being.")

PART TWO

Chapter Five: The Art of Lion Taming

Photograph of Clyde Beatty courtesy of Circus World Museum at Baraboo, Wisconsin. WA-N45BtyC. Circa 1930s.

Secrets of the Lion Tamers

85 Clyde Beatty quoted in article entitled *Raw Courage* in Clyde Beatty Cole Bros. Circus Program.
86 Kerr, Alex. *No Bars Between*. New York. Appleton-Century-Crofts Inc. 1957. Foreward p. xvi.

92 Kevin Patton in interview with author.
94 (*Don't use any forcing tactics*) Louis Roth quoted in Clyde Beatty's *Facing the Big Cats, My World of Lions and Tigers*. New York. Doubleday & Company. 1965. p. 271.
94 (*Be respectful in tone and approach. Everything works better when they are the lion.*) Jorge Barreda in interview with author.
99 Gunther Gebel-Williams. *Untamed*. New York. William Morrow and Company. 1991. p. 22.
101 Kerr, Alex. *No Bars Between*. New York. Appleton-Century-Crofts Inc. 1957.
104 Wade Burck in interview with author.

Chapter Six: Courage, the Whip and the Chair

Photograph of Clyde Beatty courtesy of Circus World Museum at Baraboo, Wisconsin. WA-N45-B. Circa 1930s.

Secrets of the Lion Tamers

113 Charly Baumann. *Tiger, Tiger, My 25 Years with the Big Cats*. Chicago, Illinois. Playboy Press. 1975.
114 Kevin Patton in interview with author.
115 Roman Proske, *Lions, Tigers, And Me*. New York. Henry Holt and Company. 1956. p. 90.
116 Joanne Carol Joys. *The Wild Animal Trainer in America*. Boulder, Colorado. Pruett Publishing. 1983. p. 251.
118 Dave Hoover quote in the Erol Morris film *Fast, Cheap & Out of Control*. Columbia-Tristar/Sony Pictures Classics. 1998.
119 Pat Anthony quoted in Bill Ballantine's *Wild Tigers and Tame Fleas*. New York. Rinehart & Company. 1958. p.78.
125 Kevin Patton in interview with author.
128 Jorge Barreda in interview with author.

Chapter Seven: The Lion's Pedestal

Photograph of Harriet Beatty courtesy of Circus World Museum at Baraboo, Wisconsin. WA-N45-BtyH-2. Image was shot by a photographer named Atwell, who was working with circus performers in the 1920s-1940s. Taken circa 1930s.

Secrets of the Lion Tamers

137 Kevin Patton in interview with author.
138 Pat Anthony quoted in Bill Ballantine's Wild Tigers and Tame Fleas. New York. Rinehart & Company. 1958.
140 Wade Burck in interview with author.
142 Carl Hagenbeck, *Beasts and Men*. New York. Longmans, Green, and Co. 1909. p. 126.
144 Hans Brick. *The Nature of the Beast*. Crown Publishers. New York. 1962. p. 3.

145 Kevin Patton in interview with author.
152 Charly Baumann. *TIGER, TIGER, My 25 Years with the Big Cats.* Chicago, Illinois. Playboy Press. 1975.

Chapter Eight: Sticking Your Head in the Lion's Mouth

Photograph of George Keller courtesy of Columbia County Historical and Genealogical Society. Bloomsburg, Pennsylvania. Special thanks to Columbia County Historical Society Photo Committee, and to Robert Dunkelberger, University Archivist, Bloomsburg University for his assistance.

Secrets of the Lion Tamers

161 Clyde Beatty quoted in Bill Ballantine's *WILD TIGERS AND TAME FLEAS.* New York. Rinehart & Company. 1958. p. 120.
163 Present the abilities of the cats rather than your own machismo. David Tetzlaff quoted in "Josip Marcan: The Man-The Legend" *American Animal Trainer.* October 2001. p. 42.
167 Clyde Beatty. *FACING THE BIG CATS, My World of Lions and Tigers.* New York. Doubleday & Company. 1965.

Chapter Nine: Lion Taming in Action

Photograph of Terrell Jacobs courtesy of Fred D. Pfening, Jr.

PART THREE

Chapter Ten: Lion Taming Is Really Lion Teaming

Photograph of Jack Bonavita. Circa 1903.

Secrets of the Lion Tamers

196 Patricia Bourne. *THANK YOU, I PREFER LIONS.* London. William Kimber. 1956.
206 Wade Burck in interview with author.

Chapter Eleven: Bringing Out the Lion Teamer in You

Photograph of Laura Roth courtesy of Circus World Museum at Baraboo, Wisconsin. WA-NP-Roth, Laura-1. Circa. 1934. This photograph came from the collection of trainer Olga Celeste from the 1930s.

Secrets of the Lion Tamers

211 Kevin Patton in interview with author.
213 Clyde Beatty quoted in Joanne Carol Joys. *THE WILD ANIMAL TRAINER IN AMERICA.* Boulder, Colorado. Pruett Publishing. 1983. p. 126.
216 Clyde Beatty. *FACING THE BIG CATS, My World of Lions and Tigers.* New York. Doubleday & Company. 1965.
218 Clyde Beatty. *FACING THE BIG CATS, My World of Lions and Tigers.* New York. Doubleday & Company. 1965.
220 Frank C. Bostock, *THE TRAINING OF WILD ANIMALS.* New York. The Century Co. 1917. p. 246.

Chapter 12: Performing in the Center Ring

Photograph of Terrell Jacobs.

Secrets of the Lion Tamers

225 Roman Proske, *LIONS, TIGERS, AND ME.* New York. Henry Holt and Company. 1956. p. 145.

226 Boris Eder. My Animal Friends. Foreign Language Publishing House. Moscow. p. 56.

232 Juergen and Judit Nerger interview with author.

237 Courtney Riley Cooper. *LIONS 'N' TIGERS 'N' EVERYTHING.* New York. Little Brown and Company. 1924. p. 17.

240 Patricia Bourne. *THANK YOU, I PREFER LIONS.* London. William Kimber. 1956.

241 Patricia Bourne. *THANK YOU, I PREFER LIONS.* London. William Kimber. 1956. p. 79.

Chapter Thirteen: Building the Lion Team

Photograph of Terrell Jacobs courtesy of Circus World Museum at Baraboo, Wisconsin. WA-np-JcbsT-41. Dates to about 1938, Hagenbeck-Wallace Circus.

Secrets of the Lion Tamers

245 Kevin Patton in interview with author.

251 Alex Kerr. *NO BARS BETWEEN.* New York. Appleton-Century-Crofts Inc. 1957. Foreward p. 53.

255 Kevin Patton in interview with author.

258 Kevin Patton in interview with author.

262 Jorge Barreda in interview with author.

263 Alex Kerr. *NO BARS BETWEEN.* New York. Appleton-Century-Crofts Inc. 1957. Foreword.

Conclusion: Take Your Bow

Photograph courtesy of Bill Biggerstaff, THE CIRCUS REPORT.

Secrets of the Lion Tamers

271 Charly Baumann. *TIGER, TIGER, My 25 Years with the Big Cats.* Chicago, Illinois. Playboy Press. 1975.

**Thanks to Erin Foley, Archivist, Circus World Museum Library at Baraboo, Wisconsin for her assistance.*

Summary of Secrets of the Lion Tamers

Part One

Chapter One: Lions Are Never Tame

1. *Lions are never tame. You need strategies to deal with that.*
2. *Lions don't bargain or reason. They fight.*
3. *Social animals need a clear decision about their social position.*
4. *Hierarchies control competition.*
5. *The signs of imminent attack are these: switching of the tail brush, sudden enlarging of the eyes with a marked increase in green color; a sudden adjustment into a crouch*
6. *There is always a bigger lion.*
7. *The lion tamer's advantage is having the intelligence to study the lions individually.*
8. *The best offense against a lion attack is a dodge.*

Chapter Two: Getting Inside the Lion's "Skull"

9. *You've got to get inside the lion's skull.*
10. *I would never understand the actions of animals unless I knew and took into account the extent to which their senses were different from mine.*
11. *The wonder is not that so many are killed but that so many remain alive.*
12. *They are killers because they know their own strength.*
13. *They don't have to be mad at you to go after you. It's just instinct.*
14. *That lions have a good visual and auditory memory is an established fact.*
15. *Lions have a faultless eye.*
16. *Intense curiosity leaders to quick attacks.*
17. *Lion's power is so much a part of its character—it is overpowering.*

Chapter Three: The Top of the Food Chain

18. *The lion is at the top of the food chain and has no need to be afraid. The lion has a "big cat mentality."*
19. *It is self-confidence in your mastery of the traits and behavior that you need, not self-confidence that you can control the lion.*
20. *Lions can run 100 yards in three and a half seconds—when you are in a forty foot cage they can nail you before you can say 'oops!'*
21. *Movements must be quick and sure, an important thing to remember.*
22. *With lions you just never know!*

Chapter Four: Bringing Out the Lion Tamer in You

23. *The number of accidents suffered is in direct proportion to the lion tamer's attentiveness.*

24. *Lions look for opportunity to test.*
25. *The quiet ones may take the most handling; the roaring ones are often not so bad.*
26. *They like the sound of their own voices.*

Part Two

Chapter Five: The Art of Lion Taming

27. *They come to see death. I don't think they wish it. That would be too horrible.*
28. *To be considered one of them you must respect their code as they do.*
29. *Getting the lion to approach you, including when you need them, is really what it's all about.*
30. *This separates the good from the bad: Do you have the patience to take it slowly?*
31. *Don't use any forcing tactics.*
32. *Be respectful in tone and approach. Everything works better when they are the lion.*
33. *Lions do not answer.*
34. *Man is almost always seen as a challenger to their rights.*
35. *Lions are hardwired as pride animals.*

Chapter Six: Courage, the Whip, and the Chair

36. *Lions can kill without killing to eat.*
37. *The steps you take and the movements you make actually provide many of the cues. It takes confidence, but not in the 'I can do anything sense'.*
38. *To know fear is not to be a stranger to courage.*
39. *When courage is self-conscious it betrays great fear.*
40. *When the lions come through the door you have three seconds to read them. Are they coming at you or going to their pedestal. And it changes every time. I am sweating. It can be thirty degrees outside and I am sweating from the physical tension, the mental stress.*
41. *It is most important that the primary movement of the cue is always the same, given from the same position with the same stance and tone of voice.*
42. *Patience is the key to lion taming. It requires many small steps, and lots of time, and then it works beautifully.*
43. *Be respectful in tone and approach; everything works better when they are the lion.*
44. *You need to prevent against lagging watchfulness. You need to know when to get out of the cage.*
45. *Think of everything you are doing and its importance.*

Chapter Seven: The Lion's Pedestal

46. *Lions always have your full attention but it is hard to keep their full attention.*
47. *If you don't get the lion to sit, you've got nothing!*
48. *Your own practices are usually what is causing the reactions of the lion.*
49. *Get them accustomed to you. Give them a definite place of their own.*
50. *You can approach a lion from any side to make him go where you want him to go; you can crowd him; even provoke him a little.*

51. *It is not all one-way. The lions learn that the pedestal or seat is where they have your attention as well.*
52. *You cannot dash and bob around haphazardly without thoroughly confusing the lion.*

Chapter Eight: Sticking Your Head in the Lion's Mouth

53. *The animal's dignity has to be respected.*
54. *Present the abilities of the cats rather than your own machismo.*
55. *A display of temper paves a sure road to an early grave*

Part Three

Chapter Ten: Lion Taming Is Really Lion Teaming

56. *Dependence on others is what makes lions different.*
57. *When lions leap through hoops of fire they don't want it to look like someone made them do it.*
58. *Many things are not what they seem.*
59. *Remember that they are wild animals...always be on your guard. And most important of all, learn to know them well.*
60. *Lions have their own sense of where they want to go and when including where they don't want to go.*
61. *Lions memorize their terrain and map out their steps.*
62. *Lions are hardwired as pride animals.*

Chapter Eleven: Bringing Out the Lion Teamer in You

63. *It is self-confidence in your mastery of the traits and behavior that you need, not self-confidence that you can control the lion.*
64. *There are forty of them, weighing nearly 20,000 pounds ... Me, I weigh 145 pounds.*
65. *I don't notice whether there are five or five thousand people watching.*
66. *Once you go through the cage door you are completely absorbed.*
67. *There is nothing they sense more quickly than fear and uncertainty in the trainer.*

Chapter 12: Performing in the Center Ring

68. *There is nothing they sense more quickly than fear and uncertainty in the trainer.*
69. *When I enter the cage I do so with no morbid thought in my head...If a trainer is afraid of tackling his animals he had better keep far away from them, for sooner or later they will do him in.*
70. *There is an emotional link—you must be willing to put yourself into it.*
71. *With lions sometimes you just never know.*
72. *It is a patient process in which the trainer, if he is a good one, grits his teeth to hold his temper smiles many and many a time when he would like to swear.*
73. *Those fractions of a second, when only the speed of reflex counts, can mean the difference between safety and disaster.*

74. *Had I been the "take it easy" sort, I would never have mastered the lions, because it is energy and keeping on the move that compels them to work.*

Chapter Thirteen Building the Lion Team

75. *Celebrate little victories as training and understanding, not as performance. What did you learn? How can it be used?*
76. *The process of preparation is where most of the work is done.*
77. *Nothing can be achieved unless mutual trust and respect are established.*
78. *Everyone has to work as a team, all with the same goal and not competing against one another.*
79. *The assistant lion tamer is also a lion tamer. Just not the one with spangles.*
80. *I would never enter the cage without knowing what kind of a day the lion is having.*
81. *Lions have few inhibitions about showing their strength at close quarters.*

Conclusion: Take Your Bow

82. *Lion tamers are presenting the lion, not the other way around.*

Index

A

accomplishments. *See* achievements
accountability, 19
achievements; communications, 193; leadership, 193; management, 193; relationships, 193
adaptive learning, 41–42, 47, 58
adjustment, 49–50, 87; adjustment agenda, 93–97
aggression, 13–14, 21, 89–90
Ames, Evelyn, 43
anger, 21
Anthony, Pat, 163
approaching, 17, 87, 92–104, 152–153. *See also* space issues
Arcaris, Joseph, 214, 217
assistants, 258–63
attention getting vs. attention using, 60, 72, 138–39
attitude, 227
authenticity, 240–42
authority, 5, 19
awareness, 227

B

Baumann, Charly, 6–7, 114–15
Beatty, Clyde, 74, 101, 111, 116, 123, 163, 214
Big Cage, The, 75
Bonavita, Jack, 94, 263
bosses. *See* lions (of the workplace)
Bostock, Frank, 118
bouncing the lion, 145–48
Bourne, Patricia, 120, 217
Brink, James T., 35
bullying, 21

C

cellular phones. *See* electronic issues
character, 19
chemistry. *See* rapport
climate. *See* environment
command, 4
commitment, 19
communication, 20. *See also* nonverbal communication; achievements, 193; personal connections, 98–101
compensation, 5
confidence, 87
consciousness, 227
contrast, 213–16
cornering, 144–45. *See* space issues
courage, 113–14, 126–27; fear and, 114–17; stress and, 118–19
Court, Alfred, 91, 115
credibility, 87

D

daisy patterns, 60–63
delegation, 19
Dhotre, Damoo, 116
discrimination, 21
disrespect. *See* respect
dominance, 4, 9, 28–30, 32, 137; fear and, 101. *See also* Lion's Four Senses

E

ego, 15, 19, 21, 165
electronic issues, 176–78
email. *See* electronic issues
environment; adaptive learning and, 58; adjusting, 90–92; considering, 59–60; focus on doing and, 59; lion tamers and, 57–59; lions and, 56–57; multidimensional thinking and, 58; up-front behavior and, 59
equanimity, 253–55

F

fear, 101–4; courage and, 114–17
fight distance. *See* space issues
flight distance. *See* space issues
focus on doing, 42–43, 47–48; environment and, 59

G

Gebel-Williams, Gunther, 99, 163, 214
Glimpse of Eden, A, 43
goals. *See* achievements

H

habit, 4
harassment, 21
Hemingway, Ernest, 123
hierarchies, 9–10, 105–7; "pride" mentality and, 206–8; social standing and, 10–11
hoops of fire. See achievements
Hoover, Dave, 101, 116

I

ignored, being, 26–27, 80
information, 5
instinctive traits, 4, 34–37; instinctive identity and, 37–46; limits and dangers of, 63–67; promotion and, 53–56; working with, 47–48
intelligence, 5
Internet. *See* electronic issues
isolation, 4

J

Jacobs, Terrell, 263

K

Keller, George, 123, 161–62
Kerr, Alex, 88, 217, 237–39

L

leaders. *See* lions (of the workplace)
leadership, 19; achievements, 193
lion taming (in the workplace); "roaring" and, 75–78; adjustment agenda, 93–98; art of, 85–87, 218–22; assistants and, 258–63; attention getting vs. attention using, 60, 138–39; authenticity and, 240–42; bouncing the lion, 145–48; communication and, 98–101; courage and, 113–19, 126–27; difficulties of, 124–25, 252–53; electronic issues of, 176–78; environment and, 56–63, 90–92; equanimity and, 253–55; fear and, 101–4; identifying lions, 14–22; instinctive thinking and, 34–50; multiple lions, 263–67; nonverbal communication and, 130–135; patience and, 88–89; patterns and, 60–63, 196–202; personal feelings, 79–81; personal investment in, 232–36; preparing for, 6, 71–72, 125; prey, the enemy, or ignored, 26–27; prides and, 104–5; public persona and, 204–6; public vs. private behavior, 73–75, 132–35, 175; recognition and, 271–73; respect and, 164–78; rules for, 8, 79–80; saying "no," 237–40; space issues and, 128–30, 137–58; trust and, 97–98
lion taming (with animals); adjustment agenda, 93–97; assistants, 259; bouncing the lion, 145–46; chairs used in, 119–24; fear and, 114–17; head-in-mouth trick, 161–64; lion's traits and, 56; rules for, 8; whips used in, 119–24. *See also* Lion's Four Senses; teaming
Lion's Four Senses; adjustment and, 228; approaching the lion and, 92; definition of, 28–30; environment and, 56, 58; fear and, 101; public vs. private behavior and, 175; rapport and, 252; using, 30–32
Lion's Pedestal. *See* space issues
lions (animals); aggression and, 13; as social animals, 10–11; contrast and, 213–14; daisy patterns and, 60–63; manes and, 202–3; overkill and, 12

lions (of the workplace); "roaring" and, 75–78; adaptive learning of, 41–42; aggression and, 89–90; as a different species, 7–8, 22, 38–41; as lion tamers, 105–7; behavior of, 13–14, 33–34; characteristics of, 3–5, 9–10, 19–21; disrespecting, 164–78; environment and, 56–63; focus on doing, 42–43; good vs. bad, 16–22; hierarchies and, 9–10; identifying, 14–16; instinctive thinking and, 34–50, 53–56; multidimensional thinking of, 38–41; need for, 5, 16; other lions and, 263–67; overkill and, 12–13; patterns and, 196; position among, 166–74; public persona of, 203–6; public vs. private behavior, 73–75, 132–35, 175; social standing and, 10–11; teaming and, 194–95, 206–8, 211–13; up-front behavior and, 43–46; weaknesses of, 63–67, 204–6. *See also* Lion's Four Senses
location. *See* space issues
loyalty, 4

M
mentoring, 19
micromanaging, 21
mistakes, 19
multidimensional thinking, 38–41, 47, 58

N
nerve. *See* courage
"no," saying, 78, 237–40
nonverbal communication, 121, 124–25, 130–35

O
office arrangement. *See* space issues
overkill, 12–13

P
paranoia, 21
patience, 49–50, 88–89
patterns, 196–202
perfectionism, 21
personal feelings, 79–81
personal space. *See* spacing issues
Peters, Jason, 267
power, 4, 215–16; perception of, 168–74
presence, 87
Prey, the Enemy, or Ignored, 26, 27, 56, 105
prides, 104–5; teaming and, 194–95
priorities, 20
Proske, Roman, 33
public vs. private behavior, 73–75, 132–35; respect and, 175

R
rapport, 27, 79, 81, 89, 93, 99, 100, 124, 139, 142, 148, 152, 155, 173, 175, 181, 184, 187, 192, 213–14, 219, 222, 225, 234, 247, 250–54, 260–61, 271–72
reaction time, 72–73
recognition, 5, 271–73
relationships, 194; building, 255–63; patterns and, 201–2
reputation, 87
respect, 20, 21, 164–78
responsibility, 19
"roaring," 75–78; reorg roar, 77–78
Roosevelt, Theodore, 263

S
Schaller, George, 12, 20
social standing, 10–11, 28–30; fear and, 101; patterns and, 199. *See also* Lion's Four Senses
space issues, 128–30; bouncing the lion, 145–48; fight distance, 142, 145–51; flight distance, 142, 145–51; Lion's Pedestal, 137–41, 185–86; office arrangement, 142–44, 153–158; personal space, 142–44

species, 7–8, 22, 87
standing up to boss. *See* "no," saying
Stark, Mabel, 89
stress, 118–19
survival, 9, 28–30; fear and, 101. *See also* Lion's Four Senses

T

teaming; art of, 221–23; building teams, 255–63; contrast and, 213–16; difficulties of, 247, 252–53; effectiveness of, 212–13; lion taming and, 191–92; multiple lions and, 263–67; patterns and, 199; personal investment in, 234–36; "pride" mentality and, 194–95, 206–8; rapport and, 226–31, 250–52; visualizing, 225–26, 248–49
temper, 21
territory, 5, 9, 28–30, 56–57; fear and, 101; patterns and, 200–1. *See also* Lion's Four Senses
training, 20
trust, building, 97–98

U

up-front behavior, 43–46, 48; environment and, 59

V

visual contact, 183
visualization, 225–26, 248–49

W

Williams, Jimy, 41

About the Author

Steven L. Katz, has worked for more than twenty years as a right-hand executive and senior advisor to leaders and executives across the worlds of business, politics, government, and non-profit organizations. From Capitol Hill and the White House to boardrooms, clients, and customers, the author has developed the art of lion taming and added it to the lexicon of leadership and the workplace. Steven L. Katz has degrees in anthropology, history, and law. He lives with his family outside Washington, D.C. For more information go to www.liontaming.com.